MORE PRAISE FOR *THE DIRECTOR*

"Though I worked for the FBI for a quarter century, I found many of the things Letersky talks about in *The Director* shockingly new, simply because no one dared speak them until now. The book rounds out what we know about J. Edgar Hoover. Yes, he was demanding, odd at times, secretive, and vindictive, but he was far more complex than most people imagine. Only could a person working by his side, who answered his phone and read his mail and dealt with his fits of pique and bursts of enthusiasm, give us this insight."

—Joe Navarro, former FBI Special Agent and
author of *Three Minutes to Doomsday*

"For a span of decades that defies belief, J. Edgar Hoover wielded more power than any other lawman in American history. Paul Letersky's rich eyewitness stories of a supercop who could be both steel-fisted and strangely soft make this by far the most illuminating portrait of Hoover I've read."

—Don Brown, former prosecutor and
bestselling author of *Travesty of Justice*

"Letersky draws back the curtain of history to offer a rare, cinematic glimpse into the psychology and motivation of the Bureau's first Director, J. Edgar Hoover. . . . A must read for anyone interested in the most celebrated of American law enforcement agencies."

—Robert K. Wittman, founder of the FBI Art
Crime Team and *New York Times* bestselling
author of *Priceless* and *The Devil's Diary*

"Anyone interested in American history will find fascinating what the book reveals about The Director and his agents. As a former member of Special Operations who learned to make maximum use of intel, I found entertaining what Letersky shows about the power of secrets."

—Tom Satterly, author of *All Secure*

THE DIRECTOR

MY YEARS ASSISTING J. EDGAR HOOVER

PAUL LETERSKY

WITH GORDON DILLOW

SCRIBNER

New York   London   Toronto   Sydney   New Delhi

Scribner

An Imprint of Simon & Schuster, Inc.

1230 Avenue of the Americas

New York, NY 10020

First Scribner hardcover edition July 2021

SCRIBNER and design are registered trademarks of The Gale Group, Inc., used under license by Simon & Schuster, Inc., the publisher of this work.

For information about special discounts for bulk purchases, please contact Simon & Schuster Special Sales at 1-866-506-1949 or business@simonandschuster.com.

The Simon & Schuster Speakers Bureau can bring authors to your live event. For more information or to book an event, contact the Simon & Schuster Speakers Bureau at 1-866-248-3049 or visit our website at www.simonspeakers.com.

Manufactured in the United States of America

1   3   5   7   9   10   8   6   4   2

Library of Congress Cataloging-in-Publication Data has been applied for.

ISBN 978-1-9821-6470-6
ISBN 978-1-9821-6472-0 (ebook)

For my grandchildren,
Charles & Liam, age 12, and Georgia & Nola, age 9.

CONTENTS

In a City of Weak Men

No one cried at his funeral.

More than twelve hundred invited guests crowded into the National Presbyterian Church in Washington, DC, to officially bid farewell to the man whose body now rested in the flag-draped coffin near the pulpit. President Richard Nixon, sitting in the front row with the First Lady, was trying his best to look appropriately solemn, even though he was privately delighted that the man in the coffin was finally dead. Nixon's long-faced, lugubrious-looking vice president, Spiro Agnew, was in the second row with his wife, while nearby sat Supreme Court justices Warren Burger and Byron White, along with House of Representatives minority leader—and future unelected president—Gerald Ford. Former US attorney general John Mitchell, now heading Nixon's reelection campaign, was there as well, while other pews were packed with cabinet secretaries, high-level presidential advisers, foreign ambassadors, big-city mayors and police chiefs, dozens of senators and congressmen, even a movie and TV star—all there to pay tribute to the strange and remarkable man in the flag-draped coffin.

And from where I sat, in a section of the church reserved for the dead man's exceedingly small group of friends and distant relatives, I couldn't see a damp eye in the house.

To anyone unfamiliar with American history it might have seemed odd that the man in the coffin would rate such a turnout of the famous and powerful, or that his funeral was being broadcast live on three television networks—this at a time when there were only three television networks to choose from. The dead man was, after all, just a bureaucrat, the head of a relatively small government agency, a man whose position in the federal table of organization technically put him on an equal footing with a deputy secretary of agriculture, or the head of the Federal Highway Administration. He'd never sought or held elected office, had never even voted; he'd never served heroically in the US military, had never been hailed as a peacemaker or served as an ambassador to foreign lands. But everyone gathered under the soaring arches and stained-glass windows in the nave of the National Presbyterian Church on this May morning in 1972 understood the truth: the man in the flag-draped coffin had transcended the ordinary rules of American political life.

Because the dead man was John Edgar Hoover—J. Edgar Hoover, for the past half century the director of the Federal Bureau of Investigation, the legendary FBI. And in terms of longevity and his cumulative impact on the national destiny, he'd been one of the most powerful men in American history.

To generations of Americans, J. Edgar Hoover was the FBI. He created the Bureau, transforming it from a small, corrupt bunch of seedy 1920s detectives and political hacks into what most people— certainly me included—considered to be the most well-trained and efficient and incorruptible law enforcement agency in the world. J. Edgar Hoover was the nation's top cop, the number one "G-man," sworn foe of John Dillinger and Alvin "Creepy" Karpis and public enemies everywhere, scourge of Nazi saboteurs and Communist spies and Ku Klux Klan lynch mobs, hero of countless books and movies and radio and TV shows in which the bad guys always lost, and the good guys always won; it was an article of faith among most Americans that J. Edgar Hoover's FBI always, always got its man.

More than that, J. Edgar Hoover was the unceasing defender of the nation against cultural rot and degeneracy, a living symbol of all those things that so many Americans wanted their nation to be—tough, strong, brave, honest, decent. He was no mere politician or bureaucrat, willing to bend to the shifting political and moral winds that swept through the nation and through Washington, DC. Instead he was, as one American president described him, "a pillar of strength in a city of weak men."

Everyone in America knew J. Edgar Hoover—or thought they did. People who would have been hard-pressed to identify the sitting vice president or the chief justice of the Supreme Court could instantly recognize his unsmiling bulldog face, his boxer's stance, his machine-gun-quick staccato speaking style. Even as he grew older, into his seventies, and the nation slid into the antiestablishment turmoil that was the late 1960s and early '70s—anti-war demonstrations, race riots, sit-ins, hippies, yippies, pot, LSD, women's liberation, gay rights, black nationalism—J. Edgar Hoover had remained an enormously popular figure. A Gallup poll taken not long before his death revealed that 80 percent of Americans strongly approved of him as FBI director, while a mere 7 percent disapproved—numbers that any public official, then or now, would kill for. If no tears were being shed among the dignitaries at the National Presbyterian Church, more than a few Americans had wept at the news that J. Edgar Hoover was suddenly dead at age seventy-seven.

His public popularity was one reason that Hoover had managed to survive through five decades of vicious Washington politics. As President-elect John F. Kennedy privately explained after deciding to keep Hoover on as FBI director in 1960, "You don't fire God"—and godlike he was, albeit a God more of the Old Testament than the New.

But there was more to it than that. Because J. Edgar Hoover's FBI was not just a national crime-fighting agency. It was also a vast domestic-intelligence-gathering organization, a spy agency if you will, a harvester of information from every corner of American life. Just as he'd collected the hundreds of paintings and antiques and assorted curios that filled his modest home in northwest Washington, DC, J. Edgar Hoover had been America's foremost collector of secrets.

It was those secrets, or the rumors of them, that had given him his power.

Over time J. Edgar Hoover's legendary "secret files" had taken on an almost mythical quality. The most lurid and sensational of those files were said to be locked away in Hoover's private office on the fifth floor of the US Justice Department building, hanging like a paper sword of Damocles over the head of any politician or anyone else who might pose a threat to the nation, or to Hoover and his beloved Bureau—which, to J. Edgar Hoover, were essentially the same thing. Sexual orientations or indiscretions, payoffs and shady business deals, political dirty tricks, career-killing associations with suspected "subversives," gossip, innuendos, slanders—every form of personal and political cancer was said to be represented in Hoover's secret files. It was assumed that almost everyone who was anyone in America, and particularly in Washington, DC, was the subject of an FBI file—including virtually every one of the dry-eyed dignitaries sitting in the front rows of the National Presbyterian Church. As one of those dignitaries, Richard Nixon, once angrily complained, "He's got files on everybody, God damn it!"

Whether that was true or not didn't matter. People believed it to be true, so the effect was the same. People who were not actually the subjects of an FBI file were deathly afraid they might be, especially if they had something to hide—which many certainly did. Even presidents of the United States, with their enormous power, were said to fear J. Edgar Hoover and his secrets. Hoover had served under eight presidents, and almost all had tried to ease him out of office, only to discover that their political courage didn't extend quite that far. Lacking that courage, they wanted J. Edgar Hoover and his secrets on their side. As President Lyndon Baines Johnson put it so colorfully, and tellingly, "I'd rather have J. Edgar Hoover inside the tent pissing out than have him outside the tent pissing in."

So while the long succession of presidents had come and gone, J. Edgar Hoover stayed on—and on, and on, and on. Even as he aged, and his once iron grip began to weaken, as it became increasingly clear that he was unable or unwilling to cope with the changes that were reshaping America in the 1960s and early '70s, even as pressure increased for his withdrawal into an honorable retirement, J. Edgar Hoover stubbornly remained. His popularity—and his secrets—protected and sustained him.

And now, suddenly, he was dead.

So rather than grief, the feeling in the National Presbyterian Church on this May morning was one of relief—relief mixed with fear. For those who'd sincerely admired and respected him, and there were many, there was relief that death had spared J. Edgar Hoover the indignity of an inevitable descent into incapacity and irrelevance. For those who'd detested him—and there was no shortage of those in attendance, either—there was relief that the old man was finally gone, that the "Hoover problem" had solved itself.

As for the fear, it was the same old dread that had surrounded Hoover for decades—that his secrets would somehow fall into the hands of one's enemies or perhaps, God forbid, the press. Even as the funeral congregants recited the Lord's Prayer and the US Army Chorus sang "How Firm a Foundation"—"When through the deep waters I call you to go / The rivers of sorrow shall not overflow"—there was a scramble to find the secret files before anyone else could, to destroy them if necessary or to keep them for use as needed. At FBI headquarters, in Hoover's home, at various FBI field offices, locks had been changed, file cabinets opened, documents shredded or carried away.

Some of Hoover's secret files would eventually surface—and ironically they'd do far more damage to J. Edgar Hoover's reputation than to those of the people named in them. But in all the world only three people had known all the secrets. Now one was dead, and the other two were sitting to my left and right in the National Presbyterian Church. They may also have been the only two people living who had, in their own ways, truly loved J. Edgar Hoover.

To my right was Clyde Tolson, who until his retirement the day after Hoover's death had been the associate director of the FBI, the Bureau's number two man. More than that, Tolson had been Hoover's closest friend, so close that there were persistent rumors that the two men had a homosexual relationship—rumors that today are widely and falsely repeated as fact. But it was true that for more than four decades the two men—neither of whom had ever married—had been virtually inseparable. Although they lived in separate residences, they rode to work together every morning, had lunch together every day and dinner together most nights, and went on annual vacations together. Wherever Hoover was, there was Tolson, and whatever Hoover knew, Tolson knew as well.

But now, at age seventy-one, Tolson was a shadow of himself. A series of heart attacks and strokes had left his once ruggedly handsome face sagging and wan, his body shrunk by forty pounds, his hands palsied and weak, his mind wandering and unfocused. He'd had to be brought into the church in a wheelchair. Sitting silently in the church, dressed in standard FBI attire—spit-shined black shoes, gray suit, dark tie, and brilliantly white shirt—he seemed to be wasting away inside his clothes. I didn't doubt that he'd loved J. Edgar Hoover in his way, but I couldn't tell it from his face. No rivers of sorrow flowed from Clyde Tolson's rheumy eyes.

And to my left, her arm touching mine, sat the only other person who knew all of J. Edgar Hoover's secrets. She was Miss Helen W. Gandy—always, always Miss Gandy—Hoover's lifelong personal secretary and executive assistant. This modest title belied her enormous influence. For more than fifty years, even before Hoover had become the Bureau director, Miss Gandy had been Hoover's guardian at the gate, controlling the flow of people and documents through his office, filing away his secrets. To his last day and beyond, Miss Gandy protected J. Edgar Hoover—bureaucratically, politically, and, in at least one case I knew of, physically. Like Hoover and Tolson, she'd never married, never had children, never had a life outside the FBI.

She wasn't a difficult or unpleasant woman. Almost everyone who knew her praised her gentle demeanor, her quick sense of humor, her unflagging dedication to Hoover and the Bureau. People said these things partly because they were all true, and partly because it was dangerous to say anything else. Because underneath that pleasant exterior was a core of pure cold steel. With a whispered aside or knowing glance or a subtle sigh, she could—and did—make or break an FBI career or change the course of FBI policy. In her way, Miss Helen Gandy was every bit as tough as her boss.

Now she was seventy-five years old, a dignified woman in a floral-print dress with a white collar and white pillbox hat, saying farewell to the man to whom she'd devoted her entire long life. And if like Clyde Tolson she'd loved J. Edgar Hoover in her own way, like Tolson she didn't show it. As the Reverend Edward L. R. Elson, pastor of the National Presbyterian Church and chaplain of the US Senate, read from the second book of Timothy—"I have fought a good fight, I have finished my course, I have kept the faith"—I didn't see a single tear course down Miss Helen Gandy's lightly powdered cheek.

And who was I to be sitting there in the "friends and family" section of the church with Miss Gandy and Tolson? I couldn't call myself J. Edgar Hoover's friend, and I certainly wasn't part of his family, which now consisted of only a few largely estranged nieces and nephews. I was FBI Special Agent Paul R. Letersky, although you shouldn't put too much weight on the "special" part; all FBI agents were and still are called special agents. Compared with the FBI top brass packed into the front pews at the funeral, some of whom were already busily scheming to take Hoover's place, I was a pretty lowly figure in the FBI pecking order. I was just a twenty-eight-year-old street agent, what we called a brick agent. I spent my days and nights doing the real business of the FBI—chasing bank robbers and airplane hijackers and dangerous fugitives and anyone else who'd done violence to Title 18 of the US Code. I had little concern for politics, within the Bureau or out.

But I'd known J. Edgar Hoover. For two years in the mid-1960s, when I was a young civilian clerk in the FBI, going to law school at night and looking forward to the day when I could become an FBI special agent, I'd been on the Director's personal staff. Working with Miss Gandy, I'd helped shuffle visitors in and out of his office, screened his phone calls, answered his mail, endured his various moods and his many eccentricities and bouts of cold, hard anger—and I'd benefited from his example. It may not sound like a particularly glamorous job, and except that I was working for the legendary J. Edgar Hoover, it usually wasn't. But it had given me a close-up view of some of the most turbulent times in our history, and an insight into the ways of powerful men, and women.

So, yes, I knew J. Edgar Hoover. And the J. Edgar Hoover I knew was kind, courteous, thoughtful, fearless, sometimes funny, a perfect gentleman, and a devout patriot. Given his public image, that may not sound plausible—J. Edgar Hoover, funny?—but it was true. And it was also true that J. Edgar Hoover could be vindictive, closed-minded, hypocritical, a man of intense hatreds and eternal grudges, a man who in his sincere belief that he was protecting his country had repeatedly violated the principles of the Constitution on which that country was founded.

He was all of those things. As I sat there at his funeral, I thought for the thousandth time that J. Edgar Hoover was one of the most fascinating and perplexing men in American history. For all his faults and failures, I admired him then—and in many ways I still admire him. But I also hoped that there'd never be another like him.

And so as President Richard Nixon stood to deliver the last eulogy for J. Edgar Hoover, I wasn't crying either.

CHAPTER 1

Mr. Hoover's FBI

August 1965, a stiflingly hot and sultry Monday morning in Washington, DC; hot and sultry is the only kind of morning they have in Washington, DC, in August. I was standing at the corner of Pennsylvania Avenue and Ninth Street, just outside the ornate art deco double doors of the enormous US Department of Justice building, already sweating in my off-the-rack gray suit and white shirt and tie. In just a few moments I'd walk through those doors and report as ordered to begin my life in J. Edgar Hoover's FBI. I couldn't help thinking once again about the odd circumstances that had brought me here.

It's funny how the course of your life can shift on mere chance. Maybe you step six inches to the left and the bullet misses you, or you step six inches to the right and suddenly you're dead. Maybe you leave a party two minutes early and you never meet the person you would have been married to for the next forty years. Or maybe you're a twenty-one-year-old college student who's planning to become a high school teacher and football coach and you just happen to get into an argument with an FBI agent—and the next thing you know you're working for J. Edgar Hoover.

That was me.

As a kid growing up, I'd never given a single thought to becoming an FBI agent. Sure, I knew what the FBI was, and that J. Edgar Hoover was the head of it—everyone in America over the age of six knew that. I'd watched some of the 1930s G-men movies replayed on TV and had seen newsreels of J. Edgar Hoover warning about

1

the Communist threat before the Saturday-afternoon matinee. But I never wore a Junior G-Man badge (actually the Junior G-Man craze had pretty much died out by the time I came of age), never dreamed of becoming an FBI agent, never had any connection to, or much interest in, any form of law enforcement. My dreams had revolved around becoming a Major League Baseball player; the only "crime" I wanted to solve was picking off a guy trying to steal second base.

I grew up in a small (population twenty thousand) industrial town called Dunkirk, in far western New York on the shore of Lake Erie. As you might have guessed from my name, my grandparents were Polish immigrants, which meant we lived in the town's "Polish Ward"—Polish butcher shops, Polish restaurants, the Kosciuszko Club, the Moniuszko Polish Singing Society, the Catholic Church with sermons in Polish. (Later, when I was undergoing the extensive background check required to work for the FBI, the Bureau had to scramble to find Polish-speaking agents who could interview my neighbors about me.) It was a solid working-class environment. My maternal grandfather—*dziazia* in Polish—worked at the True Temper shovel factory in town, my father worked as a laborer at the Briggs Dairy, and if we weren't rich, my three sisters and I never felt poor, either. To me it was sort of a *Leave It to Beaver* life, except that unlike Ward and June Cleaver, my dad never came home carrying a briefcase and my mother never cooked a meal wearing high heels.

I was born in 1943, part of the demographic cohort squeezed between the Greatest Generation, which fought World War II—two of my uncles were killed in that war—and the postwar baby boomers. *Time* magazine dubbed us the Silent Generation, and I guess we were. Plenty of things were going on in America at the time—McCarthyism, the civil rights movement in the South, the growing nuclear weapons escalation between the United States and the Soviet Union. But except for the "duck-and-cover" nuclear-war drills in school, none of those things seemed to have much direct impact on Dunkirk, New York. For me there was none of the James Dean teen angst of *Rebel Without a Cause*, or the switchblade-wielding urban violence of *Blackboard Jungle*. I guess the most rebellious thing my buddies and I ever did was when we accidentally burned an empty New York Central Railroad boxcar right down to the tracks. (It was an accident! Honest!) Fortunately, our vow of omertà—silence—somehow held up, and the FBI background checkers never found out about that caper. And I'm pretty sure the New York statute of limitations on arson has long run out.

So, no, juvenile delinquency and teen rebellion weren't my things; sports were. Basketball, track, football, and especially baseball—I loved them all, and I played them all in high school. And after graduation it seemed only natural that I'd continue to play at the college level.

I was determined to go to college. I'd spent too many days helping my father load heavy milk crates onto pallets at the Briggs Dairy to ever want to spend my life doing manual labor. So I enrolled at the State University of New York at Fredonia—go, Blue Devils!— where I majored in social studies and education. But my real major was being a jock. I made varsity in three sports, with baseball being my best, and I still harbored hopes of making it to the Bigs.

But as so often happens, eventually reality set in. In my senior year I realized that while there were thousands of pretty good ballplayers like me, in all of America only about five hundred guys actually played in the Major Leagues at any given time. I was good—but I wasn't that good.

So what to do with my life? Somehow I got the idea that going to graduate school might be the ticket. I could get a master's degree in history or political science, and besides, at the time being a full-time student got you an exemption from the military draft. This was before the big US buildup in Vietnam—most Americans had barely even heard of Vietnam—and the idea of spending the next two years of my life as a draftee sitting around some dusty army base in Louisiana or Texas didn't have much appeal.

The problem with grad school was how to pay for it. Tuition at Fredonia had been almost free (about $200 a semester), but graduate schools weren't so generous. If I wanted to go to grad school, I needed a full-time job.

Actually I had a job lined up. As I said, I was an education major, and I'd already gone through fifteen weeks of student teaching, so a local high school had offered me a job as a history and social studies teacher and coach of the football team, at a salary of $6,200 a year—which was pretty good money at the time. The coaching part sounded great, and who knew, maybe someday I'd find myself the head coach of the New York Giants. But the idea of drumming the finer points of the Missouri Compromise or how a bill becomes a law into the heads of bored teenagers for the next few years didn't sound exciting. I wondered if there could be something else out there.

I'd been told—erroneously as it turned out—that the New York State Police had a program that would pay for state troopers to go to graduate school. Again, I'd never had much interest in law enforcement, but it sounded like a good deal. I could go to grad school by day and hang speeding tickets on motorists on the New York Thruway by night. So just before my college graduation, I stopped by the state police barracks in Fredonia and talked to a captain about my plans to become a state trooper / grad student. But the captain patiently explained that I'd been misinformed, that while they'd love to have me as a state trooper, the New York State Police offered no such graduate school subsidy program. Disappointed and a little embarrassed, I thanked him, backed out of his office, and left the building.

That's when the FBI agent chased me down.

"Excuse me, young man." He flashed an ID card encased in a leather credential wallet. "I'm Special Agent So-and-So, with the FBI. I was in the office next door to the captain's, and I couldn't help overhearing what you told him. Tell me, how would you like to work for the FBI?"

I was a bit taken aback, so I stammered, "I don't know. I don't think I'm qualified to be an FBI agent."

The guy laughed. "No, you're not qualified to be an FBI *special* agent."

Now I was getting a little annoyed. This guy was in his early thirties, wearing a business suit, and he had an air of authority around

4

him, but I hadn't had a chance to completely eyeball his credentials. Maybe he was an FBI agent—special agent—and maybe he wasn't.

"If I'm not qualified, then why the hell are you asking if I want to work for them? Let me see your credentials again."

Now it was his turn to get annoyed. He grudgingly pulled out his credential case, flipped it open, and held it about six inches in front of my nose. Sure enough, the ID card said, "Federal Bureau of Investigation," and at the bottom was a tiny signature: "J. Edgar Hoover."

"Okay. But what's this business about working for the FBI?"

"Look, kid, you told the captain you're twenty-one, right? You have to be twenty-three to become an FBI agent. But after you graduate from college, we can get you a job as a civilian clerk for the Bureau, and you can go to law school at night. It's not an absolute requirement, but Director Hoover prefers his agents to have law or accounting degrees. By the time you get your law degree you'll be old enough to apply for appointment as a special agent."

Well, I was still a little suspicious of this guy, who said he was the "resident agent" in the nearby town of Jamestown—meaning he was a one-man suboffice of the FBI field office in Buffalo. Like any resident agent, part of his job was to maintain close relations with local law enforcement, which was why he was at the state police barracks in the first place.

But if I was still skeptical, I was also impressed that he'd so quickly recognized my outstanding talent and superb abilities and limitless potential. I would have been less impressed if I'd known that hitting up guys like me was also part of his job, as it was for every FBI field agent. The FBI had always said that for every man who was accepted as an FBI agent (no women were allowed to apply), another thousand applicants had tried but failed to make the grade. That wasn't quite true, but to keep the applicants-to-new-hires ratio high, agents were under constant pressure to find fresh potential applicants for the Bureau. Every field office had a quota of prospective applicants to meet, and failure to meet it meant the special agent in charge had some serious explaining to do.

They couldn't try to recruit just anybody. In addition to the college degree requirement, other critical factors were an assertive personality (I'd already demonstrated that quality to the FBI man) and the proper appearance—including the shape of the recruit's head. As I later found out, FBI headquarters sent frequent reminders to the field offices that "long-hairs, beards, pear-shaped heads, truck drivers, etc." were not to be considered for FBI employment. At the time, "long-hairs" and "beards" referred to academic/intellectual types who were thought to be too soft, while "truck drivers" was Director Hoover's shorthand phrase for men who were too rough in manner or appearance to live up to the ideal FBI image. As for "pear-shaped heads," I'm still not exactly sure what that meant, whether it referred to heads that were too big at the top and too small at the bottom or vice versa. But whatever it meant, apparently my cranial conformation wasn't disqualifying, nor was I an obvious long-hair or truck driver.

I told the FBI agent I'd think about it and gave him my mailing address. A few days later I got an application form and some brochures with titles such as "Facts About a Career in the FBI." They explained that FBI civilian clerks made an annual salary of $3,680, plus benefits, including twenty days paid vacation, and that being a clerk was an excellent pathway to becoming a special agent. To qualify as a special agent trainee, applicants had to be a male US citizen, at least twenty-three years old, with a law degree or an undergrad accounting degree with three years working experience (although as the FBI resident agent told me, there were some exceptions for college grads with special skills in language, science, and so on). As for physical requirements, applicants had to be at least five-seven "without shoes" (check—I was six-two); have uncorrected vision no worse than 20/50 in the weakest eye (check—I had 20/20); "be able to hear ordinary conversation at least fifteen feet away with each ear" (check—I assumed FBI agents needed good hearing to pick up the whispered conversations of malefactors); and, finally, "be able to perform strenuous physical exertion and have no defects which would interfere with their use of firearms or their participation in raids, dangerous assignments, or defensive tactics" (check and double-check—I was an athlete).

The more I read about it, the cooler the idea of becoming an FBI agent began to seem. Raids! Dangerous assignments! True, I'd have to slug it out as a civilian clerk for a few years, at a salary that was a couple thousand dollars less than what I could make as a high school teacher and coach. And I knew it would be a grind to work for the FBI full-time—there were no part-time jobs with the FBI—and go to law school full-time as well. (You had to be a full-time student to keep your draft deferment; part-time didn't count.) But I also knew that once I made special agent, my pay would shoot up to $10,000— and more important, it was an exciting and high-prestige job.

So my mind was made up. I was going to be a special agent of the FBI! I could already envision myself catching bank robbers, or maybe even some Russian spies. I filled out the application and sent it to the Buffalo FBI Field Office, and a couple months later, after the extensive background check, I got a letter directing me to report to FBI headquarters in Washington, DC, as a GS-4 level civilian clerk.

(A lot of people think the GS stands for "government service," but it doesn't; that would be too simple. It actually stands for "general schedule," with rankings from GS-1 to GS-15 (they used to go up to GS-18), with ten salary "steps" at each level based on an employee's time in that grade—which means that as a new guy I was technically a GS-4 Step 1 employee. As anyone who takes a job with the US government soon finds out, the first rule of the federal bureaucracy is to make everything as arcane and complicated as possible.)

Confident I'd get the job, I'd already signed up for law school night courses at the Mount Vernon School of Law in Baltimore, which was thirty-five miles away from Washington, but which was one of the few schools in the area that allowed full-time law students to also have full-time day jobs. So when the summons from the Bureau came, I loaded up my battered 1960 Mercury and headed south.

So on that steaming Monday morning in August 1965 I found myself standing outside the massive, block-long US Department of Justice building. I was young, enthusiastic, bursting with energy, and more than a little idealistic. I knew I was doing the right thing.

Without a second thought I walked through the double doors and joined Mr. Hoover's FBI.

If 1965 was a pivotal year for me, it was also a pivotal year for the nation—and for the FBI.

In January, President Lyndon Baines Johnson was inaugurated for his first (and only) elected term, this after his landslide victory over conservative Arizona senator Barry Goldwater in the 1964 campaign. In the spring, Martin Luther King Jr. and hundreds of other peaceful civil rights activists were beaten and arrested by club-wielding local cops in Selma, Alabama, while nine thousand miles away a regiment of thirty-five hundred US Marines landed at Danang, Vietnam, becoming the first American ground combat unit to be sent into that conflict. Up until then some four hundred American military "advisers" had been killed in Vietnam over the previous eight years, but in 1965 that number of American dead would grow to the thousands, and then the tens of thousands. In the summer President Johnson signed the landmark Voting Rights Act—which, coupled with the Civil Rights Act of 1964, was intended to bring long overdue justice to black Americans—but the ink was barely dry on that legislation when riots broke out in the largely African American Watts section of Los Angeles, riots that left thirty-four dead, a thousand injured, and hundreds of buildings looted and destroyed.

So it went—racist murders in the South, public draft-card burnings in Berkeley, small but growing anti-war demonstrations in the nation's capital and elsewhere. Another milestone event that year would have a profound effect on the nation—and on my career with the FBI. On New Year's Day 1965, J. Edgar Hoover celebrated his seventieth birthday.

At the time, seventy was the mandatory retirement age for most federal employees, Hoover included. (Presidents, Supreme Court justices, members of Congress, and some others were exempted.) In the months leading up to Hoover's birthday there'd been much speculation that Lyndon Johnson would allow the mandatory-retirement requirement to kick in, thus gently moving the old man out of the FBI directorship without running the political risk of firing him. But Hoover and Johnson had a long history—Johnson and his family were Hoover's neighbors in a Rock Creek Park neighborhood when Johnson was a senator—and as we'll see, Hoover had done Johnson some political favors over the years and would continue to do so. So in a ceremony in the White House Rose Garden, Johnson had announced in his Texas drawl, "Edgar, the law says you must retire next January when you reach your seventieth birthday, and I know you wouldn't want to break the law. But the nation cannot afford to lose you. Therefore . . . I have today signed an executive order exempting you from compulsory retirement for an indefinite period of time."

Despite the "indefinite period of time" caveat, there'd never again be a convenient and politically palatable way for Johnson or any other president to force Hoover out of the FBI directorship. In effect, Johnson had appointed Hoover FBI director for life—and in terms of his legacy and his standing in American history, accepting that lifetime appointment was probably the biggest mistake J. Edgar Hoover ever made.

But that was in the future. In 1965 J. Edgar Hoover was at the pinnacle of his power and success and fame. And 1965 may also have been the last year that Hoover understood the nation he'd served for so long.

Because despite the pockets of strife and turmoil described above, America in 1965 was not yet the bitterly divided nation it was soon to become. Although still shaken by the 1963 assassination of President Kennedy, and disturbed by racial violence in the South, most Americans still leaned more closely to the mores and morals of the 1950s—J. Edgar Hoover's mores and morals—than to those of the latter part of the 1960s.

According to a 1965 Gallup poll, 61 percent of Americans supported the US involvement in Vietnam, while just 24 percent opposed it, with 15 percent having "no opinion"; Johnson himself enjoyed approval ratings in the low 70s. Only 10 percent told Gallup's pollsters that they'd ever felt an urge to join a public demonstration or protest, and 72 percent said religion was "very important" to them (that figure would plummet in the next decade). Only 4 percent said they had "very little respect" for their local police. As for the Bureau, a poll conducted that year found that 85 percent of Americans had a "highly favorable" opinion of Mr. Hoover's FBI.

On the popular-culture side, America in 1965 remained remarkably "square." Less than 1 percent of Americans had ever tried marijuana, according to most estimates, and far fewer still had ever dropped LSD. (In case you're wondering, I was part of the other 99-plus percent who had not tried marijuana or LSD—and I remain so to this day. I just wasn't interested.) The top-grossing movie in 1965 was the family-friendly *The Sound of Music*, and the top-selling record wasn't some Bob Dylan–esque protest anthem but rather the nonsense song "Wooly Bully" by Sam the Sham and the Pharaohs. The top twenty shows on TV were dominated by such noncontroversial fare as *The Lawrence Welk Show* and *My Three Sons* and *The Dick Van Dyke Show*, with Rob and Laura covered neck to toe in pajamas as they crawled into their separate twin beds at night.

When it came to personal appearance, prim formality still ruled. In 1965 ladies still wore hats and gloves at social events, and most young women still sported big-hair perms and skirts with hemlines down to their knees—although a few of the more daring had begun shifting to the miniskirt, made shockingly famous the previous year by the skeletal British supermodel called Twiggy. For professional men, the gray fedoras of earlier years were out, but suits and ties and white shirts were still the order of the day. As for men's hairstyles, the short-haired "collegiate look" was still in fashion; it would soon be replaced by the hirsute styles pioneered by the Beatles and the Rolling Stones.

The point here is that in going to work for the FBI in 1965, I wasn't at odds with most of America, or even with my generational cohort. People still believed in Mr. Hoover's FBI—and so did I. I couldn't wait to become a full-fledged part of it as a special agent.

But first I had to sweat out three years as a clerk and a law school student.

At the time there were ten "divisions" in FBI headquarters, also known as FBIHQ or, for reasons lost to time, the Seat of Government (SOG): General Investigative Division, Domestic Intelligence Division, Administrative Division, Training Division, and so on, all headed by an assistant director. (In an odd twist, the second-in-command of each division was called the number one man—again, for reasons lost to time.)

I was assigned to Crime Records Division, which had little to do with either crime or records. Instead, this was the Bureau's publicity and public relations department. Staffed by about one hundred people—supervising special agents, female typists and stenographers, and civilian clerks like me (almost all of them young guys who were hoping to become special agents)—Crime Records occupied a suite of offices on the Justice Department building's fifth floor, just across the hall from the Director's office. It was a busy place, reminiscent of the newsroom of a great metropolitan newspaper: ringing phones, clacking typewriters, people hunched over desks beneath a thin blue haze of cigarette smoke. (This was a year after the surgeon general released his first report on the health hazards of smoking, but so far the warnings hadn't gained much traction; almost every office desk and living room coffee table in America had an ashtray on it. As an athlete I'd never smoked, and I never did take it up—except secondhand.)

Our duties in Crime Records were many and varied. We wrote press releases about FBI successes for newspapers across the country, created speeches for FBI brass to deliver to Elks and Moose and Rotary clubs, and produced informational brochures and booklets on such topics as prevention of juvenile delinquency and the lurking threat of Communism. The division also handled contacts with Congress and with the press, monitoring major newspapers for news stories about the FBI or on subjects of interest to the FBI. Crime Records produced the highly popular Ten Most Wanted fugitives list that was printed in hundreds of newspapers and posted on the walls of thousands of US post offices. The division also published the FBI in-house publication *The Investigator* as well as the *Law Enforcement Bulletin*, a monthly magazine on crime prevention and investigative techniques that was sent out to police and sheriff's departments throughout the nation.

And then there was the job of handling the letters from the public—tens of thousands every year, many addressed to the Director personally, others addressed simply "FBI, Washington, DC." Some were over-the-transom tips about alleged crimes, everything from a coworker allegedly dipping into the cash register to wives claiming their husbands were plotting to kill them. If a federal offense was involved, we'd pass it on to the appropriate FBI investigative division; if not, and if it seemed serious, we'd forward it to the local police. Other letters were anonymous rants against the FBI, Hoover, the government, politicians, the Supreme Court, you name it. Letters threatening violence against anyone would be sent to the FBI Crime Lab to see if they could be matched to any known handwriting sample or other evidence.

But the overwhelming majority of the letters were from ordinary people. Kids wrote to ask how they could become FBI agents. Small-town businessmen wrote to thank Mr. Hoover for his stand against the Communist threat. Housewives wrote to ask what Mr. Hoover's favorite recipes were. And on and on. Every one of those thousands of letters had to be answered with a "personal" response from J. Edgar Hoover—and part of my job in Crime Records was to help answer them.

It wasn't simply a case of stuffing a mechanically signed form letter into an envelope. The Director hated form letters. So first we'd run a name check on the person to see if anything derogatory about him or her was in the FBI's extensive files—a past arrest or conviction, membership in a subversive organization, that kind of thing; it wouldn't do for the Director to send a thank-you note to a criminal or a Communist. Then we'd dictate a response that specifically applied to the letter writer.

For example, say a hardware-store owner in Bad Axe, Michigan, sent Hoover a copy of a letter to the editor that he'd written to the local paper extolling the FBI. The response would go like this: "Dear Sir: I received your letter of September 9 and want to thank you for your thoughtfulness in writing. It is certainly good of you to furnish this material to me, and you may be assured I appreciate the favorable comments you made in your letter to the newspaper. Sincerely, J. Edgar Hoover." The response would then be typed up by a Crime Records typist, and once it was approved by a supervisory special agent, it would wend its way up through several levels of bureaucracy until it reached Hoover's office for his signature—except that Hoover didn't actually sign it. As I learned later, Miss Gandy signed Hoover's name to almost all of his correspondence. If a handwriting expert had compared Hoover's actual signature and Miss Gandy's version, he would probably have declared Hoover's signature a forgery.

This process was repeated thousands of times every year, and woe to anyone who produced a letter with a misspelling or a typo or a grammatical error—or any kind of error, however small. I remember once early on I was drafting a response letter to a kid from Duquesne, Pennsylvania, who'd written to the Director saying he wanted to be an FBI agent. "Dear Jimmy: I am delighted to learn that you wish to become a Special Agent of the Federal Bureau of Investigation. . . ." But something about the word Duquesne in the return address didn't look right to me; I thought maybe the kid had misspelled it. So I asked one of the other clerks, a guy who'd been there for a while and who hailed from Pennsylvania, "Say, how do you spell Duquesne, like the town?"

"Look it up," he said brusquely.

I thought, Well, okay, if that's the way you're going to be. "Right, I'll look it up. Thanks for the help."

The guy put down the letter he was working on and looked over at me. "Hey, Letersky, I'm doing you a favor here. Don't ever take anybody's word on something like that, because if they're wrong, it'll be your neck on the chopping block."

He looked around as if to make sure no one was listening, then went on in a low voice, "You've heard about the popovers story?"

13

"Popovers? Like the pastry?"

"Yeah. This happened a while back. Some women's magazine wrote a story about the Director that said he liked to bake popovers. So we started getting letters from housewives asking for his recipe. The Director's office gave us a recipe for popovers, and whenever we got one of those letters, we'd type up the recipe and send it to them. Then one of the supes [supervisory agents] approved a letter with the recipe and sent it up the line to the Director's office. Problem was, the letter said you needed five tablespoons of baking powder."

"So?"

"So the recipe called for five teaspoons of baking powder. Someone in the Director's office caught it before it went out, but there was hell to pay."

"About popovers? You're kidding."

The guy glared at me. "Do I look like I'm kidding? The supe and everybody else who approved it got letters of censure."

"Letters of censure?"

"Yeah. Straight from the Director's office. 'You have failed to adequately perform your duties, et cetera, et cetera.' You'll find out when you become an agent—if you become an agent. One letter of censure won't kill you, but it can temporarily hold up a promotion or a salary bump. And if you get too many, you'll find yourself freezing your ass off at the field office in Butte, Montana, or maybe bounced out of the Bureau altogether. You'll see."

"Okay, thanks for the tip," I said—then looked up the proper spelling of Duquesne.

I would soon hear other stories from other clerks and some of the special agents I got to know, stories usually told in hushed tones. Special agents who got disciplinary transfers for using a Bureau car—*BuCar* in FBI-speak—to pick up their dry cleaning. Veteran agents who were threatened with termination for being just a couple pounds over the FBI's rigid weight restrictions. Field office special agents in charge (SACs) who were summarily demoted and sent "to the bricks" as ordinary street agents because one of their subordinate agents had screwed up a single piece of paperwork.

And on and on. At the time I didn't know how many of the stories were true—actually they all were—but the point was clear: there was no room for, or forgiveness of, error in Mr. Hoover's FBI. Any violation of the rules or, worse, any action that publicly "embarrassed the Bureau" would ruthlessly be punished—and because most FBI personnel weren't covered by civil service protections, there was no appeal.

Well, all this may sound overly harsh, and even silly—and in almost any other organization I guess it would have been. But the FBI's rationale was simple. This wasn't the Department of Agriculture, or the Bureau of Weights and Measures. This was the FBI, and it was engaged in serious business; people's lives and the nation's security were at stake. Even the tiniest error in a search warrant affidavit could get an important espionage case thrown out of court; even the smallest overlooked detail could allow a fugitive murderer to escape arrest and kill again. Perfection in all things large and small was the minimum acceptable standard.

In a way that ethos made sense to me. In sports I'd always strived for perfection; even if I never achieved it, that was always the goal. The way I looked at it, if you were satisfied being anything less than perfect, you'd already lost the game. Later, as I got older and started working as a field agent, I began to realize that the Bureau's relentless demand for perfection could often be self-defeating, and at times unnecessarily cruel. But at the time I was young and a little cocky and confident in my abilities. If Mr. Hoover's FBI demanded that I know the difference between tablespoons and teaspoons and the correct spelling of Duquesne, that was okay by me.

That expectation of perfection also extended to one of my other duties as an FBI civilian clerk—serving as a guide for the famous FBI tours.

Next to the White House tour, the FBI headquarters tour was the most popular such attraction for visitors to Washington, DC. In 1965 some six hundred thousand people took the FBI tour, which works out to three thousand people every business day; people lined up in droves for the hour-long tour, during which they could gaze at various exhibits depicting the fight against gangsters and spies, peer through glass windows at the boys in the Crime Lab examining evidence with microscopes, and finally watch a live-ammunition firearms demonstration by special agents in the firing range in the basement. Over the years millions of Americans took the FBI tour, and I would guess that almost all came away with a renewed appreciation for their Federal Bureau of Investigation.

So from a public relations standpoint the FBI public tours were important. But of even greater importance were what we called "congressional" or "special" tours.

For example, say the chairman of the Jasper County, Iowa, Republican Committee wrote to his Republican congressman or senator and said that he and the missus and Buddy and Sis were planning a vacation trip to Washington, DC—and it sure would be great if the family could go on the FBI headquarters tour he'd heard so much about. The congressman's staff would forward the request to us, and after a quick name check we'd make arrangements for the family to get a private guided tour—with no waiting in line, special access to the Lab and other areas, and as much time on the tour as they wanted. As a result, the local politician would owe a small favor to his congressman, and his congressman would in turn owe a small favor to the FBI—and as those small favors accumulated, the congressman would owe a big favor to the FBI, perhaps payable at appropriations time. That was the way things worked in Washington, DC, back then—as I imagine they still do.

Of course, Mr. Hoover's FBI didn't want just anybody to guide the tours. It didn't want members of the public—and certainly not the chairman of the Jasper County Republican Committee—to come away thinking that the tour guide seemed unknowledgeable or unkempt in appearance or, God forbid, that he had a pear-shaped head. So all the tour guides had to be male civilian clerks who met the standards of the ideal FBI special agent—that is, they had to be physically fit, poised, articulate, and good-looking in a rugged all-American way. And to qualify as a "special" tour guide, you had to be all that and just a little more. At the risk of sounding immodest, I guess I fit the bill, because shortly after I reported to Crime Records I was assigned as one of the special tour guides, among my other duties.

But to be a special tour guide you had to know what you were talking about when it came to the FBI—more than just the stuff you could get from a one-day orientation. So the Bureau sent me and a few other prospective special tour guides to the FBI's training facility at the Quantico Marine Corps Base for a three-week course on FBI history, organization, and lore, taught by the same special agents / instructors who taught the new-agents classes.

It was there that I first learned the story of Mr. Hoover's FBI—or at least the story as the FBI liked to tell it.

One of the surprising things I learned during the three-week course at Quantico was that the FBI story didn't start with J. Edgar Hoover. And it wasn't even called the FBI. Instead the story began with a small and notoriously corrupt federal agency called the Bureau of Investigation, or BOI.

The BOI had a checkered history. Created in 1908 to investigate antitrust cases and frauds involving public lands, the Bureau soon found itself embroiled in a series of controversies. Amid the hyper-patriotic hysteria of World War I, BOI agents investigated alleged violations of the newly passed laws that made it a federal crime to oppose the military draft or to criticize government officials; at least a thousand people were prosecuted. BOI agents also staged "slacker raids" in various American cities to scoop up men who'd failed to register for the draft; tens of thousands of American citizens were detained, most of whom either weren't subject to the draft or who simply failed to have their draft cards on them. Still later, amid the so-called Red Scare, after a series of bombings by radical groups—including one that damaged the Washington, DC, home of then attorney general A. Mitchell Palmer in 1919—BOI agents engineered the so-called Palmer Raids, a series of sweeps directed at suspected Communists and anarchists. Thousands of people were arrested without warrants and locked up, not always gently, and hundreds of foreign-born US residents were deported.

The slacker sweeps and the Palmer Raids had initially been supported by a frightened American public and by most of the American press. Only later did the public's attitude change, after a coalition of church groups, legal scholars, and liberal politicians denounced the Bureau for trampling on people's constitutional rights and acting like some kind of national secret police force. It was part of a pattern that has followed the Bureau to this day. Alarmed by a perceived threat—anti-war activists, bomb-throwing radicals, Communists, terrorists, whatever—the American public and press and politicians demand that the Bureau use whatever means necessary to combat the threat. Then later, as passions cool, the same American public and press and politicians denounce the Bureau for going too far.

The backlash against the Bureau of Investigation following the Palmer Raids didn't matter. By then, the Bureau's reputation had sunk so low that it was in imminent danger of being abolished.

The inauguration of President Warren G. Harding in 1921 ushered in an era of almost unprecedented scandal and corruption in Washington, DC—and in the Bureau. Harding appointed as his attorney general a political hack named Harry Daugherty, who quickly put the Department of Justice and the Bureau of Investigation up for sale. Soon the BOI agents' ranks were filled with political appointees who were incompetent, lazy, or blatantly corrupt, and often all three; one particularly notorious BOI special agent was a lifelong con man who'd recently gone on trial for the murder of a wealthy elderly widow and had just barely beaten the rap.

Fortunately for the Bureau, President Harding died of heart failure while on a trip to the West Coast in 1923. His successor, Calvin Coolidge, sacked Attorney General Daugherty—who narrowly escaped going to prison—and appointed in his place a towering figure of New England rectitude named Harlan Fiske Stone. Stone in turned sacked the current director of the BOI and started looking around for a new one.

Enter John Edgar Hoover.

The Quantico instructors didn't have much to tell us about Hoover's early life. Apparently the feeling was that the Director was the Director, and what he had been like as a young boy was irrelevant—if he'd ever actually been a young boy, which to many people seemed almost impossible. But a few details about the young Hoover may be helpful here. They may explain some things.

Hoover was born in 1895, in the middle-class Seward Square neighborhood near Capitol Hill in Washington, DC; he would live in Washington for the rest of his long life. His father, Dickerson Hoover, was a midlevel employee of the US Coast and Geodetic Survey—essentially the government's mapmaking agency. Basically kindly and gentle, Dickerson Hoover was plagued by bouts of what was then called melancholia, what today we'd call clinical depression. Eventually Dickerson's mental illness would cost him his job, with no government pension, and land him in an asylum—a source of great family shame in that era. As an adult, Hoover never spoke of his father.

Hoover's mother, Annie, was strong. A descendant of a moderately distinguished Swiss family, Annie Hoover was a dominating woman, a devout Lutheran, and a firm believer in the traditional values of piety, self-discipline, and hard work—values she relentlessly imposed on her youngest son. Disappointed in her husband's lackluster career and embarrassed by his debilitating illness, Annie looked to her son to rise in the world and improve the family's social standing—and to accomplish that he would have to achieve perfection in all things. Hoover had an older brother, Dickerson Jr., fifteen years his senior, and an older sister, Lillian, but Edgar, as the baby of the family was called, was the most under his mother's spell. Hoover would live with Annie in the house on Seward Square until he was forty-three years old; only her death would separate him from his mother.

Hoover's childhood nickname was Speed, and stories about how he got the name vary. But the most likely explanation was the way he talked—a rapid-fire, machine-gun style that would become familiar to generations of radio and film and television audiences. Afflicted with a stutter, young Hoover had read somewhere that the "cure" was to speak rapidly, in short staccato bursts, as if to overwhelm the stuttering impulse through the sheer volume of words. He spent countless hours practicing that method in front of a mirror, overcoming his perceived disability through hard work and willpower—overcoming it to the point that he became a leader of his high school debate team. (It was said that the only debate he ever lost was when he tried to convince his female English teacher of the fallacies of women's suffrage.) Like many a successful man who triumphed over his own weaknesses, throughout his life he'd have contempt for other men who couldn't triumph over theirs.

Slightly smaller than average as a boy, Hoover, to his lifelong regret, wasn't an athlete. The oft-told story that his trademark pugilist's squashed pug nose was the result of a sports injury wasn't true; the distinctive Hoover proboscis was actually caused by a badly infected boil that didn't properly heal. But Hoover shone in other things. In addition to being the leader of the debate team, he was valedictorian of his high school class and a captain in the school's Cadet Corps, a spit-and-polish military-style drill team that Captain Hoover demanded had to be perfect down to the last button. He wasn't particularly popular socially, especially with girls; his dance card for one school social event didn't have a single girl's name on it. But he had an amazing ability to persuade other boys—and later, other men—that he and he alone knew what to do in any situation, and to convince them to follow him. You could say he was a born leader.

At age eighteen Hoover landed a job as a messenger for the Library of Congress while attending George Washington University law school at night, where naturally he got almost all A's. After graduation in 1917, with a law degree in hand, Hoover got a job as a clerk at the Justice Department—and began his meteoric rise within the bureaucracy. During World War I he conducted investigations of suspected anti-war activists, and later he was named head of the Department's new General Intelligence Division, which collected information on suspected radicals of the Bolshevik or anarchist persuasion. He was a key player in the Palmer Raids—for which the American left would never forgive him. In 1921 he was named assistant director of the BOI, under a director named William J. Burns, the colorful and cheerfully crooked founder of the famous Burns Detective Agency. Then Harlan Stone took over as AG.

Hoover was the sort of young man that older men of authority such as Stone noticed. Hoover came to work early and stayed late, weekends included, he consistently volunteered for additional duties, he always had the necessary facts and figures on hand, he always seemed to anticipate what the boss would want next; the man was a dynamo. A bachelor, he had no distracting social or personal life anyone was aware of. He was also, within the limits of his salary, a snappy dresser: white linen suits in summer, conservative gray suits after Labor Day, the decorative pocket handkerchief always arranged just so, his slicked-back black hair always carefully trimmed. He made a good impression.

Perhaps most important, Hoover was also known as a young man of impeccable integrity; he'd grown so disgusted with the Bureau's declining standards that he was on the verge of resigning. Then, based on recommendations from various government officials—including the secretary of commerce, and future president, Herbert Hoover (no relation to J. Edgar)—Stone decided to give the young Hoover a shot as acting director of the BOI.

As related by the Quantico instructors and endlessly repeated in articles and books, the appointment happened like this:

"Young man," Stone said as Hoover reported to his office, "I want you to be acting director of the Bureau of Investigation."

"I'll take the job, Mr. Stone," Hoover responded, "on certain conditions. The Bureau must be divorced from politics and not be a catchall for political hacks. Appointments must be made on merit. Second, promotions will be made on proven ability and the Bureau will be responsible only to the attorney general."

"I wouldn't give it to you under any other conditions," Stone growled. "That's all. Good day."

Seven months later, in December 1924, Stone dropped the "acting" from Hoover's title and made him, at age twenty-nine, director of the Bureau. No Senate confirmation was required for the position. It would turn out to be the longest-standing high-level appointment in US government history.

Hoover was as good as his word to Stone. With almost breathtaking speed he began to transform the Bureau, summarily firing the deadwood and the crooks from the agents' ranks and replacing them with young men of proven integrity, most of them holding law or accounting degrees, particularly young men who in appearance and bearing made the right impression. His rules of personal behavior were strict and strictly enforced. For example, with Prohibition in effect, Hoover made it clear he'd fire any agent caught drinking alcohol, on or off duty. He himself had given up alcohol, he said—he reportedly even confiscated Mother Annie's stash of dinner sherry—and he expected his agents to do the same.

The young Director made sweeping organizational changes as well. No longer were the heads of the Bureau's various field offices allowed to run their own little fiefdoms, with their own rules and procedures. Hoover standardized the myriad forms used by all the field offices and issued the first *Manual of Investigations*, which laid out precise regulations for conducting Bureau business—and to make sure the rules were precisely followed, he set up a system of inspectors from Bureau headquarters who'd periodically descend on field offices to examine their records and paperwork, in frightening detail. Any deviation was blamed on the special agent in charge, who'd suffer accordingly. Centralized control was the key to Mr. Hoover's Bureau.

Convinced that crime investigation was as much a science as an art, Hoover also created a nascent "laboratory" at Bureau headquarters to examine evidence in criminal cases—hair and clothing fibers, handwriting on ransom-demand letters, expended gun cartridges, and so on. Starting with a borrowed microscope in a smoking lounge at headquarters, the Bureau's Crime Lab would soon become the world's foremost forensic laboratory, examining at no charge tens of thousands of pieces of evidence sent in from police departments across the country. Hoover founded the FBI National Academy to train police officers from around the country in law enforcement professionalism and modern crime-fighting techniques; he liked to call it "the West Point of law enforcement." Hoover also began consolidating the nation's fingerprint records, which had previously been scattered at various locations throughout the country, into a central location in Washington. Now if a local sheriff had a suspicious-looking guy in the county jail on a vagrancy charge, he could simply air-express a copy of the man's prints to the Bureau's Identification Division and quickly find out if the jailbird really was just a down-on-his-luck bindle stiff or if he was an escaped murderer from Texas. The Bureau's fingerprint division began with some eight hundred thousand print cards; by 1965 it had almost 200 million.

And on and on. The young Director, we were informed by the Quantico instructors, was a man of boundless energy, an organizational genius, a paragon of personal virtue and incorruptibility. We believed it—and during that early period in the Director's tenure, it happened to be true.

Strangely enough, given J. Edgar Hoover's later thirst for publicity, for the first nine years of his directorship Hoover and the Bureau maintained a low profile, investigating federal bankruptcy frauds and crimes on Indian reservations but never grabbing the headlines. The Bureau's only jurisdiction in "street crimes" involved violations of the federal Mann Act, which prohibited the transport of a female across state lines for "any other immoral purpose."

(The Quantico instructors didn't mention this, but although the Mann Act was aimed at attacking forced prostitution, the "any other immoral purpose" clause also made it a convenient tool to use against almost anyone who'd offended public decency by engaging in interstate unmarried sex. Among the prominent individuals who'd be nabbed under the Mann Act was Jack Johnson, the first African American world heavyweight boxing champion, convicted in 1913 of transporting a white woman across state lines for consensual sex. Other alleged Mann Act violators included architect Frank Lloyd Wright, Charlie Chaplin, and Chuck Berry. Not until the late 1970s would the Mann Act be strictly limited to prostitution and child sex trafficking; until then, it had technically been a violation of federal law to take your girlfriend on a romantic weekend trip to Vegas.)

So in the early days probably not one American in a thousand had ever even heard of the Bureau of Investigation, or of J. Edgar Hoover. The Bureau was so little known that when Hoover personally went to New Jersey in 1932 to offer the Bureau's assistance in the kidnapping case of Charles Lindbergh's infant son, the famed aviator refused to even speak with him, instead entrusting the investigation to the New Jersey State Police. But several years later the Bureau would play a key role in the arrest and murder trial of the son's kidnapper, Bruno Richard Hauptmann, who was later executed.

By that time, everyone in America knew about the Bureau, and J. Edgar Hoover.

The 1920s saw a wave of crime sweep across America, as bootleggers such as Al Capone employed armies of low-level criminals to deliver and protect their products—and if necessary to murder their competitors. (Hoover's Bureau wasn't charged with enforcing Prohibition laws; that was the purview of the Treasury Department's much larger Bureau of Prohibition—which, Eliot Ness and his "Untouchables" notwithstanding, was notoriously corrupt.) As Prohibition was ending, those low-level criminals turned to other lucrative pursuits, bank robbery and the kidnapping for ransom of wealthy people chief among them; in 1931 alone there were almost three hundred such kidnappings reported, and in hundreds more cases the ransoms were paid without the local cops being informed.

But in a nation demoralized and angered by the Great Depression, many Americans didn't see robbing a bank or depriving a rich man of his money as much of a crime. Hollywood played along by producing a slew of movies in which gangsters were tragic heroes forced into lives of crime by circumstances beyond their control. Edward G. Robinson in *Little Caesar* (1931), James Cagney in *The Public Enemy* (also 1931), and dozens of others—they made criminals seem glamorous. Soon real-life criminals, not just the movie ones, became household names. Clyde Barrow and Bonnie Parker (Bonnie and Clyde), George "Babyface" Nelson, Alvin "Creepy" Karpis, Kate "Ma" Barker and her criminal brood, George "Machine Gun" Kelly, Charles "Pretty Boy" Floyd, and of course John Dillinger. Newspapers across America trumpeted their exploits, and more than a few Americans applauded.

There was no applause at the Bureau of Investigation. Hoover publicly railed against the gangsters, calling them "rats," "cowards," "scum," "these filthy degenerates with their diseased women," and he loudly condemned the "sob-sister convict lovers" who made excuses for them. Hoover's assessment of the gangsters was closer to the truth than the public's; almost to a man and woman they were simply sociopathic murderers and thugs, not modern-day Robin Hoods. But unfortunately there wasn't much the Bureau could do about the gangsters. As the 1930s began, Bureau agents weren't authorized to make arrests or even carry guns, and their jurisdiction was severely limited.

That soon changed. After the shocking kidnap-murder of the Lindbergh baby, Congress made kidnapping for ransom a federal crime, punishable by death. Later laws made it a federal offense to rob a bank, transport stolen goods over state lines, cross a state line to avoid prosecution, or assault a federal officer. Bureau agents were given the power to arrest and for the first time were issued firearms—including Thompson submachine guns, the gangsters' own weapon of choice. The changes marked the birth of the real Federal Bureau of Investigation, which became the Bureau's new official name in 1935. Armed with firepower and the force of law, Hoover dispatched "flying teams" of his top agents around the country to track down the most notorious "public enemies" and arrest them if possible or kill them if necessary.

Mostly they killed them. Baby Face Nelson, shot to pieces by Bureau agents in a gun battle outside Chicago. Ma Barker and her son Fred, shot by agents in Florida and their bodies placed on public display. Pretty Boy Floyd, shot and killed by Bureau agents in a cornfield in Ohio. John Dillinger, betrayed by a Chicago madam—

the famous Woman in Red—and gunned down outside the Biograph Theater by agents led by Melvin Purvis. Machine Gun Kelly, wanted for the kidnap for ransom of a wealthy Oklahoma oilman, captured without a fight by Bureau agents in Memphis. As the agents closed in, Kelly reportedly shouted, "Don't shoot, G-men, don't shoot!" Whether he actually called them the shorthand version of *government men* isn't certain, but the press picked it up and the *G-men* name stuck forever after.

Even Hoover himself got into the act. After a congressman publicly ridiculed him for never having personally made an arrest, Hoover flew to New Orleans to capture bank robber and killer Alvin "Creepy" Karpis, whom Bureau agents had under surveillance. Hoover reportedly grabbed Karpis as he was sitting in a car and later said the gangster shook with fear "like the yellow rat he is."

The killing wasn't all a one-way street; five bureau agents died in gun battles with the gangsters. But every killing and every arrest made headlines for Hoover and his G-men. And in an abrupt about-face, Hollywood played along. After the new Hollywood Production Code of 1934 effectively banned gratuitously violent films that glorified gangsters, Hollywood started making gratuitously violent films that glorified the G-men. The most famous was *G-Men* (1935), which ironically starred the aforementioned James Cagney as a Bureau agent battling bad guys, but there were dozens of others, with titles such as *Let 'Em Have It*, *Show Them No Mercy!*, and *Public Hero Number 1*. There were G-men radio shows, G-men books, G-men comic strips. And there were countless newspaper and magazine stories about the FBI's still-young Director—he wasn't yet forty—J. Edgar Hoover.

The instructors at Quantico didn't get into this part of it, but almost overnight Hoover became much more than just a government official. On paper he may have been a $6,000-a-year (about $100,000 today) midlevel bureaucrat, but in real life he was a celebrity. Soon his distinctive bulldog face could be spotted at star-rich venues such as the Stork Club in New York or, later, the Mocambo nightclub in LA; he was photographed with stars from little Shirley

Temple to the sultry Dorothy Lamour. The Gangster Era made J. Edgar Hoover—and the FBI.

Soon enough the gangsters were replaced by new public enemies—spies, "fifth columnists," and saboteurs. In the late 1930s, with Hitler on the march in Europe, Hoover's FBI carried out President Roosevelt's orders to investigate pro-fascist groups like the German American Bund and rolled up several Nazi spy rings operating in the United States. After Pearl Harbor, the rapidly expanded Bureau—it went from just nine hundred special agents in 1940 to almost five thousand by 1944—sent hundreds of agents into South America to combat Nazi subversion efforts there, and it also intensified the hunt for spies and saboteurs on US soil. The Bureau's most sensational World War II moment came in 1942, when FBI agents tracked down and arrested eight specially trained German saboteurs who'd been landed by submarines on beaches in New York and Florida, armed with explosives and wads of cash. After a quick trial by a military tribunal, six were hanged. The Nazi saboteurs case cemented the FBI's reputation for always getting its man; only after wartime secrecy rules were lifted was it revealed that the Bureau had gotten a lucky assist when one of the saboteurs had a change of heart and turned himself in to FBI headquarters. Still, rounding up the others had been an impressive investigative effort.

The end of World War II brought a new enemy that was actually the old enemy—Soviet-style Communism. The late 1940s and 1950s obsession with Communism may seem overblown by today's standards, and maybe it was. But Communism was undeniably a threat to freedom—ask anyone who lived in East Germany or Hungary in the 1940s and '50s. The FBI cracked numerous Soviet espionage cases, from the Julius and Ethel Rosenberg spy ring that fed purloined US atomic bomb secrets to the Soviets, to the famous Hollow Nickel Case against undercover KGB colonel Rudolph Abel. The FBI's relentless pursuit of Red spies was glamorized in popular Hollywood films such as 1951's *I Was a Communist for the FBI*. Director Hoover wrote a book about Communism called *Masters of Deceit*—required reading at Quantico—that sold a quarter million copies in hardback alone. (Much of the book was actually written by Crime Records Division.)

And so on. Gangsters, saboteurs, spies—the instructors at Quantico laid out the entire panoply of FBI successes for us.

But we didn't just learn about FBI history during our three-week course. We also had to be familiar with FBI organization and policies. We had to know that in 1965 there were 6,336 FBI special agents and 8,533 FBI civilian support personnel, distributed among fifty-six field offices and more than five hundred resident agencies, as well as in the FBI's various headquarters divisions and special units. To prepare us for the Lab part of the tour, we were instructed in the basics of spectrography and hair analysis and petrography (soil analysis). We were taught the basics of firearms identification, and the instructors even took us out to the firing range to watch a class of agent trainees go through their paces—although, perhaps wisely, they didn't let us civilians shoot anything.

One other aspect of FBI culture was drummed into us from the start—personal and professional integrity. Every FBI agent had to be above reproach, we were told; that was why the Bureau's selection process was so rigorous, and why the Inspection Division so closely monitored each agent and special agent in charge for any hint of professional misconduct or personal immorality. The Bureau did it that way because it worked.

I remember once early on, during a briefing on FBI hiring and background investigation procedures, when the agent instructor, a veteran former street agent from Chicago, called me out:

"Mr. Letersky, how many special agents of the FBI have ever been charged with a crime? Go on, take a guess."

I could tell from the way he posed the question what the answer was. "None, sir?"

"Exactly! None, as in not one. Not one serving special agent of the FBI has ever been charged with a crime. That's why the Bureau spends so much time and effort finding only the best men—not only men of mental and physical strength but moral strength as well, men who can withstand the most intensive background investigation given to any US government employee. No man with a criminal record or criminal tendencies has ever been appointed as an FBI special agent, gentlemen, and no such man ever will be. Director Hoover has a saying: 'One man didn't build the FBI, but one bad man can bring it all down.' Gentlemen, when you become agents— if you become agents—do not dishonor yourself and your family and your country and your fellow agents by being that man. Is that understood?"

"Yes, sir!"

Well, as I later found out, what the instructor said was a little misleading. True, under Hoover's long tenure no currently serving FBI agent had ever been indicted for a crime. But over the decades a few agents suspected of criminal activity had quietly been bounced out of the FBI, although they weren't prosecuted to avoid embarrassing the Bureau. And given human nature, surely there were a few bad agents who just never got caught. Still, under Hoover, no FBI agent had ever been charged with robbing a bank or shaking down a mobster or murdering his wife or selling secrets to the Russians or any other major crime. At a time when most big-city police departments were periodically wracked by police corruption scandals involving dozens and dozens of bad cops, there'd never been a corruption scandal in the FBI. This amazing achievement was a credit not only to the agents themselves but also to Hoover's management system.

So even before the three weeks at Quantico was over, I was thoroughly sold on the FBI—even more so than I'd been before. Clearly, the FBI was the best-trained, most efficient, and most incorruptible investigative agency in the world, an elite organization of honest, brave, well-educated men who were dedicated to protecting America against all enemies, foreign and domestic.

By the time I got back to FBI headquarters I was starry-eyed and eager to help tell the FBI story.

"Hello, Mr. and Mrs. Smith, I'm Mr. Letersky and I'll be your guide today. Did you have a good trip in from Jasper County? . . . Good! Congressman Jones wanted us to be sure to take good care of you, so if there's anything you need, please don't hesitate to ask. And you, young lady, you must be Sis, and you must be Buddy. Are you pretty excited about seeing how the FBI works? . . . I'll bet you are! I can tell you this, if John Dillinger had ever taken an FBI tour and seen what we can do, he probably never would have tried to take on the FBI! So if you're ready, let's begin by showing you some exhibits that tell the FBI story. Right this way."

I really enjoyed doing the tours. They took me away from paper-work, gave me a chance to meet all kinds of different people—good training for a would-be FBI agent—and to be honest, I liked the admiring, wide-eyed stares of the kids. Maybe I wasn't a special agent—yet—but I still had an FBI ID card hanging from my neck, and I looked like a special agent. For them that was enough.

So I'd take them through the various displays in the Exhibits Sec-tion: maps showing the FBI field offices, photos of the World War II Nazi saboteurs, a flowchart of the conspirators in "The Crime of the Century: The Case of the A-Bomb Spies" (the Rosenberg spy case), a section on the Gangster Era of Baby Face Nelson and Creepy Kar-pis and Machine Gun Kelly. Dillinger had a large display case all to himself, containing his death mask and the straw boater hat he was wearing outside the Biograph Theater, as well as the handgun he drew before agents shot him down. There was a wall display of "No-torious Criminals Captured by the FBI," as well as wanted posters for those currently on the Bureau's Ten Most Wanted fugitives list, a grim lineup of murderers and other malefactors that was constantly being updated. I was expected to keep up on the current stats.

"In the fifteen years since the Bureau began compiling its Ten Most Wanted list," I'd tell them, "exactly 223 of the nation's most vicious and dangerous criminals have appeared on the list, and of those, 210 of them—ninety-four percent—have been captured or otherwise located. In one-third of the cases the captures were the direct result of a member of the public seeing the Ten Most Wanted fugitive's picture in a newspaper or magazine or on the wall at the post office. In fact, not too long ago one of our Ten Most Wanted fu-gitives was apprehended after someone recognized his photograph while taking this very tour! So take a good look at those faces, Buddy, but remember, all of these men have to be considered armed and dangerous. If you happen to see anyone who looks like them, or if you see any criminal activity, don't try to do anything yourself. Ask your parents to contact your local police or the FBI, okay? . . . Good! Now, the next exhibits explain the danger to our way of life posed by Communism."

(That was a true story about one of the tour takers helping to nab a fugitive. In 1961 a nurse from St. Paul, Minnesota, recognized one of the Ten Most Wanted as her neighbor, a wanted serial murderer and rapist named Hugh Bion Morse; agents captured him the next day.)

A lot of wall displays concerned the Communist threat, with titles such as "Communism: Freedom's Enemy" and "The Built-In Deficiencies of Communism" and "Tool of Communism: Communist Party USA." There were hammers and sickles and a photo of former Soviet premier Nikita Khrushchev declaring "We will bury you!" Again, today all that may seem impossibly old-fashioned, even quaint, but in 1965 most Americans took the Communist threat seriously. The nation was only a few years removed from the 1962 Cuban Missile Crisis, which brought the world to the brink of thermonuclear war, and Communist forces were on the march in Africa, Latin America, and of course Southeast Asia. In 1965 the sight of Khrushchev's gap-toothed, porcine face declaring that the Communists would bury us was still forbidding enough to scare the bejesus out of any little kid—and his parents.

After the exhibits portion of the tour I'd load the guests onto an elevator and take them up to the FBI laboratory on the seventh floor. People on the public tours would gaze through a glass wall as special agents in lab coats peered through microscopes or pored over evidentiary documents, but on the congressional tours I'd take the guests behind the glass wall and into the Lab itself. You could never do that today, lest the visitors contaminate evidence, but things were different back then—and the visitors almost always came away impressed.

"Buddy," I'd say as we walked through the Lab's Hair and Fibers

Section, "do you see that large orange photograph on the wall there? That's a picture of a human hair magnified ten thousand times! These smart fellows in the Lab can tell an awful lot from a strand of hair—they can tell a person's age, if it's a man or woman, what race they are, and a lot of other things. The FBI Lab has cracked many a case based on a single hair left behind at a crime scene."

Then it was on to the petrology and metallurgy section, documents examination unit, spectrography unit, firearms identification unit. By today's standards the FBI Lab in 1965 would seem almost primitive, but at the time it was state of the art, and by far the most respected criminal forensics lab in the world.

Then, finally, the best part of the tour, especially for the boys, and maybe their fathers, too—an earsplitting demonstration of FBI firepower in the gun range in the basement. Firearms instructors from Quantico would squeeze off a few rounds at a man-shaped silhouette paper target with a .38-caliber revolver and then unleash an entire thirty-round magazine from a Thompson submachine. (Even though the Thompson was no longer being issued to agents, it was an integral part of the FBI mystique.) And these guys never missed; every round was in the K-5 ring, the K standing for "kill." Then they'd pull the target back in and give it to the kid with the widest eyes and the most awestruck expression; I imagine hundreds of those bullet-riddled FBI paper targets are still tucked away in cardboard boxes in attics across America.

Occasional tense moments occurred on the tours. Once I was taking a family through the Exhibits Section, and this kid, a boy about ten years old, was intently gazing at a display of an old yellowed document under glass that listed a variety of archaic crimes. Suddenly the kid looks up and says to me, "Sir, what's sodomy?"

The question kind of hung there in the air. The kid's parents looked stricken, the father flush faced, the mother biting her knuckle. I tried to act as if I didn't hear the kid, but he was relentless.

"What's sodomy?" he demanded even more loudly.

I had to give him something. "It's a crime against nature. And now if we could just step this way . . ."

But the kid wasn't having it. He gave it about one second, then demanded, "What's a crime against nature?"

The would-be FBI agent must be quick on his feet. He must be poised and articulate in his dealings with the public. He who aspires to be an FBI agent must have an answer to every question, but he must never, ever say or do anything that would embarrass the Bureau.

"Son, a crime against nature is when you go into a national forest and cut down a tree without permission."

That did it. "Oh," the kid said. I don't know if my answer caused him any minor confusion later in life, but his parents certainly looked relieved, and I'd dodged a bullet—and not for the last time, either.

Not long after that I had to dodge another one—except this "bullet" was fired by my *dziazia*, my grandfather. He'd come to Washington for a visit, and I got permission to give him a private tour, and it was going well until we got to the John Dillinger exhibit. My grandfather took one look and said, "Oh, yes, that John Dillinger was a good man!"

Did you ever notice how your grandfather's voice always got louder when he was saying something embarrassing in public? That was my *dziazia*—and he had a louder-than-most voice to begin with. Then he decided to elaborate: "Yes, that Dillinger helped poor people!"

In all the world, the last place you wanted to say something nice about John Dillinger was at FBI headquarters; it was like singing the Antichrist's praises in the Vatican. A public tour group was nearby, and already some of the gawkers were staring at us.

"That's not true, *Dziazia*," I said in a low but urgent voice. "Dillinger was a criminal. Now maybe we should move along. . . ."

"No, Pawel"—*Pawel* is Polish for "Paul"—"John Dillinger helped people out. He was a good man!"

Well, I finally got him out of there. But I never did change his opinion.

Strangely enough, there was very little mention in the tour exhibits of J. Edgar Hoover. This was in keeping with what the instructors at Quantico told us was another of the Director's favorite sayings: "The FBI is a *we* organization, not a *me* organization." Except for his official FBI portrait on a wall at the start of the tour, and a display copy of *Masters of Deceit* and some of his other writings on Communism, the Director's name and image were largely missing.

Still, J. Edgar Hoover's presence was everywhere—and people were curious about him. Two questions we often heard were "Why didn't Mr. Hoover ever get married and have a family?" and "What is Director Hoover really like?"

The married question was never asked in an insinuating way, not in 1965. It was more like "Why didn't some nice gal snag that wonderful man long ago?" With the Director now aged seventy, it was also sort of moot, but the answer to the question was simple: "Why, ma'am, the Director is married"—pause for a beat, watch the confusion spread across her face, then say—"to the FBI. And the Bureau is his family." That usually sufficed.

As for the "What's he like?" question, that was a little harder. The easy answer was something like "He's a patriot, ma'am." But a more accurate answer on my part would have been "What's the Director really like? Lady, your guess is as good as mine. I've never met him. Heck, I've never even seen him."

It was true. After working for a year in Mr. Hoover's FBI, and even though the Crime Records Division was just across the hall from the Director's office, I'd never so much as laid eyes on the man, much less exchanged any words with him. Neither had almost anyone else I worked with. It wasn't the Director's style to mix with the troops, to stride through the halls and offices doling out handshakes and impromptu pep talks. He wasn't General Eisenhower, sharing smokes and jokes with the paratroopers the day before D-Day; he was more like General MacArthur—distant, imperious, ruling from his headquarters like Zeus on Mount Olympus. It was just the Director's way of doing things.

In any event, that was how I spent my first year with the FBI—answering letters, clipping newspapers, guiding tours. At six o'clock on weekdays I'd hop in my car and hit the Baltimore–Washington

Parkway for the thirty-mile drive to the law school, where from 7:00 to 10:00 p.m. I was introduced to the mysteries of torts, contracts, rules of civil procedure, constitutional law, and criminal law. Then I'd head home, get some studying in, then catch the Johnny Carson show at eleven thirty. At six the next morning I'd get up and do it all over again.

It was a pretty hectic schedule, and it didn't leave a lot of time for socializing. But I enjoyed my work at Bureau headquarters—and when you're young, who needs sleep?

It would probably have continued that way for the next two years, except that one Friday afternoon in August 1966, my section chief, a former street agent now working his way up through the FBI management bureaucracy, called me into his small office and told me to sit down. He was a good guy, but he had a wary, nervous look that I'd later recognize in a lot of ambitious agents in their midcareers; he had too much time in the Bureau to give it up, but he was too far away from retirement to relax.

"Letersky," he said, "some of the assistant directors have been talking about you."

I'd been with the FBI long enough to know that the only reasonable response to such a statement was a silent *Uh-oh*. Out loud I just said, "Sir?"

"The Director needs a new clerk on his personal office staff. Some of the assistant directors talked it over, and they've decided you're it. They seem to think you have a good work ethic, you're quick on your feet, and you look the part. Someone from the Director's office will be over shortly to brief you on your duties. In case you're wondering, this is not a promotion; your grade and step will remain the same. This is just a reassignment of your duties. You start Monday."

"Just like that, sir?"

"Yeah, just like that. And let me make this clear. I don't know how much you've heard about the Director, but he's a lion, Letersky—a lion, and when the lion roars, you jump. Do not—repeat, do not—screw up. If you do, it will reflect badly on the assistant directors who recommended you, and then it will reflect badly on the number one men who didn't advise the assistant directors not to recommend you, and then it will reflect badly on me just for being your supervisor—and finally it will reflect worst of all on you, and your Bureau career will be over before it even begins. Have you got that?"

"Got it, sir."

Maybe something about me reminded him of himself in his younger, less nervous days. Because suddenly his tone softened, and he became sort of big-brotherly.

"Look, Paul, this could be good for you—very good. You'll be working directly for the Boss, and if you do a good job, and the Director likes you, you'll be able to write your own ticket in this organization. You know what a rabbi is?"

I knew he wasn't referring to a Jewish religious leader. It was agent and cop slang. "Yes. A rabbi is someone high up in the Bureau or a police department who watches out for you, helps your career along."

"Right. And there's no better rabbi in the Bureau than the Director. It's just that you'll need to be careful and keep your eyes open." He paused, searching for the right words. "Let me put it this way: It can be nice and warm the closer you are to the campfire. But if the wind suddenly shifts, you can get burned. Do you understand what I'm saying?"

Well, I suppose I could have tried to weasel out of it. But the honest truth is that after I'd gotten over my initial surprise, I was pleased to have been selected—no, more than pleased, I was honored. Even though the new job didn't come with a bump in rank or pay, it felt like a promotion—and I was ambitious enough to welcome anything that could boost my nascent FBI career. As for the section chief's warnings, I wasn't worried. I was too young and too confident to be afraid of anything, not even the legendary Director of the Federal Bureau of Investigation. I wouldn't screw up.

"Yes, sir," I said, "I understand. And thank you. I'll do my very best."

"See that you do," he said, stern once again.

I stood up and was heading for the door when he called after me.
"Oh, and one other thing. Watch out for the Director's secretary,
Miss Gandy. She may seem like a nice little old lady, but deep down
she's a tigress."

And that was that. My days as a tour guide and a newspaper clip-
per for the FBI were over. A woman from the Director's office—not
Miss Gandy—came over and generally explained my duties: screening the Director's calls, dealing with visitors, delivering paperwork,
running errands. Basically I'd do whatever the Director and Miss
Gandy told me to do. I packed up my few personal items and said
goodbye to the other civilian clerks, some of whom seemed envious,
while others looked at me as if I were on the way to my own funeral.

Thus amid a mix of metaphors, I prepared myself for life close
to a warm but dangerously fickle campfire, in the den of the tigress,
and in the lion's lair.

CHAPTER 2

The Director

I faced the tigress first. Despite what I'd been told by my section chief, she was hardly an example of the formidable female of the species *Panthera tigris*.

"Why, you must be Mr. Letersky," Miss Gandy said, beaming a smile. "Welcome to the Director's staff. We've heard such good things about you." She chuckled. "And I suppose you've heard more than a few things about us!"

"Thank you, Miss Gandy, it's a pleasure to be here." Naturally I ignored the part about things I might have heard about the Director's office staff.

Helen Gandy was sixty-nine years old at the time, although she looked younger. A short, distinguished-looking woman, she wore a gray buttoned-to-the-neck dress; her silver hair was curled and permed in a style that had been popular in the 1950s. Although she'd been born and raised in New Jersey, fifty years in Washington had left her with the soft, slightly Southern accent of a native-born Washingtonian. I later found out she was a GS-17 level employee, the highest-ranking—and at $36,000 annually in her later years, the highest-paid—female in the entire forty-thousand-employee Justice Department.

"Are you nervous?" she asked.

"No," I lied. Despite my brave thoughts when my section chief told me about my new assignment, over the weekend I'd had a chance to think about it—and I was nervous as hell. The night before, I'd practiced my responses to questions the Director might ask me, and this morning I'd been careful to bring a clean extra handkerchief with me in case I got an attack of sweaty palms. One of the many, many stories I didn't admit I'd heard was about the Director's aversion to sweaty handshakes. It was said that many an FBI career had been derailed by a clammy mitt. I was not by nature a sweaty-palm kind of guy, but still . . .

"There's no need to be nervous." Miss Gandy saw right through me. "The assistant directors who recommended you said you work well under pressure. You'll have no problems here. The Director will see you at ten a.m. Just be yourself and it'll be fine. Now let me show you your desk."

Actually, I'd already seen my desk—and more. On the theory that it's always wise for the visitors to check out the home team's field before the game, that morning I'd come into the Director's office suite early, before anyone else arrived, and checked out the field. There was a rather large reception room where a stream of visitors would wait to see the Director, the walls adorned with plaques, old photographs, and other FBI memorabilia; adjacent to the reception room were a couple of small offices for the Director's staff, including me. My desk, I'd been instructed, was in the "telephone room"; one of the phones, an ugly big green thing with a red bulb on top, was a direct line into Mr. Hoover's private office. Down a short hallway was Miss Gandy's office, one wall lined with locked green four-drawer filing cabinets. (Although I didn't know it then, these were where the much-feared "secret files" were kept.) Past that a door opened to a large conference room with a fifteen-foot conference table, its walls also covered with plaques and photos and memorabilia, and a row of locked filing cabinets. At the far end of the conference room was a replica of the Director's desk, flanked by an American flag and an FBI flag, and a large oval rug in front of the desk bore the FBI seal with the Bureau's motto: Fidelity, Bravery, Integrity. That was where Mr. Hoover would pose for photographs with visitors.

I even had the temerity to open the oak double doors behind the ceremonial desk and take a peek at the Director's private inner office. It featured the Director's actual working desk—a gleaming mahogany executive desk mounted on a four-inch-high dais—and full-length, windowed double doors that opened onto a small balcony overlooking Pennsylvania Avenue and toward the Capitol. There were also doors that opened onto a small half kitchen and a half bathroom, and another door to a short hallway that led to the office of Associate Director Clyde Tolson. I carefully noted the position of all the doors. I'd heard the story about one hapless visiting special agent in charge who was so flustered after a meeting with the Director that he'd tried to leave through the bathroom door; his FBI career had not prospered.

At 10:00 a.m. sharp I was at my new desk when the green phone rang—or, rather, erupted. It was the loudest phone I'd ever heard, and the red bulb on the top flashed like a nuclear attack warning. There was only one person it could be.

"Yes, Mr. Hoover?"

What came back was a growl: "Mr. Letersky, come to my office!" Click!

It was a long walk—or at least it seemed to be. Down the hall, past Miss Gandy's desk—she gave me an encouraging smile—through the conference room, a last quick palm check—perfectly dry!—and then past the open double doors and into the Director's inner office.

And there he stood, in front of his desk.

J. Edgar Hoover.

During my long career I would meet any number of famous people, from movie stars to politicians to titans of industry, people who seemed to exude glamour or power or wealth when they appeared on a film or television screen—and then when I'd see them in person, they seemed smaller somehow, more ordinary, more human. Not this man. Of course, he looked old to me, older than I'd expected, his face rounder and longer in the jowls, but that didn't mean much. When you're in your early twenties, any man over forty looks old, and any man over seventy might as well be Methuselah's big brother. But despite his age he stood ramrod straight, head up, shoulders back. He wasn't tall—officially five-ten, in reality a little less—but he seemed bigger. Despite the usual description of him, he didn't look like a bulldog to me. Instead, as my section chief had said, he looked leonine. He radiated authority, and power.

Suddenly I was conscious of my suit. The Director wore an impeccably tailored navy blue suit with a gray Italian silk tie and a blindingly white shirt with French cuffs and gold cuff links; the creases on his trousers looked sharp enough to draw blood. I wore navy blue, too, but the resemblance ended there. He was tailored Brooks Brothers, I was off-the-rack Robert Hall—and compared with his, my trousers looked as if I'd slept in them. But it was too late to worry about that. I stepped forward and extended my still-dry hand.

Firm handshake, but not the bone-crushing sort that some men use to intimidate. Penetrating stare from the dark brown eyes—not hostile, not friendly either, but coldly analytical. Then the staccato rush of words.

"Mr. Letersky, I want to welcome you to my staff. You should have been briefed as to your duties, so there is no need to waste our time reviewing your responsibilities. Just know one thing: in my office I allow no margin for error. Is that understood?"

I thought about the popovers-recipe story. "Yes, sir."

"Good. That is all. Now go to work."

He turned away, and I backed up a few steps and then turned around and successfully made it out through the correct door.

As I passed by Miss Gandy's desk, she called out to me, "Well, how'd it go?"

I made a motion as if I were wiping sweat off my brow. "It was"— I searched for the right word—"brief."

Miss Gandy laughed. "Oh, yes, get used to it. That's just the way the Director is. He's very busy, and sometimes it may seem that he's being curt with you, but you mustn't take it personally. You'll come to find that the Director is really a very kind and caring and considerate man."

Kind? Caring? Considerate? That guy? Of course I didn't say that.

Again Miss Gandy saw through me. "You'll see. Now, have you met the rest of the staff?"

I hadn't, but I soon would. The Director's personal staff was surprisingly small. There was Miss Gandy, and her assistant, Erma Metcalf, a quiet, pleasant older woman. I shared the telephone room with John Cox, like me a civilian clerk who was planning to apply for special agent training, and in an adjacent office was Nancy Mooney, a bubbly blond woman in her early forties who was the Director's stenographer. John and Nancy would become two of my closest friends, even though John, a Washington native, was a Redskins fan who scorned my beloved New York Giants.

I also got to know Sam Noisette, the office's official greeter and a kind of semi-valet for the Director. A husky African American man in his sixties, Sam had been with Hoover for almost forty years. At one point, the Director had named him an FBI special agent but it was an honorary kind of appointment; Sam never went through agent's training and had never wanted to. Sam's job was to greet visitors in the reception room, to man the kitchen in the Director's private office, and generally to do whatever Hoover needed doing. Sam was locally famous in Washington for his oil paintings, primarily landscapes, and although he was completely self-taught, they were quite good. Every year he'd hold a one-man art show at the YMCA; FBI brass were encouraged to attend.

Annie Fields was another member of the Director's staff, although not his office staff. Annie was the live-in cook and housekeeper at Hoover's home on Thirtieth Place in Northwest Washington, a job she'd had for the past thirty years. A dignified, reserved black woman in her fifties, Annie wasn't intimidated by anyone—the Director included. She knew how to handle him.

Another important member of the Director's staff was Jimmy Crawford, Hoover's chauffeur for almost thirty years, who drove the Director and Clyde Tolson around Washington, DC, in a specially built, bulletproof black Cadillac—one of four such vehicles that were stashed around the country for Hoover's use. A handsome, soft-spoken African American, Jimmy had gone through FBI special agent training in the 1940s—sadly, it was segregated training—and in earlier times many African American press outlets had referred to him as J. Edgar Hoover's "bodyguard." In those days it was a point of community pride that the country's top cop depended on a black man to protect him.

But Jimmy never called himself Hoover's bodyguard, and he never wore a badge or carried a gun—and for that matter, neither did Hoover or Tolson. Later critics would suggest that Hoover was a physical coward, deathly afraid of assassination, but as far as I could tell, that wasn't true. Except for the bulletproof Cadillacs—which I think were mostly just status symbols—and an FBI-installed burglar alarm system in his house, Hoover was remarkably casual about his personal security. On a few occasions FBI agents had staked out Hoover's house in response to immediate credible threats against him, and sometimes on his trips outside Washington the local FBI special agent in charge would assign agents to surreptitiously follow Hoover's car in case anything happened—even though there'd be hell to pay if Hoover found out about it. But unlike more recent FBI directors, Hoover never had a permanent FBI bodyguard or security detail; he said he found bodyguards "irksome." It would have been easy for assassins to bust into his house—for years his home address had been listed in the publicly available *Congressional Directory*—or to bump him off during one of his frequent walks around the neighborhood. Maybe Hoover thought fate couldn't be cheated, whatever it had in store—or maybe he just assumed that no assassin would ever have the temerity to bust a cap into God.

You may have noticed that Hoover's valet, housekeeper, and driver were all African American, which led some critics to charge that the FBI hired blacks only for menial jobs—not that Sam or Annie or Jimmy ever described their jobs as menial, at least not to me. While the Bureau had had a handful of black agents in its history, before the early 1960s the ranks of special agents had been virtually all-white, and by 1966 the FBI still had only a few dozen blacks in a total force of sixty-five hundred agents. Hoover publicly claimed the low number was because African Americans who met the basic requirements—college degree, law degree, etc.—didn't want to become FBI agents, preferring more lucrative jobs in the private sector. Maybe that was partly true; even today, despite aggressive outreach programs, only about 5 percent of FBI special agents are black, whereas about 13 percent of the total US workforce is black. But until pressured into it by the Kennedy administration, Hoover's FBI clearly didn't go out of its way to hire African American agents.

As for Hoover himself, by today's standards I suppose he was a racist. Remember, the Washington, DC, that Hoover grew up in was a Southern city, situated below the Mason-Dixon Line, by law and practice a largely segregated city—and Hoover was a product of that time and place. He certainly took a paternalistic view toward "Negroes"—as African Americans were then called, including by blacks themselves—but I don't think it's fair to say that he hated black people as a group. In the time I worked for him I never once heard him use the word *nigger* or any other racial slur, and even some of his worst critics have never claimed that he used such words. Sure, he could work up a red-hot hatred for individual black people, such as Martin Luther King—more on that later—and he could be hard on the black people who worked for him. But he hated white people who crossed him with an equal passion, and he was just as hard on the white people who worked for him as he was on anybody else. Believe me, I know.

During my first weeks of working for the Director I also got to know—or at least observe—the men around him.

Clyde Tolson was the FBI associate director, the number two man in the Bureau. A former small-town kid from Missouri who had a law degree from George Washington University, Tolson joined the Bureau in 1928 and in just two years was promoted to the number two slot, where he stayed forever after. He was usually described as Hoover's right-hand man and closest friend, but "friend" doesn't quite encompass it. It was more like he was Hoover's *alter ego*—the phrase in Latin means the "other I"—the one man who could authoritatively predict what Hoover's attitude would be on any issue, and perhaps the only man that Hoover ever fully and completely trusted.

For more than thirty years the two men had been virtually inseparable. Every morning Jimmy Crawford drove them to the Justice Department building, first picking up the Director at his home and then picking up Tolson at his bachelor apartment on Massachusetts Avenue. They had lunch together every day, usually at the Rib Room in the Mayflower Hotel, and dinner together every night at Harvey's Restaurant or Hoover's residence. They shared hotel suites during Hoover's annual vacations in California and Florida, and during their younger days they'd partied together at the Stork Club and other in-spots in New York City. That door in the Director's inner office that opened into Tolson's office made Tolson the only person in the FBI who could get to the Director without first going through Miss Gandy.

Tolson was no mere flunky. An athletic-looking man with a prominent chin and a Dick Tracy jawline, in prior years Tolson had been a key player in every facet of the Bureau's operations. Some people even said that Tolson was the real brains behind the FBI organization, but of course they never said that to Hoover. It was Tolson who meted out the draconian discipline that Hoover demanded, and most FBI agents were convinced that Tolson actively enjoyed it; after the Director, he'd easily been the most feared man in the Bureau.

There was a story about Tolson's penchant for punishments. When an FBI agent or a civilian employee was fired, it could be done with or without "prejudice." A firing "with prejudice" meant the employee was guilty of serious incompetence or misconduct, which would make it almost impossible for the person to get another government job and could even hurt his or her chances in the civilian job market; it was sort of like a dishonorable discharge from the military. The story is that Tolson came into Hoover's office one day looking depressed, and Hoover said, "Clyde, you don't look so good. Pick somebody out and fire him, it will make you feel better." And Tolson immediately brightened and said, "With prejudice?"

Well, when it comes to the Director, the story misses the mark. Hoover would fire people in an instant, but always for a good reason, or at least what he thought was a good reason; he never fired or punished people just for sport. But with Tolson, the story almost rings true.

Although Tolson's time as a street agent had been brief, like Hoover he hadn't lacked for physical courage. Armed with a machine gun, Tolson had participated in a highly publicized and controversial shoot-out with a gangster named Harry Brunette in New York City in 1936, after which Hoover gave him the nickname Killer, even though no one had actually been killed in the incident. Another nickname Hoover had for Tolson was Junior.

But now, at age sixty-six, Tolson's Junior and Killer days were long behind him. A couple years earlier he'd suffered a stroke, the first of a series of strokes and heart attacks he'd endure in the coming years. His hair had gone to gray, his jowls sagged, and when he walked, his left leg dragged on the floor. He still had his occasional good days, but for the most part he was a wraith, a specter, a gray old man lurking in the shadows. He was still feared, but not the way he had been. Most people just tried to avoid him.

Which I tried to do also, not always successfully. I regularly had to deliver memos or other documents to Tolson's elderly secretary, Dottie Skillman—she was handling most of Tolson's routine duties by this time—and on a few occasions Tolson shuffled out of his private office while I was there. I'd always give him the required "Good morning, Mr. Tolson," and he'd look in my direction—except that he wouldn't really look at me. It was as if he couldn't even see me. Then he'd wordlessly turn and shuffle back into his office. In all the time I worked for the Director, I never once heard Tolson's voice.

And there was something else about Clyde Tolson: for reasons I'd learn about later, Miss Gandy detested him—and she always had.

One thing that Tolson had never aspired to do was to replace his boss, Hoover, as FBI director; even if he hadn't suffered health problems, Tolson was the eternal number two man, content to remain in the background. That wasn't so with some of the other FBI top brass, more than a few of whom looked into the bathroom mirror in the morning and saw a future FBI director staring back at them.

One was Cartha "Deke" DeLoach, a smooth-talking Georgian in his midforties who'd spent almost his entire career at FBI headquarters. A former assistant director in charge of the Crime Records Division—he'd been my boss, although aside from "Good morning" a few times we'd never spoken—DeLoach served as the Director's personal liaison to the White House. As such, DeLoach had developed a close relationship with President Johnson—perhaps too close for Hoover's liking—and DeLoach fully expected Johnson to appoint him director if and when the Old Man ever retired.

Another aspirant was W. Mark Felt, at the time the head of the Inspection Division, the Goon Squad, whose inspectors would descend on the various field offices in search of violations of FBI rules and issue punishments accordingly. He'd replaced Tolson as the second-most-feared man in the Bureau. A tall, silver-haired, movie-star-handsome man in his midfifties, Felt was likable enough in some ways, but he was also a notorious sycophant and an insatiable schemer. Many people who knew him weren't surprised to learn years later that Felt was the Watergate leaker known as Deep Throat.

Still another who saw a future FBI director in the mirror was William C. Sullivan, assistant director in charge of the Domestic Intelligence Division. Short and somewhat rumpled in appearance, Sullivan—known behind his back as Crazy Billy—was the secret architect of some of the Bureau's most controversial activities. He was as obsequious with the Director as all the others, but Sullivan would soon develop a hatred for Hoover that bordered on the pathological—and he'd become the source of many of the most vicious stories about the Director.

A few others also had the directorship bug. As usual with rivals, most quietly despised all the others, and they were constantly on the lookout for any signs of weakness or chinks in their competitors' armor. It was almost unbelievable the lengths to which they'd go to preserve what they saw as their proper place in the pecking order.

For example, the policy was that all ten assistant directors had to be kept informed of the Director's whereabouts in case something important came up and they had to reach him. It didn't make much sense to me—if the ADs needed to find him, all they had to do was call our office—but that was the rule. So every morning after he picked up the Director and Tolson, Jimmy would call me on the Cadillac's radiophone and tell me, "He's on the way in." I then had to call and pass on this vital information to each of the assistant directors. Then, after Jimmy parked the car in the reserved spot in the basement next to the elevators, he'd call and tell me, "He's on his way up," and I'd have to call all the ADs again and tell them, "He's in the building." When the Director and Tolson left for lunch, it was "He's left the building—lunch"; then "He's back in the building" when they returned. He's in the building, he's left the building, he's in the building, he's left the building—it went on all day long until Hoover and Tolson finally left at the end of the working day, which meant that the ADs could go home as well. None of the top brass ever left the building before the Director—not if they wanted to remain among the top brass.

Mind you, these "He's in the building" calls didn't go to the assistant directors' secretaries. They went straight to the ADs themselves. Most of the time my report would be greeted by a grunt and a click!—and sometimes I didn't even get the grunt. But occasionally the AD would demand to know, "Am I the first to be notified?"

"Well, sir, uh . . ."

"I want to be the first to be notified when the Director is in the building, is that clear?"

"Yes, sir."

The problem was that three or four wanted to be the first to be notified. So I quickly learned that when they asked, the only smart thing to do was to say, "Yes, sir, Mr. Felt, you're my very first call!"

Well, I guess to claw your way up to assistant director in the FBI you had to master the ways of the bureaucracy and be attuned to even the smallest of status competitions. Still, these were grown men we're talking about. What possible difference did it make if they were the second or the fifth or the tenth one to be told that the Director had left for lunch?

Of course, I had to get along with those guys. But Miss Gandy did not. Whenever she dealt with the more ambitious FBI top brass, the tigress's claws came out.

They shamelessly sucked up to her. When they'd come in and ask to see the Director, they'd bombard her with flattery or, in a few cases, even flowers or boxes of candy, which she happily accepted. Then she'd pick up the phone to the Director's inner office and say, "Mr. Hoover, Mr. DeLoach [or one of the others] would like to see you. . . . Yes, I will ask him to wait." Outwardly it was all very nice, very cordial, but something in the way she said their names—Mr. *DeLoach*, Mr. *Felt*—was almost a hiss. It spoke volumes.

Sometimes she could be positively cruel, toying with her victims. One of the ambitious ADs would come in and Miss Gandy would smile sweetly and say, "Mr. Felt [or whomever], don't you think you should apologize to the Director?"

The AD, flustered, would say, "Apologize? For what? What did I do?"

Miss Gandy would take on a disappointed, reproving look. "Well, if you don't know already . . ." Then she'd clam up like the Sphinx. The poor ADs would spend the rest of the day trying to figure out what they'd done wrong, and what to do about it. Often the result would be a generic apology note—"Dear Boss: I apologize if I've done anything to disappoint you. . . ."—that would leave Hoover puzzled and Miss Gandy chuckling.

It was funny in a way. These men, supposedly the most powerful men in the Bureau, were being stymied and terrorized by someone who appeared to be just a sweet little old lady. At times I almost felt sorry for them.

"Miss Gandy, I know these guys are hard to take, but aren't you being a little tough on them?" I teased her one day. "Especially when they give you those nice gifts?"

She laughed. "Why turn down perfectly good flowers and sweets? Here, have some candy. Besides, they deserve it. They may think they're sitting in the Director's chair already, but it's not going to happen." Miss Gandy actually sneered. "One of them? Replace him? Never."

Miss Gandy had it right. For all the backstabbing and backbiting, for all the scheming and posturing, none of the men around Hoover would ever fill his shoes.

And neither would anyone else.

One of my duties was to screen the outside calls that came in for the Director—and they were endless. Senators and congressmen, big-city police chiefs, business leaders, prominent clergymen, FBI field agents or special agents in charge who were in town and wanted to set up a personal meeting—sometimes it seemed as if everyone in America wanted a piece of the Director's time. My job was to help decide who got it.

Sometimes it was an easy decision. Not a day went by that I wouldn't field at least one or two calls from lunatics and drunks who'd somehow managed to get past the main switchboard operators. They wanted to tell the Director that they were receiving Soviet propaganda radio transmissions through the metal fillings in their teeth, or that they'd solved the Kennedy assassination—or, rather, "sholved the Ken'dy ashashinashun." Sometimes I'd foist the calls off on the duty agents, but if I wasn't too busy, I'd listen to their stories. FBI policy was to always be polite and professional, and I tried to be: "About those radio transmissions, ma'am, have you considered consulting a dentist?" I even got to know some of the "repeaters," a few of whom would recite poems or sing songs they'd written about the Director—and in a couple of cases, songs and poems they'd written about me. My usual practice was that, once the singing started, I'd quietly put them on hold for as long as I thought the song would last, then I'd come back on and say, "Thank you, Mr. Smith, that was lovely, and I'll be sure to tell the Director." Then I'd log the call on a three-by-five index card with the notation "mental" and file it with the others in the wooden "nut box" on my desk. It was a pretty big box.

Other, more "normal" callers required a bit more discretion.

For example, if it was a field agent in town for the periodically required "in-service training" at Quantico who wanted to discuss a personal problem with the Director, I'd take down the information on a dark pink five-by-seven card and leave it with a stack of other requests on the Director's desk for him to review; seldom were such requests from field agents turned down. The process was the same with other calls from midlevel government officials or other functionaries: take down the information and pass it on to the Director. But it was different if the caller was, say, a ranking member of Congress or someone on the Director's Special Correspondents List of prominent figures—politicians, business leaders, movie stars, and other celebrities—with whom the Director was on friendly terms. Then I'd put them on hold and call the Director on the direct line.

"Sir, Congressman Jones of the Appropriations Committee would like a word with you."

"Is it him personally, or his secretary?"

"Personally, sir."

"Very well, put him through." Or more often he'd say, "Very well, put him on hold for two minutes and then put him through." The Director knew how to play the status game as well as anyone else.

There were, however, two rather prominent Americans whom I was under standing orders never to put through to the Director.

One was the gossip columnist and broadcaster Walter Winchell.

And the other was the attorney general of the United States.

Winchell was a sad case. Today he's barely even remembered, but in the 1930s and '40s and '50s he was easily the most influential newsman in America. His syndicated newspaper column—a mix of celebrity gossip, news, and political commentary—was read by some 50 million people worldwide every day, and every Sunday night 20 million would tune in to his radio show with its famous opening line, delivered in Winchell's distinctive raspy, punchy style: "Good evening, Mr. and Mrs. America, from border to border and coast to coast and all the ships at sea! Let's go to press!"

Winchell was one of the first national columnists to jump on the

G-man bandwagon in the Gangster Era, heaping praise on the Director and defending him if attacked. For example, after New York officials charged that Hoover and the FBI had been grandstanding in the aforementioned 1936 shootout with gangster Harry Brunette, 20 million Americans heard Winchell say, "Take this from one who knows how courageous the G-men are! They are man hunters, not glory hunters!"

In 1939 Winchell and Hoover even jointly arranged the sensational surrender of the notorious New York hit man Louis "Lepke" Buchalter, founder of the contract-killer group known as Murder, Inc., which was suspected of committing hundreds of murders for hire on behalf of various New York crime families. Buchalter had been on the run from state murder charges for two years when Winchell announced on his Sunday broadcast, "Attention public enemy number one, Louis 'Lepke' Buchalter! I am authorized by J. Edgar Hoover of the Federal Bureau of Investigation to guarantee you safe delivery to the FBI if you surrender!" Preferring federal justice to state justice, Buchalter, after a few miscues, did surrender to Hoover and Winchell on a dark New York street, generating front-page headlines across the country. (Hoover was later forced to turn Buchalter over to state authorities, who convicted him and had him executed at Sing Sing.)

Winchell was also a loudly supportive voice in the anti-Communist crusades of the 1950s, sprinkling his columns and broadcasts with items like this one: "Drop a thank-you note to J. Edgar Hoover's FBI. Their vigilance is one of this democracy's mightiest weapons. Subversives who have crowed that our home front would be a soft touch for their stiletto-ing have always had their arrogance shoved down their gullets—thanks to the G-men. There is never a truce in the FBI's battle against crime. And the G-men have never lost a war."

Of course, the Director loved it, and he and Winchell became fast friends, with Hoover and Tolson often being seen at Winchell's table No. 50 in the Cub Room at the Stork Club—a magnet for celebrities from every field. The personal correspondence between

Winchell and Hoover over the years ran to hundreds of pages—Winchell was "Walter," and unlike most others, Winchell always called Hoover "John." Although Hoover always denied it, he occasionally slipped the columnist bits of gossip and news that were useful to the Bureau. Hoover—or, rather, someone in the Crime Records Division—even wrote occasional guest columns for Winchell when he was on vacation.

But by the mid-1960s Winchell's career was finished—and so was his friendship with the Director. As a broadcaster Winchell hadn't survived the switch from radio to TV—he didn't have the right look and style for television—and as his columns became increasingly vitriolic and strident, one newspaper after another dropped him from their pages. His last significant gig was doing the off-camera voice-overs for *The Untouchables* TV show—which is how I remembered him.

When I first started in the Director's office, the calls came in regularly—"Hey, kid! This is Walter Winchell! Is the Man in?" Sometimes Hoover would take the call, sometimes not. When Winchell couldn't get through to the Director, Winchell would often regale me with stories about himself and the Director and old-time movie stars and politicians and gangsters; I must have heard the Lepke Buchalter story a dozen times. Mr. Winchell always sounded as if he'd enjoyed a couple or six adult beverages before making his calls, and at times he bordered on the indiscreet—which I suppose wasn't surprising for a gossip columnist.

"Hey, kid, you heard about your boss and Dorothy Lamour, right? This is back in the thirties. Oh, yeah, he and Dottie were an item. A big item! But then she married that band leader. And Ginger Rogers? Not Ginger, but her mom, Lela? Yeah, she and John had a thing going, too. I remember one time . . ."

I never knew quite how to respond. It was difficult for me to imagine the Old Man in the physical embrace of anyone, much less the sultry, sarong-wearing star of the old Bob Hope–Bing Crosby *Road* pictures. I wasn't sure if under FBI rules I was even allowed to imagine such a thing. But later I'd learn that the reports of the close friendships—romances?—with Miss Lamour and Mrs. Rogers were true.

As time went on, the Director was less and less inclined to take Winchell's calls. Finally, one day I heard the unmistakable voice on the line—"Hey, kid! Is the Man in?"—and I put him on hold and called the Director.

"Sir, Mr. Winchell is on the line and wishes to speak with you."

"Is he drunk again?"

I had to tell the truth. "He sounds to be, sir."

"Tell him I'm out of the office and you don't know when I'll return. And from now on you will always tell him I'm out of the office. Don't bother me with it again. Is that clear?"

And that was that for Walter Winchell. He must have realized that his old friend was ducking him, but he kept calling, and every time I'd have to say, "I'm sorry, Mr. Winchell, but the Director is out. Would you like to leave a message?"

"Nah, that's all right, kid, just tell him I called. Say, did I ever tell you about the time we nabbed Lepke Buchalter?"

When he died five years later, Walter Winchell was a virtual recluse, living alone in a room in the increasingly seedy Ambassador Hotel in LA. As far as I know, the Director, after instructing me to cease putting through Winchell's calls, never spoke to "Walter" again.

It was one thing to duck calls from an old gossip columnist. It was another thing altogether when the man on the other end of the line was the serving US attorney general—in this case, a forty-year-old lawyer named Ramsey Clark.

Clark, an assistant attorney general in the Kennedy New Frontier years, was the son of Tom Clark, President Truman's attorney general and later a Supreme Court justice—which is why Ramsey Clark was appointed AG in the first place. Despite his successful efforts to get the Voting Rights and Civil Rights acts through Congress, President Johnson still had, with some people, the taint of a Southern segregationist about him. So in 1967 Johnson's pal Justice Tom Clark offered to help Johnson improve that image. He, Clark, would retire from the court so that Johnson could appoint famed civil rights attorney and US solicitor general Thurgood Marshall to be the first African American ever to serve on the court. In return, Johnson would name Clark's son, Ramsay, to follow in his father's footsteps as attorney general. Johnson gratefully agreed.

Although the Director had been friends with Ramsey Clark's father, that affection didn't extend to the son. It's hard to imagine two men who were more different. Soft-spoken, mild-mannered, Clark was an intellectual type who was deeply committed to the civil rights movement and who firmly believed that the root cause of crime wasn't moral degeneracy but rather the social and financial inequities of American society. Worse, Clark naively thought that he could bring the Director and the Bureau under closer control; Clark even went so far as to suggest that LBJ appoint a high-level administrator to supervise the FBI and other intelligence agencies. (When Hoover got wind of the proposal and protested to LBJ, Johnson assured him, "Now, Edgar, ain't nobody gonna be supervisin' ya." The idea was dropped.)

Naturally, the Director detested Clark, and he made no secret of it. Although he was proper and correct during their occasional face-to-face meetings and in his official correspondence, in private Hoover referred to Clark as "that hippie," calling him a "jellyfish" and a "softie" and, for some reason, "the Bull Butterfly." And I frequently got caught in the middle. The AG's secretary, or sometimes the attorney general himself, would call and ask for the Director, and I'd have to go through the routine.

"Sir, the attorney general is on the line and wishes to speak with you."

"Tell the Bull Butterfly I'm on the Hill," the Director would growl, meaning he was testifying before Congress on Capitol Hill. Or "Tell the jellyfish I'm out!" Or "He's got a yellow belly and a jelly spine! Tell him I'm not here!"

Then I'd have to get back on the line with the AG, hoping that I wouldn't slip up and say something like "I'm sorry, Mr. Attorney Jellyfish, the Director isn't in." Finally the Director instructed me to make up a reason for his unavailability whenever the attorney general called.

Clark was always nice about it; as I said, he was a mild-mannered sort. And unlike Walter Winchell, he soon got the message. After a while the calls stopped, and the Director and Clark communicated almost solely through memos or scheduled meetings.

Well, as a budding FBI man, I was on the Director's side. It was important to protect the Bureau from interference by outside "political forces," and as presidential appointees, attorneys general were by definition political. But I was also a law student, immersed in the study of constitutional law and the orderly process of law enforcement. I wondered if it was proper for the head of any Justice Department division, even Hoover, to so contemptuously blow off the duly-constituted attorney general of the United States. In fact, I wondered if it was even legal—a thought I privately shared with Miss Gandy.

"Oh, Paul," she said—I was "Paul" to her by then—"you know the Director is just trying to protect the Bureau. Mr. Clark has some unusual ideas. Besides, if you think it's bad with him, you should have seen it when the other one was here."

"You mean Bobby Kennedy?"

"Yes, Mr. Robert Kennedy." She grimaced, as if it were distasteful for a grown man to be called Bobby. "Senator Kennedy now of course. When he came in, he wanted to change everything, and he really wasn't very respectful to the Director. And that awful phone!"

I'd heard some stories about the Bobby Kennedy days. By the time Jack Kennedy was elected in 1960 and appointed his younger brother Bobby as attorney general, Hoover had served as the Bureau director under a dozen attorneys general. With the exception of Harlan Stone, whom the Director still idolized, and a few others, Hoover's attitude was that while he had to work *with* the attorney general, he certainly didn't work *for* him. On major issues the Director preferred to deal directly with the president, either in person or through an FBI White House liaison man, effectively making an end run around the AG—and most of the attorneys general went along with it rather than butt heads with Hoover.

But it was hard to end-run an attorney general and go to the president when the AG in question was the president's brother and closest adviser. And Bobby was unlike any other attorney general the Director had encountered. He was young, for one thing, just thirty-five, half the Director's age, and he was also brash, cocky, energetic, arrogant, with his own ideas about how the Department of Justice—and the FBI—should be run. He scandalized the Director by holding meetings with his shirtsleeves rolled up, playing darts in his office, and bringing his dog—a big, shaggy black Newfoundland named Brumus—into his Justice Department office, this in clear violation of government regulations. And Kennedy infuriated the Director with his "meddling" in Bureau business, sometimes calling field office special agents in charge to discuss pending cases without going through Hoover.

Then there was the awful phone. When Kennedy first came in, he ordered a direct phone line to be installed between his office at the far end of the fifth-floor hallway and the Director's office. The direct line was installed, but the phone was placed on Miss Gandy's desk, not Hoover's. The first time Kennedy called and Miss Gandy answered, an angry attorney general made it clear that when he called the Director, he wanted to hear the Director's voice, not his secretary's. The phone was duly moved to Hoover's desk, and when it rang, the Director had to answer it—a humiliating reminder of exactly who worked for whom. The Director was careful to maintain outwardly civil relations with the attorney general, but inwardly he seethed. It didn't help that Bobby Kennedy let it be known that as soon as his brother won a second term, there'd be a new FBI director.

But that ended with six seconds in Dallas in November 1963. After the JFK assassination Bobby Kennedy stayed on as attorney general for nine months before resigning to run successfully for senator from New York, but he was a profoundly changed man— and he was no longer the president's brother.

"The first time Mr. Kennedy called after that, the Director was having a meeting in his office," Miss Gandy told me. "Mr. Hoover just let that phone ring and ring and ring, and when it stopped ringing, he said, 'Now get that damn thing off my desk!'" Miss Gandy lowered her voice when she said the word *damn*. "And for the last six months he was attorney general, the Director didn't speak with Mr. Kennedy at all. So you see, Paul, you don't need to worry about Mr. Clark. He'll be gone soon enough, just like all the others."

Actually Ramsey Clark stayed on for another two years, until the end of the Johnson presidency, after which he seemed to justify the Director's suspicions of him by becoming a noted anti-war activist and a defense lawyer for radicals of both the left and the right. And he continued to rankle the Director. After Clark wrote a book in which he mildly criticized the Director, Hoover let loose in a headline-making 1970 interview with the *Washington Post*.

"If ever there was a worse attorney general, it was Ramsey Clark," the Director said. "You never knew which way he was going to flop on an issue. . . . He was a jellyfish, a softie. He was even worse than Bobby Kennedy."

You have to remember, this was two years after Bobby Kennedy was struck down by an assassin's bullet in Los Angeles, a time when RFK was a revered figure of almost mythic proportions. Most people may not have cared that Hoover called a former attorney general a jellyfish, but to disparage Bobby Kennedy—to imply that he was the second-worst attorney general the Director had known— was heresy.

But that was the Director. He wasn't the sort who'd ever let go of a grudge—not with a jellyfish, and not with a dead man, either.

Like the phone calls, visitors to the Director's office came in a never-ending stream. Congressmen, businessmen, federal judges, military officers, heads of veterans' organizations, field agents and their families, you name it, they came (by appointment only) not so much to discuss FBI business, but simply to spend a few minutes in the glow of the legendary J. Edgar Hoover—and in most cases to have their picture taken with him by a Bureau photographer.

The Director never left anything to chance. Before each visit I'd have to write up notes with background information on the visitor—

information derived from their Bureau file if they had one, from any previous correspondence or contact they'd had with the Director, or maybe just a quick check among the tens of thousands of people listed in *Who's Who in America*. That way the Director could give the meeting a personal touch, saying things like "Mr. Smith, congratulations on being named the Dallas Rotary Club Man of the Year," or "Mr. Jones, I was pleased to hear about your promotion to executive vice president," or "Mr. Johnson, I understand you were quite a ballplayer when you were at Iowa State." In almost every case they would come away beaming, flattered beyond belief that J. Edgar Hoover actually knew them. Later they'd receive an autographed photo of the meeting—signed in Hoover's name by Miss Gandy.

The Director was particularly gracious with the women visitors. He had an old-fashioned, paternalistic view of the opposite sex, viewing women as delicate creatures who required the supervision and protection of men—unless of course the women were gangsters' molls or some other members of the criminal class, in which case they were "diseased" harlots who were even more morally degenerate than their men were. By today's standards Hoover's attitude toward "ladies" would be considered condescending at best, but by his standards, and the standards of most men of the time, he was simply being a gentleman. With women he was warm, cordial, amiable, charming—the exact opposite of what he was like during ordinary office situations.

Sometimes this could cause confusion. Later I had an agent friend who, like me, had spent a couple of years as a civilian clerk in the Director's office before becoming an agent, and he told me about the time he brought his wife in to meet the Director. For months he'd been coming home and regaling her with stories about the Director's abrupt and tyrannical ways, how the old SOB did this and the old SOB did that. Then when the wife finally meets him, Hoover starts in on how lovely she is, and how her pretty blue dress makes her beautiful blue eyes glow, and what a lucky man her husband is—and so on. My friend told me that the minute they left the building, his wife angrily turned on him and said, "How could you say all those terrible things about such a kind, wonderful man!"

When it came to Bureau field personnel, Hoover's meeting policy was generally open door—not just for special agents in charge but for street agents as well. Again, the Director wasn't the sort who'd visit a field office and glad-hand with the troops, but he liked to meet with his agents one-on-one, just to size them up; he also insisted on a personal meeting with any agent being promoted to a senior supervisory position, to make sure he was the right man for the job. I think the Director would have met with all six thousand of his agents if he could have.

As tough and demanding as he was, Hoover was actually a soft touch for the "hardship cases." Although he had a reputation among some field agents for not caring about agents' families—imposing immediate disciplinary cross-country transfers even though the agent's kids had just started school, or his wife was sick—that wasn't the Hoover I saw. Time and again I'd set up a meeting for an agent who'd come in and tell the Director that his wife had cancer and needed treatment at the Mayo Clinic, or that his daughter had a respiratory disease and needed to be in a drier climate—and within minutes after the meeting the agent's dark pink meeting-request card would be on my desk with the handwritten notation "Have Agent X transferred to Rochester," or "Have Agent Y transferred to Phoenix." Contrary to most reports, the Director did sometimes have a heart.

Still, in most cases a meeting with the Director caused considerable anxiety for the agent. As I learned when I got out in the field, some agents never wanted to be seen by the Director, on the theory that it could only hurt them, that the risk was simply too high. There were countless stories of agents who had met with the Director and exhibited some career-killing failing—sweaty palms, a few pounds over the Bureau's strictly enforced (except for the Director himself) weight restrictions, perhaps a sudden attack of stage-fright inarticulateness—that left their careers in tatters. But others, more ambitious, were willing to take the risk in the hope that if they did make a good impression, it would advance their careers. So if they were coming in from the field for in-service training sessions in the Washington area, they'd call me and ask for an appointment with the Director—and if he was available, they usually got one.

Sometimes it worked. The agents would come in and spend a few minutes with the Director in his inner office, and usually they'd lay it on a little thick—how honored they were to be part of the Bureau, how happy they were that he was the director, that sort of thing. With Hoover at this stage of his life, a little flattery—or even a lot of flattery—never hurt. If the agent made a good impression, the Director would dictate a brief memo for inclusion in the agent's personnel file: "Today I met with Special Agent So-and-So of the such-and-such Field Office. Mr. So-and-So makes an excellent, mature, and substantial personal appearance, and I would rate him above average. I think this agent has potential for advancement in the service."

And if the meeting with the Director somehow went badly? Again, there were oft-repeated stories about agents leaving Hoover's office and hearing behind them a bellowed comment to Tolson or Miss Gandy: "He's a pinhead! Get rid of him!" It didn't actually work that way—although the results were just as professionally fatal. The Director would simply dictate a memo that was the exact opposite of the one above, ending with "I DO NOT think this agent has potential for advancement in the service." The agent wouldn't necessarily be fired, but whatever dreams he may have had about one day becoming the SAC in Honolulu or San Diego were gone forever.

Interestingly, one FBI special agent always made a good impression whenever he visited. Except that he wasn't really an FBI special agent—he just played one on TV. That was Efrem Zimbalist Jr., star of *The F.B.I.* television series.

Over the years Hoover had been approached by a host of Hollywood types who wanted FBI cooperation with, and endorsement of, various film and television depictions of the Bureau. Hoover almost always declined to put the Bureau's explicit imprimatur on any Hollywood project the Bureau did not control, a standard he'd set with the 1959 Warner Bros. production *The FBI Story*, starring Jimmy Stewart, which was based on an FBI-approved book written by Pulitzer Prize–winning reporter Don Whitehead. (Hoover and Tolson made brief nonspeaking appearances in the movie.) The producers gave Hoover approval power over every aspect of the film, and it was said that, after he first saw it at a private screening, the Director had tears in his eyes—a little hard for me to believe, but maybe it was true.

So when Warner Bros. and big-time Hollywood producer Quinn Martin proposed a TV series along the same lines as the film, Hoover said okay—provided the Bureau would have veto power over the scripts, the casts, the production crew, the sponsors, everything. Everyone connected with the series underwent a background check to weed out any criminals or subversives or other undesirables, the Bureau reviewed and approved all scripts in advance, and a special agent from the Crime Records Division was assigned fulltime to the studio as a "technical adviser" and watchdog. In return, the producers were allowed to display the FBI seal in the opening credits, and Crime Records provided the screenwriters with actual Bureau criminal case histories on which to base their scripts. Although Hoover never appeared on-screen, at the end of every show a still shot said, "The producers extend their appreciation to J. Edgar Hoover, Director of the Federal Bureau of Investigation, and his Associates in the production of this series."

Zimbalist played the lead role of Inspector Lewis Erskine. (FBI inspectors were a rank above supervising special agents in the FBI hierarchy. Most inspectors conducted the periodic reviews of field office operations that so terrified the SACs—they were the aforementioned Goon Squad—but sometimes an inspector was dispatched to take over a major criminal investigation.) Hoover didn't personally choose Zimbalist for the role, but he might as well have. Zimbalist was perfect. The son of a prominent concert violinist, Zimbalist was a decorated combat veteran of World War II, a political conservative, and—rare for Hollywood—a happily married man with no record of personal scandal. And he looked like an FBI man, or at least what the Director thought an FBI man should look like: slim, handsome, full haired, with a healthy-looking tan.

Zimbalist spent a week at headquarters and Quantico before the filming began in 1965 to familiarize himself with Bureau procedures and to shoot the exterior scenes for the opening credits, which showed him driving a Ford Mustang convertible out of the Justice Department building and around various DC landmarks— the Capitol, the Washington Monument, and so on. The exterior scenes were basically the same every season, but they had to be reshot every year because the Ford Motor Company, which sponsored the show, didn't want Inspector Erskine driving around in last year's model Mustang. (Of course, in the vast fleet of Bureau cars there wasn't a single Mustang convertible; Bureau agents drove stripped-down, standard-issue sedans. But you had to make some allowances for Hollywood.) And every time Zimbalist came to town, he had a meeting with the Director; he and Hoover were on an "Edgar" and "Efrem" basis.

These visits were always something of an event. Even Miss Gandy, who over the decades had seen a host of famous people pass by her desk on the way to the Director's office, seemed a little starstruck by Efrem Zimbalist Jr.

"So nice to see you again, Mr. Zimbalist," she'd say. The actor, a nice guy, would make a fuss over her. "I'm so happy to be here, Miss Gandy. My, you're looking particularly lovely today!"

Miss Gandy would blush like a schoolgirl. "Oh, Mr. Zimbalist!"

The popular show ran for 241 episodes over nine seasons, with Inspector Erskine and associates chasing down hundreds of murderers, kidnappers, deranged extortionists, train wreckers, art thieves, mobsters, Communists, old Nazis, escaped fugitives, and other malefactors—not once ever failing to get their man. The Director watched the show at his home every Sunday night, and generally he loved it—except when it appeared that his instructions hadn't been followed. On several occasions he threatened to withdraw FBI cooperation—which would almost certainly have killed the show—if the producers didn't make changes in scripts that seemed unrealistic or contrary to the Bureau's policies or image. The producers always gave in.

Hoover was particularly annoyed when the screenwriters tried to sneak in bits of what he thought was gratuitous violence—which he made clear in a series of memos: "I understand that in the last TV script there were three killings, and it [the script] had to be returned to be rewritten. I want to make it emphatically clear that I do not want any acts of extreme violence on our TV program. There is a nationwide feeling that TV presents entirely too much violence, and I do not intend the FBI's TV program to be in that category. . . . I want no equivocation about this, either here or at the studio."

You'll note the reference to "our TV program" and "the FBI's TV program." Technically, Warner Bros. and Quinn Martin Productions may have held the rights to the show.

But there was no question who really owned *The F.B.I.*

The Director didn't run the Bureau through in-office meetings; those were mostly for ceremonial or political purposes. He actually ran the Bureau with paper—reams and reams and reams of paper. Entire forests perished to produce the paper on which the Director's office and the rest of the Seat of Government insatiably fed, with hundreds, even thousands of pages of memorandums and other documents crossing the Director's desk each day, in both directions, in and out.

Many of the incoming pages concerned minutiae. If the typists and stenographers in the Crime Records Division were producing an average of 3.40 pages per hour each with a 98.2 percent accuracy rate, as opposed to the SOG average of 2.88 pages per hour, the Director had a memo on it. If the Omaha Field Office was closing an average of 9.3 cases per agent, just over the national average of 9.2 closed cases per agent, the Director had a memo on it. If the agents in the Birmingham Field Office were commendably spending 89.9 percent of their time in the field pursuing leads instead of in the office, as opposed to the overall field office average of 88.9 percent, the Director had a memo on it. Nothing that happened in any area of Bureau operations was considered too small for the Director's attention. (Those are actual numbers. That was how precisely the Bureau's Inspection Division measured the performance of its employees—down to the first or second decimal place.)

The Director made his own extensive contributions to the paper tsunami. After every meeting or phone call with the president or the attorney general or anyone else on some issue of national importance, the Director would dictate a memo to record the conversation, some memos running into the thousands of words. (His dictation was always crisp, clear, with no *uhs* or *ums* or pauses while he searched for words, but he did have a few verbal tics. For example, the word *Communist* came out "Comma'nist," and *government* was "gov'ment.")

But other, lesser issues would also produce floods of memorandums. Was a certain junior female clerk in the Files and Communications Division still employed despite persistent poor performance evaluations? Get rid of her, the Director would demand in a lengthy memo, adding, "We must not palliate incompetency and inefficiency." (*Palliate* was one of the Director's favorite words; it means to underestimate the seriousness or gravity of a problem or an offense.) Had he received a report that some FBI civilian employees were engaging in excessive "youthful exuberance" and "loudness" while staying in Bureau-approved housing? This must cease, the Director would insist in a three-page, single-spaced memo. (The Bureau had a list of approved apartment buildings and other housing for its unmarried agents and civilian personnel to protect them from association with any undesirable elements. Naturally, male and female employees were housed as far apart as possible; sexual "fraternization" between unmarried employees was strictly prohibited and could result in termination.)

But it was simple blue ink, not dictated and typewritten memos, that inspired the most fear in the assistant directors and other brass who surrounded the Director.

In an organization with fifteen thousand agents and civilian employees, only two people were authorized to use blue ink on any Bureau documents: Miss Gandy to sign Hoover's signature, and the

Director himself. After reading through an incoming memo, Hoover would pick up his blue ink pen and scrawl notes at the bottom or in the margins. Usually they would simply say, "OK H," but sometimes the Director would let fly. "This is atrocious!" the dreaded blue ink would declare, or "This is a stupid idea!" or "I am astonished to learn that my explicit directions were not carried out!" When he was really worked up, the Director might fill the memo margins to all four corners with blue ink scrawls—what was known as a "four-bagger."

The problem was that like many people, as the Director got older his handwriting so deteriorated that it could be hard to decipher. In one case Hoover responded to a request from a special agent in charge with the handwritten notation, "No H." But the *N* and the *H* were so wobbly that the SAC thought the notation read "H OK" and he went ahead as if his request had been approved. When the Director found out—as he almost always did—the SAC barely held on to his job. That wasn't the only time that the FBI brass were befuddled by what was known as the Director's "marginalia."

Sometimes even when the handwriting was decipherable, the meaning was not. The story goes that after reading a memo on national security matters, the Director scrawled at the bottom, "Watch the borders!" This sparked a frenzy of calls to FBI offices from Laredo to Niagara Falls, demanding to know what was happening on the Mexican and Canadian borders, and why they should be watching them. Finally someone figured it out. The margins on the memo in question had been set too narrowly for the Director's standards; he wrote "Watch the borders!" but he meant "Watch the margins!" But none of the assistant directors had wanted to seem ignorant or uninformed by simply asking the Director what he meant. I don't know if this story is true, but it says something about the fearful men who surrounded Hoover at this stage of his tenure.

As you've probably realized by now, J. Edgar Hoover had his idiosyncrasies, as we all do. It was just that the Director had more than most people.

Consider, for example, the paper clips.

Did you ever notice that a paper clip has two distinct sides? Neither had I until Miss Gandy pointed it out to me. On one side there's a short loop that's enclosed in a longer loop on the other side. When the Director paper-clipped some pages together, he insisted on always having the short loop on the front, on the theory that it covered up less space at the top of the page. As a result, the paper clips in the magnetic paper-clip holder on the Director's desk always—always!—had to be positioned so that the long-loop side was facing up, ready for the Director's fingers to grab them and slide them over the papers short side up. When Miss Gandy first explained this to me, I thought she was kidding. But no.

Same thing with the small clear-plastic paperweight on the Director's desk. It had a coin embedded inside it with the Republican elephant on one side and the Democratic donkey on the other. Each night before I went home, I had to determine the party affiliation of the next morning's first scheduled inner-office visitor and flip the paperweight accordingly, then continue to do so throughout the day. Sure, the Director could have taken a nanosecond of his time and flipped the coin himself, but that was the way he wanted it. (Hoover always made a point that he was not a member of any political party and had never voted.)

Of course, there were any number of rumored Hoover idiosyncrasies that were just that—rumors and wild stories. One was that Hoover kept a wooden box in his office that he'd stand on when meeting visitors who were taller than he was. I worked in Hoover's office every day for two years—no box. Another was that Hoover had a germ-killing or bug-killing light mounted in the ceiling of his inner office to protect him from flies and bacteria and other pathogens. Again, no such light, at least not when I was there.

But perhaps the most persistent rumor of Hooverian eccentricity was the "no left turns" tale. According to the story, during a trip to California Hoover had been involved in a minor traffic accident when his driver was making a left turn at an intersection, after which Hoover issued a standing order—no more left turns! In 1975 a former FBI agent named Joe Schott wrote an amusing—and highly fanciful—book titled *No Left Turns*, in which he described in hilarious detail the efforts of the Dallas SAC to drive the Director and Mr. Tolson from the Dallas airport to downtown Austin while making only right turns.

I'm not saying that Mr. Schott made it all up. It's certainly possible that the "no left turns" rumor had spread through the SAC grapevine to the point where the SACs all believed it and acted accordingly—and none had the temerity to ask the Director if it was true. (See the "borders" story above.) But I know for a fact that when I worked for him, the Director had no bias against left turns. I know this because whenever the Director had a meeting scheduled at Capitol Hill or the White House or elsewhere in Washington, I'd have to make a "reconnaissance drive" along the proposed route the night before, writing down driving directions, which I'd give to Jimmy Crawford the next day. Never mind that Jimmy had made the drive to Capitol Hill or the White House a hundred times before; I had to make sure there were no road construction projects or malfunctioning traffic lights or anything else that might delay the Director and cause him to be late. And my driving directions always included their fair share of left turns.

But whether the Director's idiosyncrasies were of the real or imagined sort, collectively they made the same point: the Director wanted things his way. Nothing moved him to anger more quickly than not having his instructions followed to the letter.

The "pork chop incident" was a case in point.

It started when Jimmy Crawford came into my office one morning with a worried look on his face. Jimmy and I had become friends and allies; I'd been to his house, where I met his wife, Dorothea, who good-naturedly put up with Jimmy's long hours and infrequent days off.

Jimmy was usually calm and unflappable, but this day he was obviously distressed. "Paul, you gotta call Annie and warn her," he told me. "The Boss is pissed!"

"At Annie? About what?"

"About pork chops!"

It seems that the night before, Jimmy had driven the Director and Clyde Tolson to Hoover's home, where the two men had dinner, served by Annie in the dining room. Jimmy, who had to wait around to drive Tolson home, had dinner, too, but he ate in the kitchen. The thing was, Hoover had a standing order that Jimmy would always be served the same meal that Hoover and Tolson were eating. Hoover probably thought of this as an egalitarian gesture, although from today's perspective it might seem like the old "separate but equal" concept that had governed race relations in America for most of Hoover's life. But in fairness, few high-level government officials made it a practice to dine with their drivers, white or black.

Anyway, on this particular night Annie had a problem. Hoover wanted steaks, but she only had two steaks in the fridge. So she cooked the steaks for Hoover and Tolson and fried some pork chops for Jimmy.

"Then this morning I was driving them in and the Boss says, 'Crawford, how'd you like that dinner last night?' I forgot about the steaks and I told him how much I loved Annie's pork chops, and he starts getting mad and saying, 'Pork chops? We had steak!' Now he's fixing to give Annie hell when he goes home tonight."

I told Jimmy I'd try to square it, and then I called Annie.

"Thanks for the warning," Annie told me, "but don't you worry. If he starts giving me hell, I'll just do what I always do—I'll say, 'Yes, Mr. Hoover,' 'Yes, Mr. Hoover,' until he gets tired of giving me hell, and then I'll forget about it, and pretty soon he'll forget about it, too. That's what you gotta do, just let the storm pass over you and don't take it personal."

It was good advice. Unfortunately, I wasn't always able to follow it.

When he got angry, the Director wasn't a screamer; he was far too disciplined to let himself loose that way. His anger was more of a cold, controlled fury, which for its recipient was even worse than being yelled at. I found that out one day when I didn't answer the phone.

The green-phone direct line on my desk had to be manned at all times when the Director was in his office. If I had to perform some task that took me away from my desk, I would ask John Cox to keep an eye on it for me. But one day there was a miscommunication—it was my fault, not John's—and while I was away, the green phone started ringing and flashing, ringing and flashing, ringing and flashing, with no one there to answer it. Finally Nancy Mooney, in the adjacent office, realized what was happening and made a lunge for the phone, but that didn't solve the problem. As soon as the Director heard her voice, my goose was cooked. When I got back just a few minutes later, Nancy had a stricken look on her face.

"Oh, Paul, the Director's line rang while you were gone and I heard it, but I didn't know where you were so I answered it, and now he's really mad! He told me to tell you to report to his office the minute you got back! Oh, Paul, I'm so sorry!"

After reassuring Nancy that everything was okay, even though I knew it wasn't, I made the short walk to the Director's office. Miss Gandy gave a look as I passed by that was both worried and disapproving. I knocked on the double doors and was barked inside. The Director did not invite me to sit down.

"Mr. Letersky," he said, his voice calm but full of menace, "do you remember what I told you the first day you came to work in this office?"

"Yes, sir, you said—"

He cut me off. Apparently the question had been rhetorical. "I told you that in this office there is no margin for error. And you assured me that you fully understood your duties here, one of which is to ensure that the phone on your desk is manned at all times. Manned, Mr. Letersky, not womaned! A few minutes ago I called and Miss Mooney answered. Not you, not Mr. Cox—Miss Mooney! This is unacceptable. Miss Mooney has a number of important responsibilities, none of which is to step in on your behalf when you are derelict in your duties! Is that clear?"

"Yes, sir, no excuse, sir."

"You're damned right there is no excuse," the Director growled. "In this organization nothing excuses substandard performance. Nothing! We cannot and will not palliate carelessness and negligence in this office!"

It went on that way for a while. It probably lasted less than a minute, but it felt like an hour. I've blocked out much of what he said, but I remember some key words and phrases: "lackadaisical," "irresponsible," "indifferent," a "casual approach to your duties." It was a thoroughly comprehensive ass chewing. I remembered my supervising agent's cautionary words about being close to the campfire; the wind had shifted, and I was getting seriously burned.

And despite Annie's good advice, the longer it went on, the madder I got. I know, I know, earlier I said that I respected the Bureau's quest for perfection in all things—but it felt different when I was the target. Yes, it was a mistake to leave the phone unattended, even for two minutes, but the punishment seemed all out of proportion to the crime. He didn't even mention what earthshaking matter he'd been calling me about in the first place. I'd been busting my butt for this guy for six months, and now he was accusing me of having a casual attitude to my duties? It wasn't fair! By the time he dismissed me with a curt "Now get back to work!" I was red in the face and almost trembling with anger. I stormed past Miss Gandy's desk without saying anything. I was this close to quitting.

Why didn't I? Because I still wanted to be an FBI agent. And I didn't want to be a quitter.

The next morning I was at my desk when the green phone rang—and you can bet I picked it up before the first ring was over.

"Mr. Letersky, come to my office!" Click!

Oh, Lord, I thought, what now? But as I walked past Miss Gandy's desk, she gave me a mysterious, *Mona Lisa*–like smile. And strangely enough, when I walked into the Director's office, he motioned me to sit down in the chair in front of his desk.

"What can I do for you, sir?"

He waved the question away. "Mr. Letersky, it's been brought to my attention that I may have been a little rough on you yesterday. That was not my intention. My intention was simply to correct an error on your part and ensure that it will not be repeated. But perhaps in your mind I was a bit overzealous in doing so."

I could hardly believe my ears. Was the Director apologizing? No, it couldn't be.

"Not at all, sir." My anger had cooled since the day before.

"I understand that you intend to apply for appointment as a special agent after you've completed your legal training."

"Yes, sir."

"Well, *if* you are so honored"—he accentuated the *if*—"when you are assigned to the field, you will no doubt encounter a number of Bureau policies and protocols that to you may seem petty or unnecessary or unimportant. But I assure you they are not. Every word in the *Manual of Rules and Regulations* is there for a reason."

The Director leaned forward at his desk, for emphasis. "Control, Mr. Letersky! Control and supervision! All men, even the best men, must be closely controlled and supervised at all times. If they are not, if they are left to their own devices, they inevitably will start to slip. They will get lazy, they will try to cut corners, they will develop bad habits, they will make errors of judgment or action—and an error that goes uncorrected simply invites other, more serious errors. Control and supervision! That is the bedrock principle of this organization, and for the past forty-two years it has served us well—and I intend for it to continue. Do you understand?"

"Yes, sir."

"Good," the Director said. "Now, unless you have any questions"—the way he said it did not invite any—"you may resume your duties."

I got up to leave, but the Director stopped me. "One more thing. You show some promise, Letersky, given proper supervision. But don't let that go to your head. You still have a long way to go. That's all."

Miss Gandy was waiting for me when I passed her desk. "Well? What happened?"

I was still a little dazed by it all. "I'm not sure. It was like he was apologizing for chewing me out yesterday—except that he wasn't really apologizing, he was explaining. He said it had been 'brought to his attention' that I was upset. That was you, right? You made him do that, didn't you?"

She laughed and made a show of feigning ignorance. "Why, Mr. Letersky! You know my conversations with Mr. Hoover are strictly confidential. Besides, no one makes the Director do anything. One can only"—she searched for the right word—"encourage him in a certain direction."

"Well, thanks anyway. That was another thing. He called me Letersky."

We both understood the significance of that. The Director was rigidly formal in the office, referring to employees as Mr., Mrs., or Miss. (*Ms.* wasn't in common usage yet, and even if it had been, I'm sure he never would have used it.) But if you were a male employee and were in his special good graces, he'd sometimes drop the *Mr.* and call you by your last name alone. But that benediction could be withdrawn at any time. For example, if "DeLoach" or "Felt" was suddenly addressed in a memo as "Mr. DeLoach" or "Mr. Felt," they knew they were in the doghouse.

"You see?" Miss Gandy said. "He likes you."

I wasn't ready to go that far. "Yeah, maybe someday he'll actually call me Paul."

I was kidding, but Miss Gandy suddenly turned serious. "Oh, no, first names are only for the Director's most special friends." She paused, as if wondering whether to go on. When she spoke, there was a hint of sadness, of wistfulness. "You know, Paul, I've worked for him for forty-eight years, and not once has he ever called me Helen."

I was, frankly, shocked. "Never?"

"Never."

"That seems . . . a little strange," I said.

She shook her head. "No, no. That's just the way he is."

I wanted to ask her more, but I held back. I could tell from her expression that she didn't want to talk about it.

I liked Miss Gandy—a lot. She was intelligent, resourceful, fiercely loyal, and—except to meddling politicians and ambitious assistant directors—remarkably gentle and kind. But I realized that I didn't really understand her, or the man to whom she'd devoted her life and career.

I wondered if I ever would.

• • •

So far the picture I've painted of the Director is that of a stern, dour, essentially humorless man with no interests or life outside his job. Most of the time he was certainly that. But there were times the Director could stop being the legendary J. Edgar Hoover and actually be an almost-normal human being—or so I've heard.

I say "so I've heard" because I didn't really see that side of him; with one notable exception, which I'll get to in a moment, the J. Edgar Hoover I saw in the office was all business. But shortly after his death, a journalist compiled an "oral biography" of Hoover that included tape-recorded interviews with people who knew him outside work—not necessarily friends, he had very few of those, but people he occasionally socialized with. I guess *pals* is the right word. And I was amazed at some of the things they said about him.

"He got a big kick out of life and joking with people," said one.

"He was a very genial man to be with," said another.

"He was a great kidder and a man of great humor," said yet another.

That's just a sample. Of course, it's customary to say nice things about the recently dead, but even taking that into account, there's enough evidence to show that when he wasn't working, the Director knew how to relax and enjoy himself.

He enjoyed good food, although in later years his struggle with weight forced him to give up the heavy meat-and-potatoes lunches at the Mayflower and order grapefruit, cottage cheese, and black coffee instead. (Officially Hoover weighed 193 pounds, which according to the weight standards imposed on ordinary agents was some thirty pounds in excess for a man of his stated height. But unlike hefty regular agents who lived in fear of getting a "fat man" warning letter from headquarters—lose weight or else!—the Director was never forced to step on a scale.) He also liked to drink—Jack Daniel's Black Label, on the rocks with a dash of soda—but never to excess. He never drank at lunch, and not even his harshest critics ever claimed to have seen him plastered. He was far too disciplined for that.

Hoover loved animals, especially dogs and racehorses. He still kept a photo of his boyhood dog, strangely named Spee Dee Bozo, and since a young age had never been without canine companion-ship. When I worked for him, he had two cairn terriers, named Cindy and G-Boy, although technically G-Boy should have been G-Boy III, since two predecessors had borne the same name. On a few occasions I had to run out to Hoover's house near Rock Creek Park on some errand, and when I'd walk in the door, Cindy would start yapping like the house was on fire, while G-Boy barely lifted an eyelid. Jimmy Crawford often told me how Hoover would fret and worry when one of his dogs was sick, like they were his children— which, in a sense, they were.

As for horses, Hoover never owned one, and as far as I know, he never even rode one. But he loved to watch them run, at the Bowie or Pimlico or Laurel Park racecourses when he was in Washington, or at Santa Anita or Hialeah during his annual "inspection trips" to California and Florida. (Actually they were vacations, but no one was allowed to call them that.) Hoover called the races a "whole-some diversion," and he claimed he never made more than a $2 bet. During the racing season he and Tolson spent every Saturday after-noon at the track, and we were under strict orders never to call him there for any reason short of an imminent nuclear attack. If some-thing important came up, we could call him at home, or at lunch or at dinner, or when he was on vacation—sorry, on an "inspection trip"—but never when the ponies were running.

Only one time that I was aware of did anyone call the Direc-tor when he was at the races. One Saturday afternoon President Johnson called his FBI liaison man, Assistant to the Director Deke DeLoach, and told him he wanted Hoover and DeLoach to come to the White House immediately for a meeting with the president and some of his cabinet members. Knowing full well the danger in-volved, DeLoach called Miss Gandy and told her to call the Bowie racetrack and get Hoover on the phone.

"No way," she told him. "You can bother Mr. Hoover at your own risk."

So DeLoach reluctantly called the clubhouse at Bowie—and the reaction was predictable.

"You tell the president I'm in travel status and can't be reached!" Hoover snarled at DeLoach. "Tell him I'm not expected back until late this evening! Goodbye!"

When DeLoach reported this to the president, Johnson knew it was a lie. "Bullshit, Deke," he said. "I know where he is." But he gave in. After a moment Johnson said, "All right, goddamnit, but the two of you both better be in my office at ten o'clock Monday morning or you'll both be fired."

As we'll see, it wasn't often that the Director defied the president of the United States, especially when that president was LBJ. But Hoover would defy anyone who tried to bother him at the track.

He almost never attended Washington cocktail parties or social functions. Except for heading to the track and occasional Redskins and Senators games, he was a homebody—especially in his later years. Although Annie Fields lived in a room in the basement, Hoover's house at 4936 Thirtieth Place was a man's domain; it bore no sign of a woman's hand. Hoover bought the three-thousand-square-foot, red-brick Federal Colonial–style house in 1938, after his mother died, and in the three decades since then he'd packed it with an eclectic array of odd antiques and curious collectibles. Oriental rugs lay atop Persian rugs, couches and easy chairs and settees fought for space on the floors, while scores of bronze statues and commemorative ashtrays and eighteenth-century Chinese vases—even a shrunken human head from New Guinea in a glass case—elbowed one another on the mahogany and teakwood tables. To me it looked like the storage room of an upscale auction house, which in a way it was; Hoover was a frequent customer at Washington's venerable C. G. Sloan & Co. auction house. The walls of his home were literally covered with hundreds of paintings and drawings and plaques and photographs of Hoover with various famous people. There were photos of presidents he'd served under, as well as top congressional figures and foreign leaders and movie stars, most of the Old Hollywood variety—Shirley Temple, James Cagney, Jimmy Stewart, John Wayne. There were also several sketches and oil paintings of Hoover, and a bronze bust of himself stood guard at the top of the stairs.

Hoover enjoyed gifts—receiving more than giving. The gifts poured in, on his birthday (January 1), at Christmas, and on the anniversary of his being named Bureau director. For his directorship anniversary the various FBI divisions and field offices would send him bottles of Jack Daniel's, cuff links with his initials or his fingerprints engraved on them, high-quality cigars, fruit and cheese baskets, flowers—the Director loved flowers—and once, as we'll see, a trash compactor.

But it was at Christmastime that the true deluge began. Gifts would pour in by the hundreds, mostly delivered to his home, from Bureau employees, congressmen, police chiefs, movie stars, clergymen, titans of industry—even ordinary people who'd never met Hoover. Jimmy Crawford would have to load them all into the Cadillac—it looked like an armored Santa's sleigh—and make a dozen or more trips to deliver them to the conference room in the Director's suite. There Miss Gandy and I and others feverishly cataloged all the gifts, carefully assembling a manifest of senders, dates, and descriptions. Then we'd regift them, sending a necktie that the Director had received from a congressman to a special agent in charge who'd sent Hoover an azalea plant, and so on. I don't know if J. Edgar Hoover invented regifting, but he was one of its most prolific practitioners. We had to be careful, though. Once I almost committed career suicide by regifting to Hoover's pastor, Edward Elson, a set of cuff links that the good reverend had sent to Hoover. But fortunately Miss Gandy caught it in time.

As for his own gift giving, the Director was casual at best, farming most of it out to Miss Gandy, and he was more than a little cheap as well. (Although he earned a good salary—$42,500 annually in his later years, equal to about $250,000 today—the Director was notoriously tight with his own money.) I still have the two neckties he gave me, and while I don't know if they were regifts, I know the Director didn't pick them out personally, because he had a finely tuned fashion sense in men's clothing accessories, and the ties were hideous. I never wore them, but they still hang in my closet.

On the other hand, the Director could be gracious to his office staff, including me. I still have a letter he wrote and signed, personally and in longhand, saying, "Whatever success I may have attained over the years has been due to the magnificent dedication of our entire staff. In that, you as my immediate office co-workers have led the way, and for that I am immensely indebted and appreciative. Sincerely yours, J. E. H."

Hoover's tastes in entertainment were decidedly middle-class, and white-bread. His musical favorites were Lawrence Welk and the crooner Frankie Laine, both of whom were personal acquaintances. Whenever Welk was in town, he stopped in to see Hoover, and every Christmas Laine sent Hoover some dry-iced tuna steaks from a fishing boat Laine owned. (We never regifted the tuna fish.) On TV, in addition to *The F.B.I.*, the Director liked to watch westerns such as *Gunsmoke* and *Rawhide*. Hoover was also a fan of the Jack Benny and Red Skelton comedy shows. I know it's hard to imagine J. Edgar Hoover sitting at home watching Red Skelton doing his Clem Kadiddlehopper and Freddie the Freeloader sketches, but apparently he did.

The Director was an inveterate storyteller, although like many men as they grow older his stories tended to hark back to his younger days. And while he hated to be laughed at by others, at times he could be self-deprecating. He loved to tell the story about how when he arrested kidnapper Alvin "Creepy" Karpis in New Orleans in 1936, neither he nor any of the agents with him had handcuffs. They had to tie up Karpis's hands with an agent's necktie, and then as they were driving their captive back to the New Orleans FBI offices, they got lost, and Karpis had to give them directions.

Once, when Hoover was asked if he, the top cop in the land, had ever personally been the victim of a crime, Hoover said, "Yes. Once by a fellow who came door-to-door. I bought a load of fertilizer from him for my roses, and the stuff turned out to be black sawdust. And then once by the fellow they called the Birdman of Alcatraz. He had two cells, one in which he lived and another where he kept his birds. My mother was alive then and she always liked to keep a few birds, so I bought a canary from him. Only it turned out to be just a sparrow, dyed yellow. So I've been conned at least twice in my life. I guess that proves I'm human."

(As Hoover was well aware, convicted murderer Robert Stroud wasn't allowed to keep birds when he was confined in Alcatraz federal prison; he conducted his bird research while locked up in Leavenworth federal prison. But the Birdman of Alcatraz was the name that stuck.)

Obviously, the Director's sense of humor was of the understated, wry sort. And occasionally—not often, but occasionally—he brought it into the office. Once when he got a memo and a clipping from a foreign newspaper announcing that Hoover had married the mother of buxom actress Jane Russell, Hoover scrawled in the memo margin, "At least if they were spinning such a yarn they might have married me off to Jane Russell herself!" (Apparently, the newspaper had gotten the story mixed up with reports of Hoover's aforementioned relationship with Ginger Rogers's mother, Lela.) Another time a Bureau agent wrote to ask for a delay in a routine assignment so he could attend his own long-planned wedding. Hoover scribbled in response, "The ceremony without the groom would be a complete failure! Let the wedding proceed!" And once when a man in Texas wrote to ask about a supermarket tabloid photo that showed a midget dressed up like a space alien being escorted by two alleged "FBI agents," Hoover politely thanked him and wrote, "I can assure you the FBI has never had custody of a visitor from another planet."

And then there was the time I saw J. Edgar Hoover laugh out loud.

The occasion was Miss Gandy's seventieth birthday. (Unlike with Hoover, who'd been given an open-ended extension on the mandatory federal retirement age, government policy allowed yearly extensions for employees deemed "essential"—which Hoover had declared Miss Gandy to be.) As a birthday present to herself Miss Gandy had just bought a brand-new robin's-egg-blue Chrysler New Yorker, so I got a birthday card and asked one of the artists in the Exhibits Section of the Lab to draw a caricature on it of her driving the car with her head sticking out the window, grinning like a

Cheshire cat. We all signed it, Hoover included, and the next day we gathered in Hoover's inner office for some ice cream and a birthday cake baked by Annie Fields. When the Director handed her the card, Miss Gandy laughed at the caricature and said—almost coquettishly, I thought—"Mr. Hoover, would you like me to take you for a ride in my new car?" And the Director, utterly deadpan, said, "If I wished to commit suicide, Miss Gandy, I would simply jump off the top of the Washington Monument."

Okay, it wasn't exactly Don Rickles knocking them dead at the Sands Hotel in Vegas. And maybe the "women are bad drivers" theme doesn't play well today. But at the time, it was funny! We all stood there, laughing out loud—and the Director laughed, too. It wasn't a big belly laugh or anything, more of a "Heh, heh, heh, heh." Still, it was unmistakably a laugh.

But that was the only time. Again, the J. Edgar Hoover I knew was all business.

Which probably was only fitting in the serious—and in some ways frightening—times we were living in. Because beyond the walls of the Justice Department building, in the streets and on the campuses and in the jungles and rice paddies nine thousand miles away, America seemed to be sliding into an abyss.

And eventually it would drag J. Edgar Hoover and his beloved Bureau down with it.

CHAPTER 3

Nightmares in the Daytime

Thursday evening, just after 7:00 p.m. Washington time, April 4, 1968. It was one of those nights that started off as normal and routine, and then for the rest of your life you remember in precise and exacting detail where you were when you heard about it.

I didn't have any law school classes that night, so after the Director and Tolson and Miss Gandy and just about everybody else had left the fifth floor, I strolled down the long hallway to the attorney general's law library. My law school library didn't allow students to check out lawbooks, and given my schedule, I wasn't able to sit in the library and study the cases we'd be talking about in class. So I'd let myself into the AG's library, find the casebooks I needed, and haul them back to the giant Xerox Model 914 copy machine in Nancy Mooney's office. (The thing was a monster, about four feet square and weighing close to seven hundred pounds.) I'd copy the pages I needed, hoping the machine wouldn't catch fire—which it had a disturbing tendency to do—then return the books and spread out the copied pages on my desk for study.

I was sitting there, trying to absorb the salient points in the case of *Somebody vs. Somebody*, when a young female clerk from the switchboard room came rushing in and wordlessly handed me a piece of paper ripped from a teletype machine. It was from Robert Jensen, special agent in charge of the Memphis Field Office:

"URGENT, 04-04-1968 18:10 CST. TO: Director. FROM: SAC,

Memphis. SUBJECT: Martin Luther King, Jr. Information received this Division that referenced subject was shot while standing on motel balcony this city. Further details will be submitted."

For a moment I felt the same way I'd felt a little over four years earlier, when I'd heard on my car radio the first news report about JFK being shot in Dallas: a moment of shocked disbelief, followed by a feeling that it was the end of something, the end of a time in history. But I also sensed that the reaction to the MLK shooting would be far different from how the country had processed the Kennedy assassination. In 1963 there'd been a national outpouring of grief. In 1968, after all that had happened in the past few years, the outpouring would be of rage.

This moment of reflection only took a second or two. By the time I finished reading the teletype message I was already reaching for the phone.

Annie Fields answered, and a few moments later the Director came on the line.

"Sir," I said, forcing my voice to remain calm and professionally measured, "we've just received a teletype from the Memphis office advising that Martin Luther King was shot while standing on a motel balcony in that city."

There was only the briefest pause as the Director took that in. When he spoke, there was no tone of surprise or satisfaction in his voice. He was all business.

"Is he dead?"

"I don't know, sir. The teletype just says he was shot. We're standing by for more information. Would you like me to connect you directly with SAC Jensen?"

"Yes, do that." Then Hoover said something I will never forget:

"I hope the son of a bitch doesn't die. If he does, they'll make a martyr out of him."

The Director was right. The Reverend Dr. Martin Luther King Jr. died at a hospital less than an hour later, at age thirty-nine, killed by a single rifle bullet that had severed his spine—and, yes, "they" did make a martyr out of him. The bitter irony for Hoover was that the more Dr. King's martyrdom grew, the more of a villain he, Hoover, would appear to be.

The Director's distrust of the famed civil rights leader had its roots in the same fear that had obsessed Hoover since the days of the Palmer Raids and the Red Scare: fear of Communist infiltration, subversion, and violent insurrection. Whether that fear was grossly overblown on the Director's part is arguable, but no one ever doubted his sincerity. To Hoover, Communism wasn't simply a competing ideology; it was pure, unadulterated evil, a disease of the human spirit, and anyone who wittingly or unwittingly advanced its cause was the enemy.

Not even Hoover claimed that King himself was a card-carrying member of the Communist Party. But through an FBI mole in the Communist Party USA, in the early 1960s the Bureau learned that one of King's closest advisers, a white New York City lawyer named Stanley Levison, was working on behalf of the Communist Party USA (CPUSA) and its controllers, the Soviets. And at least a couple of other close King advisers had similar ties. To Hoover it was clear that King was involved in an "unholy alliance" with the CPUSA.

Hoover wasn't the only one who thought so. Both President Kennedy and Attorney General Robert Kennedy had closely identified themselves with King and his nonviolent civil rights movement, and any hint of Communist influence would have been politically damaging to them. After King failed to sever his connections with the suspect advisers, Robert Kennedy authorized the Bureau to set up telephone wiretaps on King's office and his Atlanta home, and, later, to install listening devices or bugs in his hotel rooms when he traveled.

The taps and bugs apparently never uncovered evidence of direct Communist Party control over King, or of significant Communist influence over the civil rights movement. But they did inadvertently document one aspect of King's personality—his weakness for women. Like JFK, King was young, charismatic, and handsome, and there was no shortage of women who were attracted to him. Also like JFK, the married Dr. King received their attentions with a casual recklessness that alarmed many of his friends. Graphic sex talk and the sounds of lovemaking and drunkenness showed up regularly on the taps and bugs.

Was King's sex life any of the Bureau's business? Clearly, no. But a microphone can't pick and choose what it hears. Remember, the electronic surveillance was initiated by Robert Kennedy as a "national security" matter—that is, to determine if a powerful popular movement was being infiltrated and manipulated by agents of a hostile foreign power. Despite what some critics say, the Bureau's surveillance of Martin Luther King didn't begin because Hoover was trying to uncover sexual dirt on the civil rights leader.

But when the dirt showed up, it outraged and enraged the Director. It was more than just a married man cheating on his wife. King was a minister, a man of God, and to Hoover the reverend's indulgence in drunken partying and extramarital sex was the worst sort of hypocrisy. The Director wasn't a particularly religious man; Jimmy Crawford told me that the boss almost never attended church. But he was extremely straitlaced about sexual matters—some might say repressed—and he was highly moralistic and judgmental. To him, the man who'd led the historic 1963 March on Washington and famously declared, "I have a dream," who'd been named *Time* magazine's 1963 Man of the Year, who'd been awarded the 1964 Nobel Prize for Peace, and who was loved and admired by millions—that man was a fraud, an imposter, a con man. Hoover started referring to King in blue-inked memos as a "moral degenerate" and a "tomcat."

King didn't help matters with his seemingly dismissive attitude toward the Bureau and its director. He criticized the Bureau in a *New York Times* interview, claiming that most FBI agents in the South were Southerners with segregationist attitudes, and that because agents had to work closely with local police to solve ordinary crimes, they were reluctant to intervene when civil rights workers were harassed or attacked.

The first part wasn't true; most of the agents in southern field offices were Northern-born and raised. The second part was partly true. A one-man resident FBI agent in some small city in Mississippi or Alabama did have to cooperate with local cops and local people to solve federal crimes and apprehend fugitives. But as Hoover repeatedly insisted, under current laws the Bureau's authority to intervene in civil rights cases was severely limited. Besides, he argued, the Bureau was an investigative agency, not a national police force or a federal protection service. If civil rights workers needed protecting, that was a job for the local or state police or the US Marshals or the National Guard or federal troops—not the FBI.

During the 1950s the Bureau had enjoyed generally good relations with the civil rights movement and African Americans in the South; in contrast to many local cops, the feds were the good guys, the people African Americans could trust. And the Director was widely admired in the black community. For example, an article in the popular black-oriented magazine *Ebony* called Hoover "the nation's foremost law enforcement officer" and praised his "deep sense of values in dealing with his fellow man." Now King was publicly attacking the Bureau—and by extension, J. Edgar Hoover.

It should have been a minor flap, quickly forgotten. But months later, still seething, Hoover brought up King's allegation during a press briefing with a group of women reporters in the conference room, saying, "In my opinion Martin Luther King is the most notorious liar in the country"—a comment that was blazed across newspaper front pages throughout the nation. "J. Edgar Hoover Calls Rev. King 'Liar,'" a typical headline read. King in turn subtly questioned Hoover's mental state, saying he was "faltering under the heavy burdens and responsibilities of his office."

Finally, at President Johnson's insistence, King and Hoover agreed to a face-to-face "clear the air" meeting in the Director's office. Hoover was gracious, even though King and his entourage arrived a half hour late; Hoover again warned King about some of his associates, but he made no threats or demands, nor did he mention any of the sex stuff. King, for his part, was conciliatory, claiming that his remarks about the Bureau had been distorted. But that was all for show. Hoover still saw King as a national security risk, and King was later heard on an FBI wiretap saying of the Director, "That old man talks too much." King had repeatedly been warned that he was under Bureau electronic surveillance, so he must have known that his comment would get back to Hoover—which it did. But King didn't seem to care.

Over the coming months and years Hoover and the Bureau would wage a virtual war against the civil rights leader—bugging his hotel rooms, spreading the word about his sexual indiscretions, pressuring universities not to award him honorary degrees. Assistant Director William Sullivan anonymously sent a copy of a "King sex tape" to the reverend's home, along with a letter urging King to kill himself or face public exposure. Much of what the Bureau did regarding King was unethical, some of it was only quasi-legal, and some of it was illegal as hell. It was all top secret, but naturally it eventually came out. And when it did, the revelations would prove far more damaging to J. Edgar Hoover than to Martin Luther King.

But that was in the future. In the meantime, King was having his own problems, not related to the FBI. By the mid-1960s, King's policy of nonviolence and working for change within the system was being eclipsed by more radical calls for revolution and "black power." Some black leaders were denouncing King as weak and out-of-date; some others, such as Malcolm X, had called him an "Uncle Tom." By 1968 even the Bureau's attentions had largely shifted away from King to other, more radical black organizations and leaders—the Black Panthers, Stokely Carmichael, H. Rap Brown. Martin Luther King was in danger of becoming irrelevant.

And then—Memphis.

King and his entourage had come to the city to support black municipal garbage workers who were striking for better pay and working conditions. King was under surveillance in Memphis—but not by us. Instead, the Memphis Police Department planted a member of its security division in a city fire station across the street from the Lorraine Motel, where King and his group were staying. The cop's role was to keep an eye on King, not to protect him; the cop was acting in an intelligence-gathering capacity, not as a guard. From his vantage point, he couldn't see the rifle sticking out the window of a communal bathroom in a boardinghouse across the street from the motel. But when the shot rang out and King fell, the cop immediately called Memphis PD headquarters, which immediately called FBI SAC Jensen. That was how I got the teletype report of the shooting so quickly and was able to notify the Director before it broke in the news.

After calling the Director I stayed around the office for a couple of hours, waiting to see if I'd be needed. Hoover remained at home to monitor the situation by phone, but a number of agents and several of the assistant directors came rushing back to their offices. There was no sense of satisfaction or joy that Martin Luther King had been killed. Whatever personal feelings anyone had about King, everyone knew this was going to be a shitstorm—and the Bureau would be right in the middle of it.

In fact, I was already in the middle of a minor shitstorm, courtesy of Assistant to the Director Deke DeLoach. DeLoach was furious when he found out I'd called the Director as soon as I got the teletype from Memphis. Red-faced, he cornered me in my office and loudly insisted that I should have called him first so he could break the news to the Director. It was like his demand that he be first on the "He's left the building" calls; the guy went on and on about it. DeLoach was the number three man in the Bureau then, so there wasn't much I could say except "Yes, sir." But when Miss Gandy later found out about the chewing out he'd given me, she was furious. I told her it was no big deal, not to worry about it, but she waved me off. She was the tigress protecting her cub.

"Don't you worry about Mr. DeLoach," she hissed. "I'll take care of him." I don't know what she did, or if it was related, but sometime after that the Director temporarily dropped the friendly "DeLoach" form of address and started addressing his number three man in memos as "Mr. DeLoach."

Anyway, even though the King murder wasn't a federal crime, President Johnson immediately directed the Bureau to take over the investigation, acting under authority of an old Reconstruction-era federal law against conspiracies to violate a citizen's civil rights.

Legally it was thin, and the potential penalties under the federal law were too weak to fit the crime, but it was enough to get started. (After the JFK assassination Congress had made it a federal crime punishable by death to kill a president, a vice president, or certain other high-level federal officials. But the murder of a civil rights activist, even an iconic one, technically remained an ordinary local murder.)

Later, some critics would suggest that because of Hoover's contempt for King, he ordered the Bureau to slow-walk or stall the assassination investigation; others would even claim that Hoover and the Bureau were coconspirators in King's murder. The second allegation is absurd—and so is the first. Anyone who believes it didn't know J. Edgar Hoover. The Director may not have cared very much that King had been killed, but he cared a lot about finding his killer. Failure to do so would damage the Bureau's reputation and seriously embarrass the Director—perhaps to the point of costing him his job.

And there was another factor. After the JFK assassination, the Warren Commission, which was appointed to investigate the president's murder, had mildly criticized the Bureau for not alerting the Secret Service before the assassination that Lee Harvey Oswald was living in the Dallas area. (As a double defector, once to the Soviet Union and then back to America, Oswald was a legitimate target of FBI scrutiny. FBI agents had interviewed Oswald and his wife, Marina, but he displayed no hostility against Kennedy and was not considered a threat.) But to Hoover there was no such thing as "mild" criticism of his Bureau. This time he wanted no slipups.

The daily pressure on Hoover to find King's killer—from the president, from Congress, from the press and public—was enormous, and naturally that pressure rolled downhill. In the following weeks the Director was even more short-tempered and demanding than usual with his subordinates—and the blue ink flew in the memo margins. "This is unacceptable!" "Follow up on this immediately!" "Why hasn't this been done already?" Hundreds of agents spent tens of thousands of man-hours tracking down leads, interviewing witnesses, examining fingerprint files. It was the biggest

FBI investigation since the JFK assassination, but unlike the JFK case, in which local cops had nabbed the suspected assassin within hours, this was a far more difficult whodunit situation involving an unknown suspect.

Eventually the Bureau got its man. I won't go into all the details, but the Bureau identified the killer as James Earl Ray, a racist prison escapee and drifter with a host of aliases. A worldwide manhunt ensued—Ray's photo was even shown on *The F.B.I.* TV show—and with key assistance from authorities in Canada and Europe, Ray was arrested in Great Britain two months after the crime and returned to Tennessee to face state murder charges. The Bureau had built a virtually open-and-shut case against Ray, so to avoid the death penalty he pleaded guilty and was sentenced to ninety-nine years in prison, where he died in 1998.

What Hoover did to Martin Luther King in the years before his death may have been a low point in Bureau history. But identifying and tracking down Martin Luther King's killer was one of the Bureau's finest hours.

So in the murder of Martin Luther King, justice was done. But unfortunately, in the streets of America, some people hadn't been willing to wait for it.

The trouble started that first night, April 4. The nation had witnessed major race riots before—in Watts in 1965, in Cleveland in 1966, in Detroit and Newark in 1967, among many others. But in scale and intensity, there'd never been anything like this. Looting and burning and battles with police broke out almost simultaneously in more than a hundred American cities; by the time it was over, more than forty people were dead, three thousand were injured, and twenty thousand people had been arrested.

Washington, DC, was particularly hard hit. Thirteen people died, more than twelve hundred buildings were burned to the ground, and violent crowds got within two blocks of the White House before being turned back. With the DC police overwhelmed, twelve thousand federal troops were called in; marines mounted machine guns on the Capitol steps, and phalanxes of army soldiers surrounded the White House. I remember trying to make my way home in my brand-new 1968 British racing-green MGB convertible—I'd bought it fresh off the boat in Baltimore—and thinking how surreal it all was. A curfew had been imposed, and except for military vehicles the streets around the Justice Department building were largely deserted. (My FBI identification got me past the roadblocks.) But the air was thick with the smell of smoke and tear gas, and in the distance I could see the glow of fires and hear the sounds of gunfire. It was as if the city, and the nation, were coming apart.

Most federal workers in the city were told to stay home, but at Bureau headquarters it was business as usual; the Director wasn't about to let his FBI be shut down by a bunch of race radicals and street hooligans. But the atmosphere was tense—and that tension led to a bizarre incident.

It happened the second day, Friday, when hundreds of buildings were aflame and pitched battles were being fought in the streets. Miss Gandy happened to look out a window toward the roof of the National Archives Building across Ninth Street, and suddenly with a short, frantic cry she ran—ran!—through the conference room and threw open the doors to Hoover's private office. Startled, Erma Metcalf and Nancy Mooney and I followed her, and when we peeked inside, we could hardly believe our eyes.

There was Miss Gandy, standing on tiptoe in front of the windows facing out across Ninth Street, her arms stretched up protectively, shouting at the Director at his desk, "Get down! Get down! There's a sniper on the Archives Building! With a gun pointed at you! Get down!"

And what did the Director do? Did he hurl himself to the floor or clamber under his desk? Of course not. That would have been backing down in the face of the rioters, and J. Edgar Hoover never backed down from anybody. Besides, it would have been undignified, and I'm convinced that Hoover would have preferred death to indignity. So instead he looked up from the memo in front of him, calmly glanced around Miss Gandy, and barked, "Get away from that window, woman! There's no sniper up there! Go back to work!"

Woman? Woman? Not *Miss Gandy*, certainly not *Helen*, but *woman?* It was so dismissive, so callous, so damnably rude. Miss Gandy stood there for a moment, deflated, her face flushed. Then she ran out of Hoover's office, crying.

We couldn't have been any more surprised if the Director himself had suddenly burst into tears. Miss Gandy simply didn't cry— but here she was, weeping uncontrollably.

"There was a sniper!" she said through the tears. "I saw him! I saw him!"

I looked out the window at the Archives roof; no sniper that I could see. I called the duty agent, who called the Archives security police, but they didn't find anybody on the roof either. Probably there was nothing to find. But there was no question that Miss Gandy believed there was a sniper—and that she'd been absolutely willing to trade her life to protect Hoover's.

Miss Gandy was still crying, so we all gathered around her, making "There, there" sounds and keeping her supplied with tissues, while she kept saying, "How could he? How could he?"

Finally I said, "Now Miss Gandy, don't have a nightmare in the daytime."

That was one of her favorite phrases. Whenever someone was overly worried or excited or upset, she'd always say, "Don't have a nightmare in the daytime." The line brought a wan smile and a short laugh, and the tears stopped. Sniffling, Miss Gandy went back to work, and so did we.

But we were all pretty pissed off at the Director, like kids who are mad at Dad because he made Mom cry. How dare he treat her that way? We didn't say anything directly, of course, but for the next week or so we were all just a little more terse, a little more formal in our dealings with him than usual. But it seemed as if the Director didn't even notice that we were giving him the cold shoulder; if he had, he would probably have thought that we were all simply being more efficient in our jobs.

Later, after things settled down a little, I had a chance to talk to Miss Gandy about what had happened. She came into the office every Saturday to check the mail and incoming memorandums and decide if anything was important enough to send to the Director at his home by courier. After I'd been in the Director's office for about six months, she'd asked Hoover—and me—if I could sit in for her for a couple of hours on Saturdays so she could attend to some personal business. The personal business, she explained to me, was getting her hair done.

"I don't have many excesses," she told me, "but I'm always so rushed on Saturdays. It would be so nice just to relax at the salon for a while."

I didn't mind coming in on Saturdays. It was a quiet place to study, and the AG's library was down the hall. So I'd brown-bag lunches for the two of us and come in around 10:00 a.m., and then Miss Gandy would come in at about 2:00 p.m. I'd always comment on how nice her hair looked, which seemed to please her, although to be honest I couldn't see any difference; as far as I could tell, her hairdo hadn't changed since 1952. Then we'd sit around for a while, chatting about Bureau gossip or the affairs of the day. A week or so after the "sniper" incident, I brought it up.

"Miss Gandy, I'm curious about something."

She smiled. "You're always curious about something."

It was true, I tended to ask a lot of questions. But I didn't think that was a bad trait in a would-be special agent of the FBI.

I pressed on. "The other day, when you thought you saw a gunman on the roof of—"

She cut me off. "There was a sniper," she said coolly. She'd believe it to her dying day—and, again, it didn't make any difference if the sniper had actually existed or not.

"I know, I know," I said. "What I meant was, when you saw the sniper, why did you do what you did? Standing in front of the window like that? I mean, it was brave, but—"

She waved that away. "Oh, no, Paul, I'm not brave. Haven't you noticed? I'm just a little old lady." She smiled innocently; we both knew she was anything but just a little old lady.

"Well, whatever you want to call it, your first thought was to protect him—not yourself, not anybody else, but him. You must really
love the guy to do something like that."

She seemed to stiffen at the word *love*. "My first thought," she
said evenly, "was to protect the Bureau. It's what I've been doing for
almost fifty years."

"Protect the Bureau? By taking a bullet for him?"

"It's the same thing, Paul. I thought you'd understand that by
now. And I'd expect you to do likewise."

I didn't respond to the last part. I respected the Director, but
intentionally catch a bullet for him? I didn't think so.

"So it's just about loyalty then?" I said. "That's the most important thing?"

She seemed puzzled by the question. "Of course it is, Paul. Loyalty is all we have."

I wasn't quite buying it. *Loyalty* wasn't a strong enough word to
explain what she'd done. When a soldier throws himself on a hand
grenade to save his buddies, is that mere loyalty? No, it's something deeper, something closer to that other L-word that seemed
to bother Miss Gandy—the sense of unconditional selflessness that
we often define as love. By that definition, I had no doubt that Miss
Gandy loved the Bureau, and that she loved the Director—as she'd
said, to her they were the same thing. But I wondered if there was
or ever had been something beyond that, something more—personal. I didn't ask her though, not then anyway. It was never wise to
press Miss Gandy too hard. I changed my tack.

"You know, we were all pretty upset that he made you cry."

Her face reddened slightly. She was still embarrassed by the display of emotion.

"Well, Paul, like you said, I was having a nightmare in the daytime. It doesn't happen often."

"No, it doesn't. But he shouldn't have spoken to you that way."

She shrugged it off. "Oh, that's just the way he is. You just have
to get—"

"I know, I know, get used to it. You told me that my very first day here, remember?" I didn't wait for an answer. "Did he ever apologize?"

That brought a small smile. "Paul, you should know as well as anyone that the Director never says he's sorry, at least not in so many words."

We both recalled the non-apology apology he'd given me the year before; I assumed he'd done something of the same with her.

Miss Gandy paused for a moment and then she said, "He noticed, you know."

"Noticed what?"

"The way you were all sulking around and being so stiff with him. I noticed it and he did, too. He notices everything. You really shouldn't have done that."

Her tone was reproving, but I could tell she was secretly pleased that we'd stood up for her, even in such a small, silent way.

"So what did he say? Was he mad?"

"Oh, no. All he said was 'Loyalty among colleagues is an admirable quality, Miss Gandy, as long as it doesn't interfere with their duties—and so far it has not.'"

"Loyalty again, huh? So does that mean he's not going to transfer us all to Butte, Montana?"

She laughed. "Not yet anyway. But if you don't get out of here and let me get to work, Mr. Letersky, I'll have you transferred to Butte, Montana! And don't you think I couldn't do it!"

I didn't think that. I didn't think that at all.

I didn't think there was anything in the FBI that Miss Helen Gandy couldn't do.

The weeks that followed were a blur of the dramatic and the routine. The flames from the riots were out, the armed troops dispersed, but the charred skeletons of burned-out buildings still stood as reminders. The Director continued in his usual schedule—"He's in the building," "He's left the building"—but as time passed, the pressure to solve the King murder grew more and more intense.

Then, two months after the King assassination, and just two days before the triumphal arrest of James Earl Ray, the Bureau was drawn into the assassination of yet another of the Director's old enemies—Bobby Kennedy.

RFK was shot at the Ambassador Hotel in Los Angeles just after midnight on June 5, soon after he won the California presidential primary; he died twenty-six hours later. The shooting occurred in the early-morning hours on the East Coast, so I wasn't in the office, and I don't know how Hoover reacted to the news. I'm sure he didn't shed any tears, but as with the King killing, I seriously doubt that he expressed any satisfaction that Kennedy had been mortally wounded. I imagine his first thought was the same as it always was when anything big happened—that is, How will this affect the Bureau?

Like the JFK and MLK assassinations, the RFK killing was not a federal crime, and this time the LAPD and local prosecutors took charge of the case. (With an apparent knack for belatedly closing the barn door, it was only after the RFK murder that Congress made it a federal crime to assassinate a major presidential candidate.) But unlike in the King case, the suspect, an apparently deranged twenty-four-year-old Palestinian immigrant named Sirhan Sirhan, had been tackled immediately after the shooting, with the gun still in his hand; this was not a whodunit, and there'd be no international manhunt. The FBI's role was to help determine if Sirhan was a lone gunman, or a member of a conspiracy. After thousands of interviews and hosts of forensic tests, both the local authorities and the Bureau concluded that Sirhan was just another murderous nut with a gun, acting alone—the same conclusion drawn by every other legitimate inquiry since then.

But of course, conspiracy theories persist—that there was a second gunman, that Sirhan had been hypnotized *Manchurian Candidate*–style to commit the murder, that Bobby Kennedy was the victim of a conspiracy by the Mob or the CIA—or by the FBI and Hoover, who supposedly had Kennedy killed because he knew if RFK won the presidency, he would fire the Director. Well, I can't speak for the Mob, or the CIA, but I can promise you the Bureau

had nothing to do with it. The Director and the Bureau didn't oper-
ate that way, and besides, if the Director had wanted to destroy the
Kennedy name and derail RFK's presidential bid, there were other
ways to do it. As we'll see, the Kennedy brothers had given Hoover
plenty of ammunition over the years.

Still, the Director would not, could not, forgive the brash young
man who'd humiliated him. After Bobby Kennedy's death, Hoover
ordered a telegram sent to his widow, Ethel, extending condolences
and saying, "His passing leaves a great void in the hearts of the nation." Hoover wouldn't have viewed that as hypocritical; to him it was
simply being polite. But a few days after the assassination, I handed
the Director a personal invitation from Attorney General Clark to an
in-house Justice Department memorial service for the slain former
attorney general. Hoover read it, grimaced, and put it aside.

The in-house memorial service for Bobby Kennedy was held in
the courtyard of the Justice Department building, just a few steps and
an elevator ride from Hoover's office. The Director did not attend.

There were no riots following Bobby Kennedy's murder, and no
more major political assassinations that year. But it would be wrong
to say that things returned to normal.

Because this was 1968. And nothing seemed normal anymore.

America in 1968 had changed since I first went to work for the FBI
three years earlier. It seemed that almost every day in those few
years some long-held standard of behavior or morality came under
assault, some old belief system began to crumble. Some of the
changes in fashion and music and culture were transitory and silly,
but other changes were fundamental and long-lasting.

And if there was anything that J. Edgar Hoover hated more than
criminals and Communism, it was change.

As so often with cultural shifts, this one was youth driven, fueled
by the millions of post–World War II baby boomers who were coming of age. *Life* magazine called it "the counter-culture" and said that
the movement "has its sacraments in sex, drugs and rock [music]."
The magazine had it right. In its attitudes toward sexual freedom

and drug use, and its taste in music and fashion, this culture was counter to almost everything most Americans had known and believed in. "Make love, not war"; "Tune in, turn on, drop out"; "Never trust anyone over thirty"—those were the watchwords of the day.

Although they never constituted more than a fraction of the youth population, the *hippies*—a new word—set the tone and style. With long hair, beards, bell-bottomed jeans, sandals, old army field jackets with flowers embroidered on them, the hippies embodied counterfashion, and soon kids across the country were emulating them. In 1967 a hundred thousand hippies—also known as flower children—descended on San Francisco's Haight-Ashbury for the "Summer of Love," a celebration of casual sex and uninhibited drug use that spread to other cities as well. Naturally this shocked and horrified most Americans over a certain age—according to a 1968 Gallup poll, two-thirds of adult Americans still thought that sex before marriage was immoral—but the young people didn't care. There was no such thing as AIDS, the contraceptive known as the Pill easily prevented pregnancy, and the young had no patience with older generations' outdated "hang-ups" about sex.

As for the drugs they were using, it wasn't limited to just pot anymore; former Harvard professor Timothy Leary was one of many who popularized a new drug, lysergic acid diethylamide—LSD or acid, for short—which promised to "expand your mind." Minds were expanded en masse at "acid tests" staged by writer Ken Kesey and his band of Merry Pranksters, among others. The "psychedelic" trend found its way into music with the Grateful Dead, Jimi Hendrix, the Doors, and countless others; the Beatles sang they'd like to turn you on in the *Sgt. Pepper's Lonely Hearts Club Band* album; and in the LSD-inspired song "White Rabbit," Jefferson Airplane exhorted listeners to "feed your head."

The "new permissiveness," as it was called, was everywhere. Despite official efforts to ban it as obscene, the 1967 Swedish film *I Am Curious (Yellow)*, which featured startlingly graphic sex scenes, went mainstream, becoming the highest-grossing foreign film ever in the United States. *Life* was the most popular magazine in

America, but *Playboy* wasn't too far behind; every month 4 million copies of the glossy skin mag were sold for the reading—or rather, viewing—pleasure of American men. The musical *Hair* opened on Broadway, with its brief but controversial "full frontal nudity" scenes and its hopes for the dawning of the Age of Aquarius, the time when peace would supposedly guide the planets, while love would somehow steer the stars.

Yet for all the talk of peace and love in the air, on the streets and on the campuses there was something else—anger. Not since the Civil War had America seen widespread popular protests against an ongoing war, but now the protesters collectively numbered in the millions. In 1967 more than three hundred thousand people turned out to protest in New York City, while in Washington that year fifty thousand people sought to stop the war by mentally "levitating" the Pentagon; Abbie Hoffman, cofounder of the Youth International Party, promised that "girls will run naked, and sorcerers, swamis, witches, warlocks, medicine men, and speed freaks will hurl their magic at the faded brown walls." College campuses saw "be-ins" and "teach-ins" and "sit-ins" as students took over administration buildings; thousands of young men burned their draft cards.

In the war itself, LBJ and his generals kept promising a "light at the end of the tunnel," even as they poured hundreds of thousands more Americans into the conflict. From eighteen hundred Americans killed in the war in 1965, more than six thousand died in 1966, and more than eleven thousand were in killed in 1967—along with tens of thousands of Vietnamese. In January 1968 the Vietcong and North Vietnamese launched the Tet Offensive, which for the Communists was a military defeat but a psychological victory. After one battle in a provincial capital, a US military officer seemed to sum up the futility and madness of it all by declaring, "It was necessary to destroy the town in order to save it." CBS News anchorman Walter Cronkite, "the most trusted man in America," told the nation there was no light in the tunnel, that the war was lost, and people believed it. For the first time, a majority (52 percent) of Americans in a Gallup poll said the war had been a "mistake." Anti-war Democratic candidate Senator Gene McCarthy made a strong showing against LBJ in the 1968 New Hampshire primary—strong enough to force Johnson to quit his race for reelection, and strong enough to lure another anti-war Democratic senator, Bobby Kennedy, into the presidential contest.

It wasn't only the war that sparked protests. In 1968 more than two hundred women demonstrated in Atlantic City against the "objectification of women" at the Miss America pageant; some of the women burned bras as symbols of male oppression. Mexican Americans in the Chicano movement began demanding their seat at the table, and César Chávez cofounded the United Farm Workers to fight for fair treatment. Native Americans founded the American Indian Movement (AIM) in 1968 to protest chronic poverty and centuries of broken treaties.

After the hopeful years of the early civil rights movement, black-white relations in America were on a downward spiral. The "long hot summer" of 1967 saw race riots erupt in dozens of American cities, and the King assassination riots of 1968 added to the destruction. Heavyweight champ Muhammad Ali coupled the war abroad with the fight against racism at home, refusing to be drafted into the military and declaring, "No Vietcong ever called me nigger." Martin Luther King did the same thing with different words, calling America "the greatest purveyor of violence in the world today" and encouraging African Americans to resist the draft. At the 1968 Olympics in Mexico City two black American athletes raised their fists in defiant black-power salutes during the playing of "The Star-Spangled Banner"—an action reminiscent of today's take-a-knee movement, except that in 1968 it was something new and shocking and, to more than a few Americans, frightening.

For many Americans, fear was the order of the day. The murder rate went up 40 percent from 1965 to 1968, with corresponding increases in reported rapes, assaults, robberies. A Gallup poll found that one in three Americans said they lived in or near an area where they'd be afraid to walk at night. To many people the Supreme Court of Chief Justice Earl Warren seemed to be on the criminals' side, issuing a series of rulings that expanded the rights of defendants in criminal cases—including throwing out the conviction of a confessed Arizona rapist named Ernesto Miranda on grounds that police had not informed him of his right to remain silent. Mass killings and serial murders horrified the nation. In San Francisco in 1968, the Zodiac Killer began a series of random murders, taunting the police and public with cryptic notes promising more victims. (The killer was never caught.) That summer an ex-con named Charles Manson and his "family" of strays and runaways were in Death Valley, preparing for the "Helter Skelter" murders that would soon terrorize Los Angeles, while in Chicago another ex-con named Richard Speck had raped and tortured and stabbed to death eight young student nurses.

Political violence was on the rise as well. New Left anti-war groups such as the Students for a Democratic Society and others shifted the emphasis away from peaceful protest tactics to active resistance, a shift that ultimately led to the creation of the violent Weather Underground faction. In 1968 alone there were more than forty on-campus bombings and arsons, many targeting Reserve Officers' Training Corps (ROTC) buildings. Anti-war activists like Daniel and Philip Berrigan and others broke into local Selective Service offices and burned or poured blood on draft records. At the Democratic Convention in Chicago in 1968, protesters pelted police with rocks and bottles, prompting a response that was later described as a "police riot"; more than four hundred protesters and two hundred cops were injured. At South Carolina State University police shot and killed three black protesters and wounded almost thirty others—a prelude to the shootings of students at Kent State University and Jackson State College two years later. The newly formed Black Panther Party openly rejected nonviolence and preached armed resistance, with "Off the pigs!" as their rallying cry; in the coming years more than two dozen cops would be killed in ambushes or shootouts with the Panthers or offshoot groups, and dozens of black nationalists would be slain by police or in internecine power struggles.

And then there were the assassinations. Malcolm X, shot down by members of a rival Nation of Islam faction in New York City in 1965.

American Nazi Party founder George Lincoln Rockwell, shot down outside a Virginia laundromat by an embittered former follower in 1967. Martin Luther King Jr., killed in April 1968, and Robert F. Kennedy, shot and killed in June.

So that was the America that J. Edgar Hoover saw when he read his reports from the field offices or watched the TV news or gazed out from his office windows on the fifth floor—an America beset by sexual promiscuity and drug use and crime, by hippies, draft resisters, white revolutionaries, and black revolutionaries, by angry braless women and angry spoiled young men. And he didn't like what he saw one bit. In interviews and speeches he railed against the "moral degeneration" of American life, the "coddling" of criminal "scum," the "filth" in contemporary music and films, the "mental halitosis" of liberal anti-war "pseudo-intellectuals."

Certainly the Director wasn't about to let the changing social mores infect his Bureau, as he made clear in a speech to the Society of Former Special Agents of the FBI. "Maybe those of us in the FBI are narrow-minded when we frown on indiscretions involving unmarried couples," Hoover told his receptive audience. "Maybe we are old-fashioned when we frown upon extreme hairstyles and wearing apparel. But we have exacting standards in the FBI, and we apologize to no one for them. We have no intention of compromising these standards to accommodate kooks, misfits, drunks, and slobs."

Hoover wasn't alone in his disdain for the dramatic shifts in America life in the late 1960s. If you're a baby boomer, chances are your father felt the same way. But the tragedy for J. Edgar Hoover was that he didn't see hippies and anti-war protesters and pseudo-intellectuals and the other "kooks, misfits, and slobs" as simply agents of unwelcome and uncomfortable change. Instead he saw them as a national security problem, an existential threat to the American way of life.

They were J. Edgar Hoover's nightmares in the daytime. And they led him and the Bureau into some dark and secret places.

CHAPTER 4

Secrets

It was no secret that the Federal Bureau of Investigation had secrets—millions of them, all safely tucked away in what were collectively known as Bufiles (for "Bureau files") or simply "the files." But when it came to the Bureau, the term *file* could be a little misleading.

Every document that passed through FBI headquarters was assigned a classification code number based on its subject matter—kidnapping, extortion, espionage, administrative and employment records, and so on. Each individual case within each classification would have a numbered file, and each document within that file would be individually numbered or "serialized" as well. By the late 1960s about 6 million such files were on hand, covering everything from organized crime investigations to background checks on applicants for federal jobs. The files contained the names of some 20 million people, but that didn't mean that everyone whose name was in the files had been investigated by the FBI, or that the FBI "had a file on" the person. The names in the files also included crime victims, witnesses, people who were interviewed by field agents, and so on.

(The general files are not to be confused with the Bureau's fingerprint-card file system, which in 1968 held almost 200 million fingerprint cards, although many of those were duplicates. The Bureau's fingerprint records included criminal as well as "civil" fingerprint files—that is, fingerprints collected by the military and other federal agencies, fingerprints submitted voluntarily by citizens for identification purposes in case of accidents or amnesia, etc.)

At the time, virtually all Bureau files were considered confidential, accessible only to Bureau personnel. Although Congress passed the Freedom of Information Act (FOIA) in 1966 to make government documents more open to the public, initially the law was weak; it specifically exempted from public scrutiny any government documents concerning national security and criminal investigations or matters of personal privacy, and it gave senior officials wide latitude in deciding what documents would and wouldn't be released. As you might expect, J. Edgar Hoover took the position that Bureau files were the Bureau's business and nobody else's.

So in the late 1960s the Bureau closely held all of its secrets. But some secrets were more closely held than others.

Especially sensitive investigative files—files on espionage and high-level organized crime cases, for example—were kept in a limited-access Special File Room in the basement of the Justice Department. A few files on pending criminal or intelligence cases were kept in some of the assistant directors' offices for quick reference. But the most sensitive documents—most sensitive to Hoover, at any rate—were kept in the Director's suite of offices.

Those documents constituted the legendary "secret files of J. Edgar Hoover."

That the Director kept "secret files" in his office had long been an article of faith in Washington and beyond. As for what was in them, most people imagined that they contained derogatory—and probably salacious—information on congressmen, senior public officials, journalists, celebrities, even presidents. But no one knew what was in his or her FBI file, or if the Bureau even had such a file. And of course the Bureau wasn't saying. If asked, the Bureau would say that the rumored "secret files" were figments of overly fevered imaginations, that they simply didn't exist.

But they did exist—although not in Hoover's private office. They existed in a half dozen olive-green four-drawer locking metal filing cabinets in Miss Gandy's office, in drawers marked "Personal/Confidential" (P/C) and "Official/Confidential" (O/C). Only two people had access to those file cabinets—the Director and Miss Gandy. Even an assistant director who wanted to see something in those files had to get Hoover's permission—and the file had to be read inside the Director's suite of offices and immediately returned to Miss Gandy.

Naturally I had heard the rumors about the so-called secret files. In fact, I occasionally handled some myself.

As I mentioned earlier, on Saturdays I would come in to the office to fill in for Miss Gandy while she got her hair done. My instructions were that if a courier came in with any envelopes marked CONFIDENTIAL, I was to place them in the in-box on top of a filing cabinet so she could look them over and decide if there was anything important she needed to immediately notify the Director about. If not, Hoover would review them later and decide whether they should be assigned to the Personal/Confidential or Official/ Confidential files. The envelopes were sealed and Miss Gandy always kept the file drawers locked, so I didn't know what was in them—but I can't say I wasn't curious.

(The sealed envelopes weren't unusual. To prevent prying eyes, particularly sensitive documents were usually sealed in envelopes before being handed to a clerk for delivery somewhere in the building. That was especially true with materials filed under the Interstate Transport of Obscene Materials category—magazines, books, photos, and so on. To protect innocent Bureau employees from such "filth," as Hoover put it, those envelopes were taped shut and clearly labeled OBSCENE—which to me seemed more like an invitation than a warning. Once when I was retrieving some files from the Identification Division, I noticed that many of the files labeled OBSCENE had layer after layer of Scotch tape on them, as if they'd repeatedly been opened and retaped by libidinous employees—which they had been.)

Obviously I couldn't just come out and ask Miss Gandy what was in the secret files in her office. But I did hint around about them.

"I suppose a lot of people are curious about what's in there," I said to her one Saturday afternoon, glancing toward the filing cabinets.

She followed my look. "Some people are too curious for their own good," she said. "Remember what happened to the curious cat."

"I know, but that must really be some secret stuff."

She gave me a reproving look. "As you know, Paul, all of our Bureau files are confidential."

"But some are more confidential than others?"

That earned a smile. "I suppose you could say that. The Director feels that certain . . . sensitive materials need to be closely monitored, just in case anyone gets overly inquisitive."

I thought about the much-taped OBSCENE files in the Identification Division.

"As for those"—Miss Gandy nodded toward the filing cabinets— "it's really not what some people seem to think. For the most part, they'd be disappointed."

I noticed she said "for the most part."

Neither of us could know it at the time, but eventually some of the documents in the Director's Official/Confidential files would be opened to public view—and as Miss Gandy said, for the most part they'd be disappointing to people looking for a vast trove of sleaze and scandal. (More on those documents later.) But there were other Personal/Confidential secrets in those olive-green filing cabinets that would never come to light. Miss Gandy would see to that.

For now, though, all of the secret files in Miss Gandy's office remained secret. But one thing about those files puzzled me. Although Miss Gandy kept the file drawers locked, and she locked her office door at night, to me they didn't seem all that secure.

"Miss Gandy, I have to ask. If the files are so . . . sensitive, why keep them here? I mean, what if somebody walked in while you weren't here, or they broke in at night? It wouldn't take long to pick those little locks."

She flashed a look. "They wouldn't dare!"

Actually, there'd come a time when someone would dare to break into an FBI office and steal reams of secret documents—not from the Director's office but from a small FBI resident agency in Pennsylvania—and the consequences for Hoover and the Bureau would be catastrophic. Security at FBI offices was tightened after that, but in the mid-1960s the Bureau's security measures were surprisingly lax by today's standards. Employees who worked in the Justice Department building came and went as they pleased, no one checked your briefcase when you left at the end of the day, and frankly the GSA (General Services Administration) guards responsible for the building weren't exactly a crack security force. But at the time that wasn't unusual. Looking back, it's a little hard to believe, but in the 1960s airline passengers still boarded planes without ever being screened, constituents could stroll into a congressman's office on Capitol Hill unannounced and uninvited, and even people taking the White House tour never passed through a magnetometer.

So maybe it wasn't a surprise that the same sort of casual approach to security was applied to another set of highly secret documents in the Director's office—that is, the "tech manual."

One of my daily tasks was to make sure that the black three-ring binder notebook we called the technical manual was placed on the Director's desk each morning, then put back on a bookshelf in the conference room at the end of the day. That may not seem like a dramatic or important job, and it wouldn't have been if the tech manual had been what it sounded like—a repair guide for a piece of equipment, like that seven-hundred-pound Xerox copy machine in Nancy Mooney's office.

But in Bureau-speak words took on different meanings. In this case, *technical* referred to "technical surveillance," which in turn meant electronic eavesdropping in its various forms—*telsurs* for "telephone surveillances," *misurs* for hidden "microphone surveillances"—in other words, wiretaps and bugs. (Collectively, they were also known as *elsurs*, for "electronic surveillance.") That three-ring binder the Director wanted on his desk each day was a catalog of the who, what, when, where, and why of every warrantless wiretap and bug that Bureau agents were operating at any time—and as such it was a legal and political ticking time bomb.

So did I ever open it up and take a peek? Of course I did! But to tell you the truth, the documents in the binder didn't make for very interesting reading. There were a lot of code words and symbols, and I didn't see any names that I recognized. Almost all the taps and bugs in operation seemed to be connected to espionage or organized crime cases—which made it surprising to me that the three-ring binder wasn't kept under closer wraps. Anybody with after-hours access to the conference room—say, for example, me— could easily have copied it or absconded with it and sold the information to the KGB or the Gambino family. Obviously, I never gave that a thought; I'm just saying it was possible.

And there was another surprising thing about the catalog of wiretaps and bugs. It was surprising how thin that three-ring binder was, how few electronic surveillances were being conducted by agents of the FBI—only a few dozen at any time.

A lot of people assume that J. Edgar Hoover's FBI was an Orwellian domestic spying agency that kept thousands or even tens of thousands of Americans under electronic surveillance, that there was an FBI tap on every phone and a microphone was disguised as an olive in every martini glass. But it just wasn't so.

That was partly for practical reasons. In those days, before keyword-recognition and speech-to-text computer programs, every tap and bug had to be continuously monitored by agents who would record conversations and keep written logs of pertinent information; important conversations would then have to be transcribed. To monitor thousands of taps and bugs would have required several times that number of agents—this at a time when there were only about sixty-five hundred agents in the entire FBI. Another problem was that for every minute of useful conversation by a targeted subject, the listening agents would usually get two hours of the subject's wife talking on the phone to her mother. In short, wiretaps and bugs required enormous amounts of manpower, often with limited results.

And there was another reason Hoover kept the number of electronic surveillances strictly limited. Believe it or not, he just didn't like taps and bugs.

That attitude dated back to when he was first appointed Director in the 1920s. Hoover wanted to disassociate the Bureau from the sleazy tactics of the old private gumshoes of the day, who were notorious for tapping phones to steal business information or to nab cheating husbands. So Hoover issued the following directive in the Bureau's *Manual of Rules and Regulations*, under the heading "Unethical Tactics": "Wiretapping . . . in connection with investigative activity will not be tolerated by the Bureau." Later, at the urging of Justice Department officials, Hoover amended the rules to allow wiretapping in cases involving espionage, sabotage, the safety of kidnap victims, and cases of "major law enforcement importance." But all wiretaps had to be approved in advance by FBI headquarters, and Hoover made it clear he considered wiretapping to be a "lazy man's investigative tool."

That began to change just before and during World War II, when the Bureau's mission was expanded beyond crime fighting to domestic-security intelligence gathering and counterespionage; by necessity, electronic eavesdropping became a standard Bureau technique. During the war hundreds of FBI wiretaps and bugs were planted in the embassies and consulates of governments considered friendly to the Axis powers and were deployed against people suspected of espionage or sabotage. The practice continued during the 1950s and into the mid-1960s, when the Bureau routinely wiretapped and/or bugged Communist Party members, organized crime figures, Klansmen, neo-Nazis, and suspected "subversives" such as Martin Luther King and others—all under the category of "internal security" and all without a warrant.

And the Bureau was good at it. Every major field office had a team of "soundmen," agents who were specially trained in wiretapping and the use of an increasingly sophisticated array of listening devices. They were also trained in lockpicking, safecracking, defeating alarm systems, and other skills necessary for black bag jobs or surreptitious entries—that is, breaking into someone's home or office to install a wiretap or plant a bug or photograph documents. (Agents didn't always have to break in. Most telephone companies cooperated with Bureau requests for wiretaps in national security cases, and often a friendly building superintendent or hotel detective would simply let the agents into an apartment or office or hotel room when the occupant was away; sometimes a super would give the agents a copy of the key so they could enter the premises anytime to remove a bug or replace a battery.)

None of this was exactly legal—but under the federal laws at the time it wasn't exactly illegal, either. In 1934 Congress passed the Communications Act, which made it illegal to "intercept and divulge" telephone and radio communications, and later the Supreme Court ruled that intercepted phone conversations could not be used as evidence in a criminal trial. But the court left open the issue of government wiretaps being used in foreign-espionage and other "national security" investigations—a loophole that President Franklin Roosevelt used to permit extensive FBI wiretapping of suspected "subversive activity" by pro-Communist and pro-Fascist groups in the years before World War II. As for hidden microphones, the laws were even less clear. In the 1950s the Supreme Court ruled that evidence gained through the warrantless installation of a microphone could not be used in court—but again, it left open the issue of whether a president could authorize buggings in national security investigations when the purpose was to gather intelligence, not evidence for trial. President Eisenhower's Justice Department took the position that such buggings were permissible when done "in the national interest," even if the installation of the bug involved "trespass"—that is, a black bag job or burglary—which was clearly illegal under state laws.

The problem, obviously, was what "in the national interest" meant. Most people would agree that planting a bug in the Soviet embassy was permissible; that was simply how the spy game was played, and besides, the Russians were doing the same thing to us. Wiretapping and bugging organized crime figures could also arguably be considered "in the national interest." But what about tapping and bugging alleged "subversives" such as Martin Luther King Jr.? Was that in the national interest? It was a debatable point.

But it was not a point that Hoover wanted to have debated. For decades he managed to keep the extent of FBI taps and bugs largely secret from the public. And he took extreme steps to make sure that his agents didn't get caught in bugging or wiretapping operations—

which would have "embarrassed the Bureau" and thus Hoover as well. All field office requests for electronic surveillance still had to be personally approved by the Director, and every request had to be accompanied by a "feasibility study" explaining in precise detail the precautions taken to ensure the surveilling agents wouldn't get caught. Hoover also kept the numbers of electronic surveillances strictly limited, on the theory that the more taps and bugs the Bureau had going, the more likely it was that one would be discovered; to keep the total numbers down, for every new wiretap that was approved, another had to be discontinued. Also, all correspondence concerning electronic surveillance devices—which were euphemistically referred to as "highly confidential anonymous sources"—was marked DO NOT FILE or JUNE, a code word meaning the document would not be entered in the Bureau's general investigative files and eventually it would routinely be destroyed. That way, if a defense attorney or a court demanded to know if a criminal defendant had been electronically surveilled, the Bureau could say with a straight face that "no record" of such surveillance was in the files. That may not have been ethical, but again, under the law at the time it wasn't necessarily illegal.

But even Hoover couldn't keep all of the Bureau's tappings and buggings secret forever. In the mid-1960s a series of court cases exposed incidents of wiretapping and bugging of US citizens by various government agencies, including the IRS, the National Security Agency, and the FBI. (One FBI case involved bugs planted in the count rooms at Las Vegas casinos to gather intelligence on the skimming of untaxed cash by organized crime.) The revelations prompted an outcry from the public and press about electronic invasions of privacy, not only by the government but by private business as well. "The Big Ear: Today It Can Be Anywhere and Everywhere," one headline said, the accompanying story explaining that in addition to government and police electronic eavesdropping, private companies were bugging office watercoolers and bathrooms to find out what their employees were saying.

The furor prompted President Johnson in 1965 to issue a directive prohibiting federal agencies, including the Bureau, from tapping and bugging—although again "national security" cases were exempted. It also prompted no less than five congressional subcommittee hearings on electronic invasions of privacy, including one in which an electronics expert wowed the politicians and the press with a bug in a martini glass disguised as an olive with a toothpick as the antenna. (That wouldn't have worked in a real martini: the bug would have shorted out in the gin.) Hoover managed to ward off any congressional probe of FBI electronic surveillances, but he could read the writing on the wall. In 1965 Hoover notified the attorney general's office that "in view of the present public atmosphere," he was severely curtailing the number of Bureau taps and bugs and virtually eliminating black bag jobs.

He was as good as his word. To the dismay of many agents and Bureau supervisors, by 1966 the total number of Hoover-authorized wiretaps in place at any time numbered a few dozen or less (the total number for the year was less than two hundred), and the number of bag-job microphone surveillances was officially zero; the number of wiretaps decreased even further in subsequent years. Hoover watched those numbers like a hawk—which was why I had to put the three-ring-binder tech manual on his desk every day. If, say, the president of the United States wanted to know how many electronic surveillances the Bureau had going, the Director had the numbers at his fingertips.

This didn't necessarily mean that Bureau agents in the field were abandoning electronic surveillances. A field agent could always resort to a "suicide tap"—that is, an unauthorized wiretap or bugging that would spell career suicide if the Director found out about it. A field agent could also ask friendly local police detectives, who routinely conducted warrantless taps and buggings in bookmaking and narcotics cases, to either install a tap or provide information from one already in operation.

Still, despite what people may think, J. Edgar Hoover clearly tried to limit electronic surveillances of American citizens to what he considered a necessary minimum, and he disapproved more field requests for taps and bugs than he approved. In fact, after Hoover's death there were far more FBI electronic surveillances than when he was alive. In 1978 Congress passed the Foreign Intelligence Surveillance Act, setting up the first workable system for the FBI and other agencies to request court-issued warrants for electronic surveillance in national security cases. In the first four decades of its existence, the so-called FISA court approved more than forty thousand electronic surveillance warrant requests, while denying fewer than one hundred. In other words, in forty years the FISA court handed out four times as many electronic surveillance authorizations as Hoover did in his entire career as director.

Don't get me wrong. I'm not trying to tell you that Hoover and the Bureau were ceaseless champions of civil liberties. When confronted by something they considered a threat to America's security, Hoover and the Bureau could certainly play fast and loose with some of the finer points of the Constitution. We did it with Martin Luther King—and we also did it with a series of secret Bureau operations collectively known as COINTELPRO.

I'd seen the phrase written on Bureau documents a number of times over the years, with various subheads: "COINTELPRO—White Hate Groups," "COINTELPRO—CPUSA" (Communist Party USA), "COINTELPRO—Black Nationalists," and later in my time in the Director's office "COINTELPRO—New Left." It didn't take a genius to figure out what COINTELPRO meant in Bureauspeak. It stood for "counterintelligence program." But I couldn't quite figure out what those counterintelligence programs entailed.

So I did what I often did when I had a question about Bureau operations and what was going on in the field. I asked J. P. Mohr.

John Philip Mohr was the assistant to the director for administration, which made him the number four man in the Bureau, below Hoover, Associate Director Tolson, and Deputy Associate Director Deke DeLoach. Although Mohr had once been a Tolson protégé, Miss Gandy liked him, at least partly because he wasn't one of those ADs who saw a future director in the bathroom mirror; I'd often see them talking in conspiratorial tones in Miss Gandy's office, as if planning which of the other ADs Miss Gandy would torpedo next. And I liked him, too; he was easily my favorite among the various ADs. A stocky man in his mid-fifties, Mohr never demanded to be first on the "He's left the building" call list, and he didn't have the arrogant, superior manner that so many ADs displayed. Like the other ADs, he could be obsequious and subservient when dealing with the Director; to survive as an AD in Mr. Hoover's Bureau he had to be. But unlike most of the other ADs, he never demanded obsequiousness from people below him. He was a little gruff, but he had a sense of humor, and you could actually talk to the guy.

For some reason he took an interest in me, maybe because despite the difference in age and rank we came from similar backgrounds. The son of a steamfitter, he was raised in New York State, a high school athlete who'd gotten a scholarship to American University and then went to law school at night. He'd often stop by my office and ask how things were going, and he was quick to offer career advice and insights into the way the Bureau operated in the field. With thirty years in the FBI, most of it at SOG, there wasn't much that went on in the Bureau that J. P. Mohr didn't know about.

So whenever I had a question about the way the Bureau worked, I'd ask him. How do we do this, and why do we do that, and how does this work? It was only natural that one day not long before I was scheduled to begin New Agents Training, I asked him about COINTELPRO.

"Mr. Mohr, I keep seeing references to counterintelligence programs, COINTELPROs—'White Hate,' 'Black Nationalists,' 'New Left.' What's that all about?"

He gave me a sharp look. "Whoa there, Paul. All that stuff is closely held, not to be discussed outside the Bureau."

I was on good enough terms with him to be a little impertinent at times. I glanced at our surroundings. "But, sir, right now we're inside the Bureau."

"Don't be a wise guy," Mohr said.

I didn't say anything more; my initial question still hung in the air. I think I already instinctively understood that sometimes an interrogator's best weapon was silence. Most people want to tell you things, but sometimes you just have to give them a moment to think about it. Mohr understood the technique as well as anybody, but it still worked.

"Okay," he said after what seemed like a full minute of conversational void. "You're going to run into some of this when you get out in the field anyway. So let me explain it this way. You know the difference between intelligence and counterintelligence, right?"

"Sure. Intelligence is when you gather information on the enemy. Counterintelligence is when you prevent the enemy from gathering information on you—catching spies and things like that."

Mohr nodded. "That's correct as far as it goes. But counterintelligence—active counterintelligence—goes beyond that. With that kind of counterintelligence you take direct actions against the enemy. You try to confuse him, disrupt his operations, sow dissension in his ranks, ruin his morale, steer him in the direction you want him to go without him knowing that he's being manipulated. That's what COINTELPRO does. It started back in the fifties with CPUSA and SWP"—he meant the Socialist Workers Party—"and it grew from there."

"But how does it work? What kind of 'direct actions' are we talking about?"

Mohr shrugged. "Depends on what group you're dealing with. With the CP, maybe we'd get hold of their membership records— I'm not going to say how we'd get hold of them, but—"

"Black bag jobs?"

He seemed surprised. "You do have big ears, don't you? I'm not going to get into it, but you get hold of the membership rolls and you start calling people—friends, employers, landlords, whatever, and you tell them, 'Hey, did you know so-and-so is a card-carrying member of the Communist Party?' Maybe you pass the names on to the IRS for audits, or you get some citizen to file a complaint about the building where they have their offices so the local building inspectors will drive them crazy with code violations. Or you put informants in there to stir things up, spread rumors, sow dissension.

It's pretty effective. Twenty years ago CPUSA had fifty or sixty thousand members, and now it's down to about five thousand at most."

(I have to inject a word about the term *informant* here. An informant was not an undercover Bureau agent who posed as a sympathizer and infiltrated a targeted group. The Director seldom approved the use of Bureau agents as undercovers, partly because of the danger to the agents and partly because of the fear that an agent would have to commit illegal acts to protect his cover—acts that might later be brought out in court and "embarrass the Bureau." And despite the sinister sound of the word, most Bureau informants were simply ordinary people who casually passed on things they'd heard just to be helpful—cabdrivers, journalists, college administrators, businessmen, small-town mayors, local cops, even an occasional movie star. But some of the Bureau's active informants were civilians who worked under an FBI agent's direction to provide information on specific investigations or in some cases to infiltrate and report on a targeted group. Those informants did so for various reasons. Some were criminals looking to work their way out of a pending criminal charge. Others were paid for their services, sometimes quite handsomely; an informant who helped the Bureau crack a major case might get $10,000 or $20,000, although usually the pay was far less. At any time the Bureau had thousands of full- and part-time informants working in criminal as well as counterintelligence capacities—and the pressure was always on the field agents to find more. The Director adhered to the widely shared belief that an investigator was only as good as his informants.)

"So that was it?" I said to Mohr. "Just harassment? No rough stuff?"

"Depends on how you define *rough stuff*. Sometimes we had to, like with the Klan." He paused for a moment. "You remember Medgar Evers? The Birmingham church bombing? The three civil rights workers?"

I did. Black civil rights leader Medgar Evers was shot in the back and killed in his driveway in Mississippi in 1963. That same year a bomb killed four young black girls at a Baptist church in Birmingham, Alabama—one of a series of racist bombings that earned the city the nickname Bombingham. In the summer of '64 three civil rights workers, two white and one black, were kidnapped and murdered by Klansmen near Philadelphia, Mississippi. I knew about those cases—everybody in America knew about them.

"We knew who the killers were in every one of those cases," Mohr said. "We had technicals, misurs"—he meant wiretaps and bugs—"informants, forensics from the Lab. We knew who they were, but we didn't have jurisdiction in murder cases, and the locals wouldn't do anything. Even if they filed state murder charges, what happened? The Evers case? The shooter got two hung juries and then the locals dropped the case. The Birmingham church bombers? The locals convicted them on state charges of illegal possession of dynamite and they got hundred-dollar fines—a hundred bucks. The MIBURN case—that's the three civil rights workers? We could only get 'em on civil rights violations, not murder. And then last year some redneck political-appointee Mississippi federal judge gives them three to ten years—three to ten, for murdering three people!"

(An historical update: Byron De La Beckwith, Medgar Evers' killer, was finally convicted of state murder charges in 1994 and sentenced to life. Years after the Birmingham church bombing, three men were convicted in state court and sentenced to life—the last of them in 2002. Of the seven Klansmen convicted in 1967 of federal civil rights violations in the MIBURN investigation—Bureau-speak for "Mississippi Burning"—none served more than six years.)

"The point is," Mohr continued, "the Klan was laughing at us. Worse, they were threatening us, saying they were going to shoot our agents or blow us up. So Crazy Billy came up with a plan."

Crazy Billy was the aforementioned William Sullivan, the AD in charge of the Bureau's Domestic Intelligence Division. It was a measure of Mohr's trust in me that he would use Sullivan's behind-his-back nickname with me—a nickname earned by Sullivan's combative, sometimes explosive personality and his frequent off-the-wall ideas.

Mohr went on, "This is three, going on four years ago. Sullivan says, 'Hey, why wait for these guys to commit a crime and then investigate them? Let's destroy these redneck bastards beforehand, using the same sort of tactics we used against CPUSA in the fifties.' It was time to take the gloves off. That was the start of 'COINTEL-PRO—White Hate.' He liked the idea."

I could tell from the way Mohr said "he" that he meant the Director.

"So we went after these guys. At one point we had hundreds of agents in Mississippi alone, following Klansmen around, taking down license plate numbers at their cross-burning rallies, knocking on their doors at night, showing up at their workplaces to interview them, day after day and week after week. Wherever they went, we'd be practically stepping on their heels, and we weren't shy about it. We wanted them to know we were there, and that we knew who they were."

Mohr smiled. "We'd send these anonymous postcards to their house or their work with a drawing of a guy in a hood and the message 'Klansman! Trying to hide behind your sheet? We know who you are!' We must have sent out thousands of those. It drove 'em nuts. That was the idea, to mess with them. Maybe we'd put it out that this Klansman was sleeping with that Klansman's wife, or that this other Klansman was stealing money from the coffers, or we'd put a snitch jacket on them."

"A *snitch jacket*?" I hadn't heard the term.

"Yeah, you let it leak out that a certain Klansman is working for us, the Bureau, that he's an informant, even though he isn't, so the rest of his Klan buddies won't trust him. The thing is, a lot of these guys *were* our informants. We buried the Klan in informants. Most of those guys down there are poor, uneducated, and we had all the money we needed—Mr. Hoover saw to that—so we never lacked for informants. Remember the Viola Liuzzo case?"

"Sure." Everybody in America knew about the case. In 1965 a thirty-nine-year-old white civil rights worker named Viola Liuzzo was riding in a car with a young black man near Montgomery, Alabama, when she was chased down and shot and killed by four Klansmen in another car. Like so many others, the crime shocked and horrified most of the nation.

"We bagged those guys within two hours," Mohr said. "And how? One of those four Klansmen was one of our informants! He was riding in the car! He didn't do the shooting, and he couldn't stop it, but he gave up the other three. That's how deep we're into these guys."

Mohr lowered his voice. "This really is confidential, Paul, so keep it to yourself, but according to Sullivan, one out of every five Klan members on their rolls is actually working for us. But the funny thing is, according to our informants, most of the Klan members think the number's even higher, that something like half of their Klan buddies are on the Bureau payroll—and that most of the rest of them want to be, for the money. Same thing with the American Nazi Party and the National States' Rights Party and the other 'white hate' groups we've gone after. Nobody trusts anybody else in those groups anymore; that's how effective COINTELPRO has been."

"It sure sounds that way, Mr. Mohr. But I have to ask—is it all legal?"

He smiled benignly. "Oh, that's right, I forgot, you're still in law school—which means you're still an idealist. Let's just say that most of our COINTELPRO tactics are extralegal—not regulated by law. Is it illegal to make an anonymous call? Or to send a postcard? No. Our operating principle is 'do unto others as they have done unto others.' The Klan's been harassing and intimidating and murdering people for years, and the law, the local law, wasn't doing anything about it—so we did. You asked about rough stuff. I'm not saying that if somebody threatened one of our agents that he wouldn't get a pretty serious talking-to from our guys. And our informants aren't always angels. When you get on the bricks, you'll learn that informants almost never are. Maybe some of them crossed over the line. But we never killed anybody."

Technically, that was true. FBI agents never killed anybody in connection with COINTELPRO. But as I would later learn—as everyone would later learn—people had gotten killed as a direct result of the counterintelligence programs. That was especially true with the Bureau's "COINTELPRO—Black Nationalist Hate Groups" operations directed against various radical African American groups—the Nation of Islam, Black Panther Party, Black Liberation Army, and others. Paid Bureau informants heavily infiltrated those groups, spreading dissension and distrust between factions, putting snitch jackets on other members, at times encouraging— or at least not discouraging—violent attacks on rival organizations. Although the Black Panthers and others were idealized by the political left and much of the news media, the truth was that many of their members were criminals and ex-convicts. So they dealt with rivals and suspected snitches the way criminals and convicts do— they killed them. Those killings didn't prompt any tears within the Bureau. After all, the Panthers openly called for the murder of cops and other "establishment" figures—the party "training manual" advised using high-powered rifles to "knock the pig out of his shoes at a distance of three blocks"—so the Bureau's feeling was that they had simply reaped what they had sown. But as Mohr had said, I still had traces of the idealist in me.

"So the end justifies the means?"

Mohr gave me a disappointed look. "That's a simplistic way of putting it." Then he thought for a moment. "But, yeah, sometimes, when it's for the right reasons, the end does justify the means— within limits. Look, Paul, these are tough guys out there. They're not playing around. The Klan, the Panthers—they'd kill you in a minute if they had the chance. Remember that when you get into the field."

"Yes, sir." Then I had another thought. "What about 'COIN-TELPRO—New Left'? What's that about?"

Suddenly Mohr looked uncomfortable. "Oh, that's mostly SDS"— he meant the Students for a Democratic Society—"the war protesters, the campus agitators, the radical professors. People like that."

"And it's the same sort of thing? Disruption, spread dissension, all that stuff?"

"It's a national security issue," Mohr said a bit defensively. "He thinks they're all controlled by the Communists." Mohr glanced around conspiratorially. "For God's sake don't tell anyone I said this, but he's obsessed with Communists. Obsessed."

Again, I didn't have to ask who "he" was. The Director's bedrock belief was that all the protests and demonstrations against the war were the work of Communist agents in service of the Soviet Union, Red China, North Vietnam. He would believe it to his dying day.

"So they aren't? Controlled by Communists?"

Mohr shook his head. "Not by the CPUSA, that's for sure. Those guys are so compromised they couldn't organize a party picnic, much less control the anti-war movement. The Soviets? They certainly aren't unhappy about what's going on, the protests and all, but they don't know how to handle a bunch of pot-smoking hippies and pampered college students any more than we do. I know, a lot of these SDS types will wave Mao's *Little Red Book* and quote Fidel and Che"—Castro and Guevara—"and talk about the Marxist revolutionary struggle and all that crap. But they don't have enough discipline to be real Communists. But they're extremists, and some of them are violent. So they're fair game."

Mohr didn't specifically mention the violent Weathermen break-off faction of the SDS, for the simple reason that they didn't yet exist; the Weathermen, later known as the Weather Underground, wouldn't be formed for another year. But as I mentioned earlier, already in 1968 there'd been dozens of campus bombings and arsons, along with other acts of political violence.

"The problem," Mohr went on, "is that we can't seem to tell the difference between a kid who wants to build a bomb and a kid who just wants to wave a protest sign. We can't tell the difference between a college professor who's against the war and a dangerous radical who wants to destroy the country. So we're going after all of them. It's the same problem the army is having over there." He meant Vietnam. "They can't tell who the enemy is, so pretty soon everybody is the enemy. And that's when things get out of hand."

"Are they? Out of hand?"

"Yes. We're going too far." Mohr stopped, as if he feared he'd already said too much.

"Look, Paul," he said after a moment, "let me give you some advice. You're young, and you look younger, and you'd fit in on a college campus. So when you get in the field, they may try to draw you into some of these counterintelligence things. Try to avoid it if you can."

"Okay—but why?"

"Because if this COINTELPRO stuff ever gets out, it's going to blow up in our faces—all of us, from the Director on down. And you don't want to be a part of it."

As it turned out, Mr. Mohr was prescient, on two counts. Soon I'd be drawn into the Bureau's COINTELPRO—New Left operations. And, yes, eventually the "stuff" would get out—COINTEL-PRO, the wiretaps, the bugs, the bag jobs, all of it.

Most Americans wouldn't be too concerned about the Bureau playing hardball with a bunch of red-necked Klansmen, or some tired old Stalinists and Trotskyites in the CPUSA and the Socialist Workers Party. They wouldn't be alarmed by the Bureau's tapping and bugging and harassing the mobsters of La Cosa Nostra. (Organized crime was never an official COINTELPRO target, but some similar tactics were used.) And for many people, the Bureau's use of extralegal or illegal tactics against cop-killing Black Panthers and bomb-making Weathermen could be understood, if not completely justified.

But when it was revealed that the Bureau had waged a COIN-TELPRO war against college professors and students and generally peaceful protesters—their own sons and daughters!—well, the public outrage would be deep and long-lasting. The Bureau would be portrayed as a kind of American Gestapo—that's the word many critics used, Gestapo, the Nazi secret police—with the Director playing the role of a modern-day Heinrich Himmler. It would come close to destroying the Federal Bureau of Investigation—and it would play a major role in the posthumous lynching of J. Edgar Hoover's reputation.

But the critics almost always ignored one thing. Hoover wasn't acting on his own. Since before World War II, every president he'd served—those revered by the left and those revered by the right—knew what Hoover and the Bureau were doing in domestic security and surveillance. They may not have known all the details—most didn't want to know the details—but they knew the general outlines. Every one of those presidents could have made Hoover stop what he was doing or fired him outright.

But for their own reasons, not one did.

The popular conception these days is that J. Edgar Hoover was a manipulator of presidents, that he was a puppet master looming darkly over every sordid episode in mid-twentieth-century American history, that he used his power, and his secrets, to blackmail presidents and bend them to his will. But I never saw Hoover blackmail a president. Actually, it was the other way around.

During my entire time in the Director's office the president was Lyndon Baines Johnson. Whenever he called the Director—the calls came from the president's secretary—I was under strict orders to inform the Director immediately, no matter what. Even if the Director was enjoying his customary postlunch nap and the NO CALLS card was propped up by the phone, if the president's office called, I had to wake him up.

That only happened a couple of times. I'd call the Director's inner office on the green phone and he'd answer groggily and grumpily, "I said no calls!" ·

"Sir, the president's office is calling."

He'd tell me to put it through at once. Hoover always understood who the boss was.

Of course, I wasn't privy to what was said during those presidential calls. But on a few occasions I'd have to bring some documents to the Director's desk while he was on the line with the Oval Office, and I'd hear his side of the conversation. And mostly what I heard was "Yes, Mr. President." "Yes, Mr. President." "I'll take care of that right away, Mr. President." To me the Director sounded less like a presidential manipulator than a husband being browbeaten by his domineering wife—which in the case of LBJ was an apt analogy.

The Director's relationships with presidents had varied widely over the decades. When he was first named director, Hoover was just an obscure midlevel bureaucrat in the Justice Department, so President Calvin Coolidge probably couldn't have picked him out of a lineup. The Director's relationship with President Herbert Hoover was cordial, but again, the Bureau wasn't yet the high-profile crime-busting agency it would later become, and thus not worthy of much presidential attention.

Ironically, it was the liberal Democrat Franklin Delano Roosevelt, not some right-winger, who did the most to expand the Bureau's—and Hoover's—authority and power. Roosevelt pushed the series of congressional "anti-crime bills" in the mid-1930s that greatly extended the Bureau's criminal jurisdiction. He also expanded the Bureau's role beyond crime fighting and into domestic intelligence and internal security. Roosevelt, who like Hoover was an inveterate collector of intelligence, and gossip, ordered Hoover to investigate political groups on the left and the right—Communists, Fascists, America First members who opposed US involvement in the war in Europe, and other political opponents of the president—and FDR secretly gave Hoover the authority to use wiretaps in "national security" cases. When Roosevelt took office in 1933 the Bureau had fewer than four hundred special agents in its ranks; by the time Roosevelt died in 1945, that number had grown more than tenfold, to forty-five hundred agents. Hoover enjoyed frequent and easy access to the Roosevelt Oval Office, a symbol of the Director's growing influence—but Roosevelt often ignored his advice.

(To cite just one example of his rejected advice, after Pearl Harbor, and acting under presidential directive, the FBI detained more than fifteen thousand "enemy aliens"—that is, German, Italian, and Japanese nationals—who had previously been investigated by the Bureau and placed on the Custodial Detention List of potential spies and saboteurs. But Hoover strongly opposed the shameful mass "relocation" of Japanese American citizens from the West Coast, calling it "utterly unwarranted" and the result of "public hysteria." Under political pressure, Roosevelt overruled Hoover, and more than one hundred thousand Americans of Japanese descent were sent to detention camps. Critics who portray Hoover as an unrestrained trampler of civil liberties usually ignore that episode.)

Hoover's close presidential relations ended when Harry Truman took over. Truman made it clear from the start that if he wanted to communicate with the FBI, he'd do so through his attorney general—a snub that Hoover never forgave or forgot. (When Hoover died, he had photographs in his home of every president under whom he'd served, with one exception—Harry Truman.) Truman often expressed to aides his fear that the Bureau would become a Gestapo-style secret police agency, but that didn't stop him from re-authorizing the Bureau's warrantless wiretapping practices and ordering Hoover to investigate certain of Truman's political enemies. He also charged the FBI with investigating the "loyalty" of many current and would-be federal employees, thus adding many thousands of new "secret files" to the FBI file room

The Director fared much better under Dwight D. Eisenhower, who met with Hoover shortly after the 1952 election and assured him that he had Eisenhower's complete support. I already mentioned that it was Eisenhower who, through his attorney general, authorized warrantless FBI taps and bugs in national security cases, even when a bag-job break-in was required. Eisenhower also issued the now-infamous Executive Order 10450, which broadened Truman's loyalty program and required all federal employees to be investigated by their department heads—with FBI assistance—for "any behavior, activities or associations which tend to show that the individual is not reliable or trustworthy," including "sexual perversion." Some five thousand gay federal employees were dismissed under the order, and thousands more were denied employment, on the theory that their sexual orientation made them prime targets for blackmail by foreign espionage agencies. That sounds appalling now, and it was, but at the time it was the harsh societal reality.

The point of all this is that while Hoover and the Bureau conducted operations that were later widely criticized, he was careful to ensure that those activities always had the expressed or tacit approval of the current president. Although Hoover had varying degrees of influence over various presidents, he never controlled them, and he certainly never "blackmailed" any of those strong and powerful men. If he'd tried, Roosevelt or Eisenhower would have fired him, and Truman would probably have had him arrested. Hoover was kept on as director by a long succession of presidents because he was popular with the public and Congress, he was efficient—and he was useful to the presidents.

Despite a host of conspiracy theories, even John F. Kennedy was never the target of Hooverian blackmail—although the youthful president provided plenty of opportunities for it with his relentless and often reckless pursuit of women. (Kennedy reportedly once said that if he didn't have sex at least once a day, he would get a migraine.) The Bureau never directly investigated Kennedy, but his name came up in several Bureau investigations unrelated to him. The first was in 1942, when the Bureau was investigating a strikingly attractive Danish national and alleged Nazi spy named Inga Arvad, a former model and actress who was working as a reporter for the *Washington Times-Herald*. With Roosevelt's approval the Bureau tapped Arvad's phone, which ultimately revealed that she was having a torrid affair with a young navy ensign in the Office of Naval Intelligence—that is, John Kennedy, son of the wealthy former ambassador to Britain Joe Kennedy, a longtime Hoover acquaintance. The Bureau did not open a separate investigation of the young Kennedy; in Bureau terminology he was just a "walk-on," someone who is inadvertently picked up on a surveillance. In fact, Hoover specifically ordered that Kennedy not be investigated by the Bureau; his affair with the suspected spy was the navy's problem, Hoover said— a problem the navy solved by shipping Kennedy to the Pacific theater, where he later won fame as the heroic commander of *PT-109*. As for Arvad, she was never proven to be a German spy—although that didn't mean the Bureau's investigation wasn't a legitimate counterespionage operation.

Kennedy next came to the Bureau's attention in 1960, after he won the Democratic Party's presidential nomination. As you might expect a national security organization to do, the Bureau assembled a dossier on the potential next president, most of it from public sources such as newspaper articles, but some from Bureau files. (The Bureau did the same thing with Kennedy's opponent, Richard Nixon.) The confidential dossier noted that then-senator Kennedy and his family had always had "friendly" relations with the Bureau and that he'd been "conscientious and sincere" in his Senate duties, and the file assessed his stands on various political issues such as Communism and civil rights.

But the dossier also noted that Kennedy had long been known for certain "immoral activities," not only with Inga Arvad but with numerous other women as well—a practice that Kennedy carried with him into the White House. Not that that was any secret in Washington. The young president's long string of sexual affairs— including a likely but never-quite-proven tryst with Marilyn Monroe—was common knowledge among Washington insiders and the press. That the stories didn't come out while Kennedy was alive indicated how delicately the press treated presidents back in those days.

Hoover never put the president under surveillance or tapped his phones—even if Hoover had wanted to, it would have been too difficult and too risky—but he certainly was aware of the stories. For the most part he ignored them. Hoover generally enjoyed a distant but friendly relationship with the president, who unlike his kid brother Bobby treated the aging Director with deference and respect. But there was one Kennedy sex story that couldn't be ignored—and once again it happened when Kennedy was a "walk-on" in an unrelated investigation.

In the early 1960s the Bureau was conducting an organized crime investigation into Chicago mob boss Sam Giancana, who was intimately involved with a woman named Judith Campbell, a stunning LA "party girl" who also had affairs with Frank Sinatra and other famous and powerful men. Through informants and electronic surveillance of Giancana and other mobsters, the Bureau learned that Sinatra had introduced Campbell to Kennedy in 1960, and that ever since then Kennedy and the young woman had regularly been "shacking up," as the mobsters put it—this at the same time that Campbell was also still sleeping with Giancana.

Well, what is the director of the nation's premier internal security agency supposed to do when he inadvertently learns that the president of the United States and the head of the Chicago mob are sharing a girlfriend? This was clearly a national security threat: What if the Mob planned to blackmail the president? So in March 1962, two days after learning of the Kennedy-Campbell connection, Hoover sat down with Kennedy at an unrecorded meeting at the White House and told him what the Bureau had discovered. Kennedy apparently ended the relationship with Campbell that very day.

Later critics would suggest that because Kennedy was widely believed to be planning to fire Hoover at the start of his hoped-for second presidential term, Hoover was using the Campbell story to blackmail Kennedy in an effort to hold on to his job. But if blackmail was Hoover's intention, why do it in 1962, when Hoover's position as director was not in danger? Why not hold the information until it was necessary to use it? Or leak the story to the press or anti-Kennedy members of Congress and thereby ensure that there wouldn't be a second Kennedy term? Even the deferential members of the Washington press corps probably wouldn't have been willing to sit on the story of a president and a mobster's moll— and various congressmen certainly wouldn't have. So, no, J. Edgar Hoover didn't blackmail John F. Kennedy. Hoover did him a favor and kept quiet about it. The Judith Campbell story didn't come out until years after Kennedy's death.

The truth is that if there was any president with whom Hoover was involved in blackmail, it wasn't JFK but rather Lyndon Baines Johnson—and it was Johnson, not Hoover, doing the "blackmailing."

The Director had known Johnson personally since 1943, when the congressman and later Senate majority leader and his family moved into a house on Thirtieth Place NW across the street from Hoover's home. Hoover occasionally had dinner with Johnson and his wife, Lady Bird, and Hoover was also friendly with Johnson's young daughters, Lynda Bird Johnson and Luci Baines Johnson, who viewed Hoover as a sort of kindly old uncle. They'd often knock on Hoover's door and ask for help in finding their dog named Little Beagle Johnson—clearly, Johnson had a thing about the LBJ theme—help that the dog-loving Director of the FBI would cheerfully give.

The personal relationship—and the mutual fondness for dogs—continued into the Johnson presidency. Johnson had two beagles in the White House, unimaginatively named Him and Her. (Johnson got in trouble with animal-lover groups when he demonstrated for reporters how to test Him's "hunting voice" by lifting the dog by his ears until he howled.) Sadly, in 1966 Him was chasing a squirrel across the White House lawn when he was run over and killed by a Secret Service car—which prompted no end of snickers and snide comments at FBI headquarters. I was told that when the Director heard about it, he growled, "Protect the president? The Secret Service can't even protect the president's dog—from the Secret Service!"

Anyway, after Him's untimely demise, Hoover ordered a replacement beagle from a breeder in Georgia and had it sent to the White House—which led to another of Hoover's favorite stories:

It seems that one day Hoover and Johnson were walking across the White House grounds when . . . well, let the Director tell it.

"One day I was visiting at the White House," Hoover would say, "and the president said, 'Let's go look at the dogs.' We were walking along when all of a sudden he hollered, in his big Texas voice right in my ear, 'Edgar! Edgar! Where are you, Edgar?' I was confused, so I said, 'I'm right here, Mr. President,' and he looked at me and said, 'I don't mean you, I mean the dog.' I was still confused, but the president explained, "I named the dog Edgar!'"

The Director's avuncular relationship with the Johnson daughters also followed them into the White House—and it led to another rather amusing incident. In 1966 the twenty-two-year-old Lynda Bird began a very public romance with Hollywood actor George Hamilton, being seen on his arm at the Oscar awards and other glamorous events—and her daddy wasn't happy about it. He was understandably suspicious of the movie star's motives. Hamilton, then twenty-seven and a star in such films as the beach-party comedy *Where the Boys Are*, could have had his pick of any number of beautiful Hollywood women, while Lynda Bird—well, she was a bright and charming young woman, but she wasn't exactly known as a ravishing beauty. So Johnson did what any worried father who happened to be the president of the United States would do—he called in the FBI.

With Hoover's permission, Assistant to the Director Deke De-Loach, then the FBI liaison with the White House, ordered a discreet background check on Hamilton. To the president's frustration, it failed to yield any derogatory information on the actor—no criminal history, no allegations of homosexuality, nothing beyond the fact that some of the folks in his hometown thought he was a "spoiled brat." Eventually the romance fizzled of its own accord, but not before Lynda Bird and Hamilton dropped by the Director's office for a visit, apparently so Lynda Bird could show off her handsome boyfriend to "old uncle Edgar."

It was quite a day at the office. Hamilton showed up in a blue blazer and immaculate white slacks with his trademark ten-thousand-watt perpetual suntan in full glow, looking a bit bewildered to find himself in the nerve center of the Federal Bureau of Investigation. It was a long way from Hollywood. Although he tried to be charming to the staff—"It's so very, very nice to meet you!"—he came off as slick and unctuous; as soon as he turned away, Miss Gandy looked at me and rolled her eyes dramatically. What was funny about it was that the young couple were accompanied by a pair of silent, unsmiling Secret Service agents, who stood guard in the reception room while the Director met with the couple in his private office. As I said earlier, ever since the Kennedy assassination there'd been considerable bad blood between the Bureau and the Secret Service, and it was a little insulting that the Secret Service thought the president's daughter required protection while she was meeting with the Director of the Federal Bureau of Investigation. Never one to let an insult pass unanswered, Hoover made certain that two equally silent and unsmiling Bureau agents were also conspicuously standing guard in the reception room—standing guard over the Secret Service agents!

Despite their personal relationship, Hoover hadn't exactly been thrilled when Johnson became president. I had it on good authority, from someone who was in the room, that when the Director first got word that Kennedy had been pronounced dead in Dallas, Hoover's response was "Jesus Christ! Now Johnson is president! He couldn't run a dog show, how the hell is he going to run the country?"

Hoover underestimated the man. Johnson may not have had much executive experience, but as a political manipulator he was unmatched. To get what he wanted he would lie, beg, threaten, flatter, cajole, shout, scream, pound the table, and even weep, and in the process he managed to get Congress to pass landmark legislation that the Kennedy administration could never have gotten passed— the 1964 Civil Rights Act, the 1965 Voting Rights Act, Medicare, Medicaid. But Johnson was also deeply paranoid and suspicious, especially when it came to Bobby Kennedy and the "Kennedy crowd" LBJ had inherited, and to the growing protests against the war he hadn't started but now owned. "Hey, hey, LBJ, how many kids did you kill today?" the protesters shouted, and it seemed to drive him mad. When Johnson wanted to lash out at his enemies, he turned to Hoover and the FBI.

More than any other preceding president, Johnson tried his best to turn the Bureau into his personal private detective agency—usually under the guise of "national security," but often for clearly political purposes. There were numerous examples. Fearful that civil rights activists led by Martin Luther King Jr. might try to disrupt the 1964 Democratic National Convention, Johnson ordered Hoover to send a team of Bureau agents to Atlantic City to monitor—that is, wiretap and bug—King and others and report back to the Johnson campaign. When longtime Johnson aide Walter Jenkins was arrested by Washington, DC, police for a gay sexual encounter in a YMCA bathroom just before the 1964 election, Johnson ordered the Bureau to investigate whether it was a "frame-up" orchestrated by his opponent, Arizona senator Barry Goldwater. (It wasn't.) Just before the 1968 election, when Johnson was backing Vice President Hubert Humphrey against Richard Nixon, Johnson ordered the Bureau to wiretap and physically surveil the South Vietnamese embassy in Washington and to check certain Nixon campaign phone records to see if Nixon was conspiring with the South Vietnamese to sidetrack peace talks with North Vietnam. Throughout his presidency Johnson ordered Hoover to conduct "name checks" in Bureau files on various anti-war congressmen and their staffs, as well as journalists and suspected "leakers" of confidential information.

Hoover also kept Johnson well supplied with ordinary gossip, which Johnson relished even more than Hoover did. Was a local call girl bragging to an FBI informant about various congressmen she'd slept with? Had a local cop told his Bureau contact about pulling over a prominent senator for drunk driving the night before? Had the Bureau heard reports that a certain sixty-eight-year-old Supreme Court justice was having an affair with a twenty-two-year-old college student? Hoover would pass on the juicier bits to Johnson, who'd gleefully pass them on to everybody else. Trading in gossip may not have been particularly admirable, but it was hardly unusual; almost everybody did it, at every level of government. In Washington, DC, gossip was currency.

Nevertheless, Hoover tried to resist some of Johnson's more overtly political demands; the Director scrawled, "The Bureau should not be involved in this," on at least one memo concerning a Johnson order. That was probably less out of concern for civil liberties than the fear that the Bureau's activities on Johnson's behalf would leak to the press or to Congress and destroy the Bureau's reputation. For forty years Hoover had fought against the politicization of the FBI, and to a large extent he'd succeeded.

Still, he usually acquiesced to Johnson's politically motivated orders. Johnson was, after all, the president of the United States, and Hoover had never thought that his power was greater than any president's. The racetrack incident notwithstanding, Hoover never thought he had the authority to defy a firm presidential order, especially one issued in the name of "national security." Despite

Johnson's waiver of Hoover's mandatory retirement, Johnson made it clear that the director of the FBI served at the president's pleasure—and Hoover knew that if he didn't follow Johnson's orders, Johnson could simply find someone who would. Johnson never wanted to fire Hoover—as he'd said, it was better to have "Hoover inside the tent pissing out than have him outside the tent pissing in"—but to use Johnson's terminology, he had the "balls" to do it if he had to.

As tough as the Director was, in some ways he seemed overwhelmed by the force of Johnson's personality. To give you a flavor of how LBJ dealt with his FBI Director, here's a transcript of a call from Johnson to Hoover in February 1968. (I didn't listen in on the call, but Nixon wasn't the only one who secretly taped his Oval Office calls and conversations; Johnson did it, too, although much less extensively.) Johnson was convinced that some anti-war congressmen and staff members were leaking information to the Communists in Vietnam, and he wanted Hoover to find out who they were—and he didn't seem to care how Hoover did it.

"I don't want anybody to know I called you," Johnson said in his slow Texas drawl, "but I want you personally to do one big job if you never do anything else. I want you to watch with all the care and caution and judgment you've built up over the last forty years to see what those who are dedicated to overthrowing us are doing. I want you to watch it like nobody's business"—Johnson pronounced it "bid'ness"—"and make it the highest priority to see who they're talking to and what they're saying. There's so many things getting out now, every movement our troops make, they tell the other side before they move. When [Secretary of Defense Robert] McNamara goes up and testifies before [anti-war senator William] Fulbright that we are breaking the North Vietnamese codes and a goddamn Commie sympathizer goes out and tells it, they just change the codes! So I want you to take personal charge of this and have your [FBI agents] chase down every damn lead and see who they're talking to and when and how. You're the only guy in government who's watching it, and I think we'd have already lost our government if you hadn't been. So I just want to order you now to be more diligent with this than you've ever been in your life."

Hoover's sole contribution to this conversation was to say, "I'll give it my personal attention, Mr. President."

So after reading that, I ask you, Who was the boss of whom?

Less than a year after that conversation Johnson would be gone, driven from office by the war, his great liberal legislative accomplishments ignored. J. Edgar Hoover would be passed on to his eighth—and last—president with a ringing endorsement from the seventh. At a White House courtesy meeting with President-elect Nixon, Johnson told him, "Dick, you will come to depend on Edgar. You will rely on him time and time again to maintain security. He's the only one you can put your complete trust in. He is a pillar of strength in a city of weak men."

As it turned out, Nixon even more than LBJ would try to turn the Bureau into his personal political intelligence and counterintelligence arm. Because of Hoover, Nixon would fail—and in the process would destroy himself.

But I wouldn't be around to watch J. Edgar Hoover set the stage for Nixon's downfall. Because my days in the Director's office were coming to an end.

Friday, September 20, 1968, was my last day in the Director's office. After three long years I'd finally finished law school and received my formal appointment to attend the New Agents Training Class at Quantico, starting Monday morning.

Now all I had to do was say goodbye.

I stopped by Mr. Mohr's office, and he wished me good luck in New Agents Training. I gave Nancy Mooney a little hug, promising that we'd stay in touch, which we did. I shook hands with John Cox, chiding him once again about the Redskins' poor showing in the previous season and predicting a similar lack of success in the coming one. Sam Noisette took my hand and wished me well, and Jimmy Crawford sent me off with a "Now you be careful out there, you hear?" I was saving the Miss Gandy goodbye for last.

As for the Director, I wasn't quite sure. You've probably realized by now that Hoover wasn't particularly sentimental when it came to his staff, so I didn't know if I should formally say goodbye or just quietly fade away. Then late that afternoon, as I was packing my few belongings into my briefcase, the green phone on my desk erupted.

"Come to my office!" the Director barked at me for the thousandth time, and for the thousandth time I made the long walk down the hall. Just in case a handshake would be involved, I once again made sure my palm was dry.

The Director was at his desk talking on the phone with one of the ADs when I came in, and he motioned me to take a seat. I watched him as he talked, and it was strange. I remembered the day two years earlier when I first met him, and he still had the same proud bearing, the same rapid-fire speech, the same impeccable style of clothing. But something was different. He was a little older, of course, now seventy-three, but that wasn't it. When you see someone almost every day you don't notice the person aging; the process is too slow. No, what was different was his eyes. They looked . . . weary, like the eyes of a man who'd fought too many battles. I'd witnessed some of those battles, and in that moment I wondered if he'd be able to fight—and win—the new battles that were sure to come.

The Director ended his call and turned to me. "Letersky"—happily I was still just "Letersky"—"I understand this is your last day here with us."

"Yes, sir. I start New Agents Training Monday."

"Good! Study hard, keep your nose clean, and I'm sure you'll do fine."

"I'll do my very best, sir."

"Of course," he said brusquely, as if doing one's very best was merely the minimum expectation—which to him it was. "I want you to know that I have observed your development over the past two years. You have grown, you've matured, you've continued to present a good appearance, and—with a few exceptions—the work ethic you've displayed has been excellent."

A few exceptions? I remembered the chewing out he'd given

me, and the occasional brief complaint he'd growled out—and obviously he remembered them, too. He remembered everything.

"Your progress has been noticed and appreciated by all," the Director continued. "I know Miss Gandy will miss your presence here, as will I and the entire staff. I'm confident that in due time you will be back here at the Seat of Government."

What he meant was that after six or seven years in the field, I'd return to FBI headquarters as a supervisory agent and begin the long climb up through the FBI bureaucracy. He meant it as a compliment, an endorsement of my potential, but I wasn't at all sure that was what I wanted. I was young, and I wanted to be a street agent, not a bureaucrat. But of course I didn't say that.

"Thank you, sir. I want to say that it's been an honor for me to be here. It's been a great experience, and I want to thank you for giving me the opportunity."

"Yes, yes," the Director said. He paused for a moment, and when he spoke again, his voice was gentle—or at least as close to gentle as that gruff, raspy voice could be.

"Letersky," he continued, "before you go, I'm going to give you some advice. It concerns principles I have always tried to follow, and which have served me well during my long career—some would say my too long career."

There was the barest hint of a smile. Already there had been rumblings in some of the newspapers that Hoover was getting too old for the job.

"First, always be strong in your opinions, especially in crisis situations. Only a man of strong opinions can lead other men. Second, always be loyal to your superiors, even when you disagree with them. If you strongly disagree, choose your battles very carefully, but once you take a firm stand, never back down. Never! If you do, you will lose your dignity and your self-respect—and in the end, dignity and self-respect are all that any man really has. And finally, make as many friends as you can, but never be afraid to make enemies. There's a remark I like to make in explaining my philosophy on this matter: 'A man is honored by his friends, but he is distinguished by the nature of his enemies'—and I have been very distinguished."

With that the Director stood up, walked around the desk, and extended his hand, and I stood up and extended my—still dry!—hand as well.

"Godspeed," the Director said.

"Goodbye, sir."

Then we both turned away. As I walked back down the hallway, I stopped at Miss Gandy's office.

"Well, how'd it go?"she said—the exact same thing she'd said after my first meeting with Hoover two years earlier.

I tried to recall the words she'd used back then. "He was kind, caring, and considerate—just like you told me two years ago."

She remembered. "You see? I told you so!"

"Well, he was this one time, anyway. He also said you'd miss me."

"And the Director never lies!" She laughed. Then she turned serious. "I will miss you, Paul. You're a fine young man, and it's been wonderful having you here."

"I'll miss you, too, Miss Gandy. I just want to . . ."

I stopped, unsure what I wanted to say. Even after two years there were still things I wanted to know, questions I wanted to ask—about the Director, about her, about the Bureau, about the way things were and how they got to be that way. I'd never quite had the nerve to ask before, and now wasn't the right time. I hoped that someday I'd get another chance.

"I just want to say how much I appreciate everything you've done for me, how much you've taught me, how you kept me out of trouble—"

"That was a full-time job!"

"Yes, I know. But I do appreciate it."

There was a brief silence, then Miss Gandy did something that surprised me. She stood up, walked over, and gave me a hug. It was a bit awkward—neither of us was a big hugger—but it meant a lot.

"Paul," she said, releasing me, "I want you to come by and visit when you can, all right? Promise? . . . Good! Now go out there and make your mark in the Bureau. And don't forget, we'll be watching you!"

I stayed in my office until the Director and Miss Gandy left for the day, and I made my last (thankfully!) series of "He's left the building" calls to the ADs. Then I went into Hoover's office to retrieve the tech manual. I lingered there for a moment, by his desk, thinking.

I can't say I was sad to leave. I was eager and excited to move on to the next chapter in my Bureau career. But as I thought about all the things I'd seen and heard and done in the past two years, and all the things I'd learned about the ways of powerful men—and women—I knew that my time in the Director's office had fundamentally changed my life. I hadn't been lying to the Director. It was a unique opportunity—and, yes, an honor—to have worked for this strange, enigmatic, difficult, inexplicable, and remarkable man.

But enough thinking. I put the tech manual back onto the shelf in the conference room, grabbed my things from my office, turned out the lights, and shut the door.

I left the building.

CHAPTER 5

On the Bricks

I moved swiftly but cautiously past the row of commercial storefronts and toward the bank. My Smith & Wesson .38-caliber revolver was still holstered, but I had my hand firmly on the grip. I knew bad guys were lurking here and I wanted to be ready.

And suddenly—there! Off to my left and slightly behind me, a man jumped up in the open window of the bank building! I whirled, drawing my weapon out of the holster, and quickly fired a single round—*bam!*—that hit the suspect dead center in the chest. I was satisfied with my quick draw and accurate shooting—until a half second later, when I realized to my horror that the "suspect" was a kindly looking older gentlemen in a three-piece suit with a watch fob stretched across his ample belly.

I'd killed the president of the bank.

"Letersky!" Special Agent George Zeiss shouted at me later. "Why did you shoot that banker?"

I had to think fast. "He looked suspicious to me, sir! I think he was embezzling funds!"

That got a laugh from everybody, including the special agent—although given his position, he had to quickly give me a stern "Don't be a wiseass, Letersky!"

Of course, I hadn't really killed a banker. What I'd "killed" was a realistic-looking, man-size pop-up target in Hogan's Alley, a movie-set-style urban street that was used for training new agents at the FBI Academy at Quantico. Named after an 1890s comic strip set

141

in a rough New York City neighborhood, Quantico's Hogan's Alley featured a long row of facade-type buildings—a bank, a post office, a restaurant, an apartment building, and so on.

Hogan's Alley was designed to give new agents a feel for what it was like on the street, and this live-ammo training exercise was meant to test our "shoot–don't shoot" reaction time. When a target popped up in a window or from around a corner, you had to decide if it was a threatening bad guy—shoot!—or an innocent civilian—don't shoot! But if you waited too long to shoot a bad guy, or if you shot too quickly and killed an innocent civilian, your score was lowered accordingly.

The banker wasn't the only innocent civilian I shot that day. I also severely wounded a nice-looking young woman holding a baby, and I winged a priest. But I also bagged my share of bad guys—"bad guys" being targets depicting big, ugly, mean-looking men pointing guns—so I felt pretty good about myself.

And it was fun! Not just the shooting exercises, but all of the fourteen-week FBI New Agents Training program—or almost all of it anyway. Sure, there was a lot of bitching and moaning among some of the agent trainees about the long hours and the discipline and the heavy study requirements, but I wasn't among them. After three years of commuting to law school at night while working full-time at FBI headquarters—two of those years under the demanding scrutiny of J. Edgar Hoover himself—my three and a half months in 1968 New Agents Training Class No. 4 was a relative breeze.

Initially fifty trainees were in my class, from all parts of the country, but we certainly didn't represent a cross section of America. We were all men, for one thing—the first female agent trainees wouldn't be accepted until shortly after Hoover's death in 1972—and we were also all white. From today's perspective that's embarrassing to admit, but the truth is that while the Bureau was making some progress in the equal opportunity area, at the time there were still only a few dozen African American special agents and even fewer Latinos and Asian Americans and other minorities. Unlike the vast majority of young male Americans at the time, we were also all highly educated. Most of us had law degrees, and the ones who didn't had undergraduate college degrees, usually in specialized fields such as science or languages or accounting; there were also a number of college-graduate former military officers and men with previous police experience. None of us was too short or too fat or, frankly, too ugly; I think you've noticed by now how important a "good appearance" was in Mr. Hoover's FBI. None of us were drug users or had criminal records, or even any record of serious conflicts with teachers or neighbors or anyone else; the extensive "full field investigation" background checks we'd all undergone had made certain of that.

In short, we were different from most of our generational cohort—and as the instructors constantly drummed into us, not just different but special! The elite! The one-in-a-thousand young American men who were qualified to be special agents of the Federal Bureau of Investigation! When you hear that often enough, you tend to start believing it.

A few of us had worked as Bureau clerks for a few years, which gave us a step up; we were already familiar with many FBI policies and procedures. But for almost all of the class members, New Agents Training was their first real contact with the Bureau. They'd been recruited by various field office SACs and resident agents, just as I'd been recruited by the resident agent from Jamestown, New York, and they arrived at New Agents Training with little idea of what they were in for. For some, the military-style discipline and regimentation came as a shock.

Surprisingly though, unlike in many elite training programs, such as the navy SEALs school, the washout rate at the Academy was extremely low. That was partly because of the extensive pre-screening, and partly because the Bureau wanted us to successfully complete the training. If we didn't, it would reflect badly on the SAC who recommended us, on the instructors and class counselors who were responsible for us, and ultimately on the Bureau itself. If we washed out, it would mean the Bureau had made a mistake—and we've seen just how little tolerance Mr. Hoover's Bureau had for mistakes. As I recall only a few members of the class left, either because they decided that the FBI life wasn't for them or because the instructors found some shortcoming. No explanation was ever given, at least not to the rest of us in the class. They simply didn't appear one day, and their names were never mentioned.

Our training sites alternated between the Old Post Office Building in Washington, DC, and the FBI Academy at the Quantico Marine Corps Base a half hour's drive south of the city. (The Old Post Office Building—now the Trump International Hotel—also housed the Washington-area FBI field office, which was separate from FBI headquarters. The old Quantico Academy facility was replaced in 1972 by a sprawling new FBI Academy complex on the marine base, and since then all agent training has been conducted there.) At Quantico we were housed in six-man rooms in redbrick barracks-style buildings, and the food in the chow hall was surprisingly good. We were told very specifically what to bring with us: two sets of long-sleeved gray shirts and trousers, a navy blue baseball cap with a piece of white tape on the back with our last name printed on it, thick-soled black work shoes, shower slippers, gym shoes and gym shorts, and an athletic supporter with "plastic or aluminum protective cup." As a former jock I was well supplied with those. (Required attire for classroom training in Washington was the standard suit and tie and white shirt.)

We were all young and in pretty good shape, so there wasn't much emphasis on physical conditioning—no up at 5:00 a.m. for a ten-mile run and calisthenics. We were extensively trained in hand-to-hand defensive tactics, but they didn't try to make us experts in judo or jujitsu or anything like that; there wasn't time. Instead the training concentrated on how to subdue a resisting suspect and put handcuffs on him, using choke holds and "pain compliance" holds if necessary; those were perfectly acceptable, at least back then. We spent hours practicing defensive tactics, usually against one another, and being competitive young men, we weren't gentle about it. Many a night I went to bed aching and covered in bruises; my only consolation was knowing that the guy who gave me those bruises was hurting even worse than I was. As I said, it was pretty competitive.

Despite all the hours spent in defensive-tactics training, Bureau policy was to avoid physical struggles with a suspect whenever possible. Instead, we were taught that an agent's most effective tools in getting compliance from a suspect were not his fists, but his physical bearing and his voice. The theory was that if an agent projected an air of authority and spoke in a "command voice" when he said, "FBI, you're under arrest," the suspect would quietly give up, awed by the power of the Bureau's reputation and the agent's calm but firm demeanor. Most of the time it worked. But if it didn't, physical confrontation with a suspect was the second-to-the-last resort.

The absolute last resort was to use our firearms. As you might expect, we spent a lot of time on the firing ranges—which for me initially was the most challenging part of the training. Even though I came from largely rural western New York, none of my family members had ever been into hunting or guns, and neither had I. In fact, I'd never fired a gun in my life.

Still, I was confident. I'd seen it done thousands of times in the movies and on TV. Point the gun, pull the trigger, the bad guy drops dead. How hard could it be?

Pretty hard, as it turned out. My first shot on the firing range with a .38-caliber service revolver not only missed the K-5 "kill zone," it missed the entire target by a good six feet. It didn't get much better as the day progressed. Finally I took my concerns to Special Agent George Zeiss, the chief defensive-tactics and firearms instructor.

"Big George"—he stood six-five and weighed about 240—was a legend in the Bureau. Not only could he split a bullet on the edge of an ax blade and hit two targets placed on each side of it—it wasn't a trick, he could actually do it—but in defensive-tactics training he could toss around even the biggest trainees as if they were rag dolls. That was why Special Agent Zeiss had been handpicked as one of two agents dispatched to London to pick up Martin Luther King assassin James Earl Ray and bring him back to Tennessee. If Ray had started making trouble on the plane, Big George could have broken him like a twig. But as tough as he was, Big George would always give you a hand up after he tossed you onto a mat, and he was always ready to offer encouragement.

"Sir," I said to him after that disastrous first day, "I don't know what's wrong. I don't think I could hit Kate Smith in the ass with a bag of rice at ten feet." (Ms. Smith was a then-popular singer and radio and TV star known for her stirring renditions of "God Bless America" at sports events—and for her excessively broad posterior.)

Big George laughed. "Aw, that's all right, son. Guys like you who don't know anything about firearms are the easiest to train. We don't have to break you of any bad habits. Don't you worry, you'll be fine."

He was right. After some skilled coaching, and after expending some five thousand rounds of ammunition, I was more than qualified with all of the Bureau's standard-issue weapons—.38-caliber revolver (being equally accurate with both right and left hands), 12-gauge shotgun, .30-caliber semiautomatic rifle, and the 40-millimeter tear-gas-canister gun, which looked like a small hand-held cannon and had a brutal, shoulder-numbing recoil kick. Even though it was no longer standard-issue, for old times' sake we also got to fire the 1930s, Gangster Era Thompson .45-caliber machine gun. I was not and would never be a gun nut, but I have to tell you, squeezing off a drum-magazine-ful of rounds from a Thompson was a visceral thrill.

The classroom instruction wasn't as exciting as the gun range, but it was interesting. Investigative procedures, interrogation techniques, evidence handling, fingerprint identification, record keeping, and report writing, not to mention Bureau history and lore—there were a million things to learn, and not much time to do it. (I'd gotten a taste of some of those subjects during my three weeks at Quantico when I first joined the Bureau in 1965.) On the legal side, we were immersed in the finer points of the Fourth Amendment case laws regarding search and seizure and the Fifth Amendment rules concerning self-incrimination and the due process of law. (We were not—repeat, *not*—given any instructions in wiretapping, bugging, bag jobs, or any other Bureau "dark arts." We were all much too new and green and naive for those things to even be mentioned. We wouldn't learn about those "special investigative techniques" until we got out in the field.)

We were also required to study in detail all of the federal laws that came under FBI jurisdiction—more than 150. Some of those federal crimes were obviously FBI business—kidnapping, bank robbery, interstate transport of stolen goods, racketeering, copyright infringement. But many of the laws that FBI agents were required to enforce were more obscure.

For example, were you aware that the FBI has jurisdiction over dangerous refrigerators? Neither was I until I went through New Agents Training. It seems that after a wave of reports of children being suffocated after accidentally getting trapped in refrigerators with outside locking door latches, Congress passed the Refrigerator Safety Act of 1956, which criminalized the interstate transport of refrigerators that couldn't be opened from the inside. Naturally the Bureau was charged with enforcing the prohibition. Same thing with switchblade knives. After the public grew alarmed by depictions of switchblade-wielding juvenile delinquents in popular films such as *Blackboard Jungle*, Congress enacted the Federal Switchblade Act of 1958, prohibiting the interstate transport of such knives—and once again enforcement of the law was dropped into the FBI's lap. Both of those measures passed despite formal opposition from the Department of Justice and the Director, who thought the Bureau had better things to do.

Which it did. I never knew a single agent who built a criminal case involving unsafe refrigerators or the interstate transportation of switchblades. However, the Bureau did occasionally find it useful to use a seemingly minor federal law to go after a vicious criminal.

For example, as part of its Top Hoodlums anti–organized crime program, in 1962 the Bureau was conducting a "crash investigation" of a Cicero, Illinois, Mob boss named Joey Aiuppa, a former hit man for the Al Capone organization. A crash investigation was sort of like a COINTELPRO against a mobster. It involved close physical surveillance by agents—*fisurs* in Bureau-speak—examination of his IRS returns, and sometimes wiretaps and bugs. This was before the Racketeer Influenced and Corrupt Organizations (RICO) Act, which made it easier to prosecute organized crime figures, so the

Bureau didn't have enough evidence to charge Aiuppa with a serious crime. But through informants the Bureau learned that Aiuppa, an avid bird hunter, had shot far more than the legal limit of mourning doves during a hunting trip in Kansas—a violation of the federal Migratory Bird Treaty Act of 1918, for which the Bureau had jurisdiction. At the Bureau's behest, federal wildlife agents caught Aiuppa with more than four hundred dead doves in the trunk of his car, and eventually he was sentenced to three months in jail and a $1,000 fine. It wasn't much time, but the case made the mobster's life miserable for a while—and he was mockingly known ever after in Mob circles as Joey Doves.

Anyway, the New Agents Training program was tough and demanding, and we were frequently tested on our knowledge. But the instructors usually managed to let us know generally what was going to be on the tests. Again, they wanted us to get through training—and eventually we did.

There was no formal graduation ceremony, with the Director making a speech while our family members proudly looked on. That wasn't the Bureau's way. Instead, the big day for us was when we found out where each of us would be assigned to our first field office.

From the beginning of his directorship Hoover's policy had been to send all new agents as far away as possible from their hometowns, on the theory that they'd be less susceptible to "bad influences" by people they'd grown up with. It was a sound theory. The NYPD and other big-city police departments had no end of troubles with cops who hadn't quite severed their relationships with questionable family members and guys they'd known back in the hood. So I knew I wouldn't be assigned to the Buffalo, New York, Field Office—and I also knew that I probably wouldn't be assigned to a high-profile field office such as Washington, DC, or New York or LA; new agents seldom were. I had no idea where I was going, but I have to admit that I secretly hoped that Miss Gandy or Mr. Mohr—or maybe even the Director himself!—would make sure that their "fair-haired boy" was sent to some desirable posting.

So it was more than just a surprise when I opened up the letter notifying me of my assignment and I read—

Cincinnati?

Cincinnati?

No offense to the good people of Cincinnati. It was a perfectly fine town of half a million souls, pleasantly situated on the north bank of the Ohio River. But I'd been with the Bureau long enough to know the score. The Cincinnati Field Office was a disciplinary office, a place where agents were sent if they made a serious mistake or had accumulated too many letters of censure. It wasn't as much of a dreaded disciplinary field office as Butte or Anchorage, Alaska, but it was still a punishment posting. The Cincinnati Field Office had that reputation because of its succession of special agents in charge who were mean, nasty, agent-devouring sonsabitches—so much so that even agents who were from Cincinnati didn't want to be assigned to Cincinnati. And as far as anyone could remember, no new agent had ever been sent there for his "first office" assignment—until me.

Some "fair-haired boy" I was!

For a brief, angry moment I thought about calling Miss Gandy or Mr. Mohr and asking for an explanation, or even a change of assignment. But that impulse quickly faded. If they were aware of my assignment—which I had no doubt they were—I figured they must have had a reason for approving it, and someday I'd find out what that reason was. I didn't want to look like a scheming manipulator who depended on his connections, not his abilities, to get ahead—and besides, most "first office" assignments were only for a year. So, no, I wouldn't go whining to Miss Gandy or Mr. Mohr. If the Bureau told me to go to Cincinnati, then to Cincinnati I'd go.

However, I still had one more aspect of my FBI training to get through. And it came perilously close to costing me my job and another man his life.

No one in the Bureau thought that three and a half months of training made new agents fully prepared to take up their duties on the street. It took months and years of experience to become a truly effective street agent. Before we were sent out to the various field offices, the Bureau wanted us to have at least an introduction to what it was really like "on the bricks." So they sent us to the Washington, DC, Field Office for a week to tag along with some veteran agents and watch how they worked.

When I reported to the field office Monday morning, I was told that the agents in the squad to which I'd be attached were having breakfast in a nearby diner and I should hook up with them there. I went in and introduced myself, and while the four veteran agents were friendly enough, it was pretty clear that my job was to sit down, shut up, and listen and learn.

Most of the breakfast talk centered on the Redskins, who to my quiet satisfaction were having another terrible season, and about where the agents planned to meet for lunch. I started thinking that this looked like an easy job. Then one of the agents was called to the pay phone at the back of the diner, and when he came back, it was all business.

The field office had gotten a tip from MPD—Washington Metropolitan Police Department, the city cops—that a federal fugitive was holed up in an abandoned house on U Street. He had a long rap sheet—*rap* stands for "record of arrests and prosecutions"—for crimes ranging from attempted murder to rape to robbery, but there was nothing current on him except a federal warrant from another jurisdiction. The locals wanted us to arrest the guy, and they'd back us up. Oh, and one other thing. The MPD said the guy might have a sawed-off shotgun.

Today in such a situation the field office's Special Weapons and Tactics (SWAT) team would be called in to make the arrest; they have the specialized gear—helmets, bulletproof vests, battering rams, flash-bang grenades, and so on—to do the job with less risk to their safety. But at the time we couldn't call on a Bureau SWAT team because there wasn't one. The Bureau did have specially trained snipers for certain situations, but the Director wouldn't have allowed his agents to don that kind of SWAT gear or fill that kind of role. We were investigators, not cops, and if somebody needed to be arrested, you walked up and arrested him.

So it was up to us—or rather, it was up to them, the veteran agents I was with. I was just along for the ride—or so I thought.

We piled into a couple of BuCars and headed for the informal command post the cops had set up at the end of the block near the fugitive's location, where a plainclothes MPD cop filled us in on the suspect. Black male, mid-thirties, average height, reported to be in a house eight doors down the block; the cop repeated the part about the possible shotgun.

I was just standing there, wondering what, if anything, I was supposed to do. I was too green, or maybe too dumb, to be scared. I was excited. An armed-fugitive arrest! On my first day!

Then one of the veteran agents turned to me. "Hey, kid—what was your name again?"

"Letersky, sir." I didn't have to call him sir because technically we were the same rank—special agent. But only technically.

"Okay, Letersky, you take the back, in the alley. There's supposed to be a door and some windows there. If he tries to come out, drop him. Go!"

I didn't have time to ask the agent exactly how I was supposed to drop him. I guess he figured they had taught me that much at Quantico. I walked quickly down the side street and ducked into the alley.

This section of the U Street corridor wasn't the Washington, DC, of the Lincoln Monument and the Capitol and the stately town houses of Georgetown. This was block after block of urban cancer—boarded-up squatter houses and apartment buildings with no electric power or running water, abandoned hulks of cars, uncollected garbage strewn everywhere; the alley reeked of rotting food and human waste. To add to the unpleasantness, it had started to sleet—this was December—and the stinging icy particles were being blown sideways into my face. Fortunately it was still pretty early, which along with the bad weather meant there were no people around.

I took up position at an oblique angle to the back door and a badly cracked window a few feet away from it, my .38 revolver drawn and ready. I was tense, keyed up, but as the minutes passed—five, ten, fifteen minutes—I started worrying less about the suspect and more about my personal situation. I was freezing! My lightweight *Columbo*-style trench coat didn't offer much protection, and I didn't have any gloves. I kept having to shift the revolver from one hand to the other and putting the free hand in my coat pocket to warm up.

Then, just as I was promising myself that next time I'd have gloves—somebody was opening the window! From my line of sight I couldn't see who, but I could hear someone struggling with the sash, which suddenly gave way and flew up with a thud. I stepped away from the building to get a better view, and there, in the gloomy recesses behind the open window, I saw the dim, shadowy figure of a black man in street clothes holding a short-barreled shotgun. It wasn't pointed at me, but that's what it was.

"FBI! Drop the weapon!" I called out, just like they'd taught us.

Then I heard a loud, almost panicked cry. "I'm a cop! I'm a cop! Don't shoot!"

I had a fleeting thought of that "banker" and all the other innocents I had gunned down in Hogan's Alley, and for a moment I felt weak in the knees. But I had to be sure.

"Come to where I can see you!" I called out. "Don't move the weapon!"

The man moved closer to the open window, and now I could see it—a silver MPD shield attached to a cord around his neck; he was holding it out in front of him like a talisman.

There was a shout from the end of the alley. It was one of the veteran agents. "Hey, kid! Come on back! We got him!"

"Sorry!" I called out to the no-doubt-relieved MPD cop, then I trotted back around to the front of the building. The veteran agents already had the fugitive cuffed and sitting in the back of a BuCar. They'd taken him without a struggle—he was sleeping off a drunk when they came in, and they didn't even have to kick in the door, since there wasn't one, just an old blanket tacked across the doorway. They hadn't found a shotgun, which was why the DC cop was searching the room behind the window. This was a squatter building, with no working toilets, so apparently he'd opened the window to let in some semifresh air while he looked around. Frankly, he should have known that the back door would be guarded and announced himself as a cop before he opened the window. I didn't think I'd done anything wrong.

Still, I had come this close to a blue-on-blue shooting—on my very first day on the job.

This wasn't Hogan's Alley anymore. This was real.

And I still had a lot to learn.

I made my first mistake at the Cincinnati Field Office at 7:48 a.m. I remember the time so precisely because the time was the mistake.

Normal working hours were 8:00 a.m. to 5:00 p.m., but agents were expected to work roughly two hours of "voluntary overtime" (VOT) per day. Most agents actually worked far more overtime than that, on stakeouts or late-night meetings with informants or whatever, but this being the government, the overtime had to be strictly documented. To make that easier, by informal agreement the first agent to arrive at the field office was supposed to write "6:03 a.m." on the sign-in register, no matter what the actual time of day was. Then when each agent came in, he would sign in with two or three minutes added to that time—"6:05 a.m.," "6:08 a.m.," "6:11 a.m.," and so on—again no matter what their actual arrival time was. That way all the agents could "document" an hour or two hours of VOT. This was how it worked in every field office, and everybody knew it.

I said that everybody in the Bureau knew how it worked, but I should have said everybody except for brand-new agents like me. Nobody ever mentioned this in New Agents Training since technically it involved the falsification of a government document. No, not technically; it *was* falsification of a government document, albeit for a sound practical reason.

Anyway, when I came in that first day, I checked my watch and wrote "7:48 a.m." on the sign-in sheet. And then every agent who came in after me looked at the sheet and said, "Goddamnit!" or "What the hell?" or something along those lines. Obviously they couldn't write down "6:10 a.m." for their arrival time when the guy whose name appeared above their names indicated he had arrived at 7:48 a.m. Even though the goons from the Inspection Division knew how the sign-in system worked and generally looked the other way—they had been street agents once, too—they wouldn't be able to ignore that kind of discrepancy in the records. So unbeknownst to me I'd screwed my fellow agents out of their VOT for the day.

I didn't know it at the time, but that explained the frosty looks as my supervisor introduced me to the members of my assigned squad in the Criminal Investigative section, and the way other agents were giving me the fish eye all day. Finally one of the older agents, one who had enough years in the Bureau to retire if necessary, took me aside.

"Hey, kid, let me explain how this works. . . ."

He was taking a chance. What if I refused to go along and complained that he was suborning me to falsify a government document? That could cause a stink that could blow all the way back to SOG. But they didn't have to worry on that score. I quickly grasped the practical wisdom of the arrangement, apologized for screwing it up, and assured the veteran agent that it wouldn't happen again—which it didn't.

I'd passed the first test. But it wasn't the last.

I'd known from the start that as a former aide to the Director I'd be under close scrutiny, not so much from the SAC as from the other agents. They'd wonder if I was a spy, an informer, sent by SOG to rat them out for any violations of Bureau rules. If I wasn't a spy, then why was I the first new agent in memory who'd drawn an assignment to this disciplinary field office? Was I a screwup who couldn't be trusted to watch their backs in a dangerous situation?

I couldn't blame them for thinking those things. If I'd been them, I would have done the same. It would take weeks and months for me to win their confidence and convince even the most suspicious of them that I wasn't a rat—or a screwup.

(When I talk about not wanting to be a rat and a snitch, I'm talking about not ratting out other agents for minor bureaucratic stuff. It wasn't like the infamous "blue wall of silence" that was standard in many police departments, where if a cop ever turned in any of his colleagues, even for the most serious acts of corruption, he was branded a "cheese-eating rat" and permanently shunned. If I'd ever witnessed a fellow agent stealing a suspect's money or seriously abusing a handcuffed suspect or otherwise acting corruptly—which I never did—I'd have turned him in in an instant. And my fellow agents would have backed me up. Remember, we considered ourselves a better class of law enforcement agency—we were the FBI!)

As my fellow squad agents got to know me, I also got to know them. And I began to understand something about the Bureau, something I hadn't learned in New Agents class or in my time at SOG. An FBI disciplinary field office didn't necessarily get the worst agents. In many, maybe most, cases the hundred or so special agents assigned to the Cincinnati FO were the *best* agents, guys who knew what they were doing and got things done, even if they ran afoul of their supervisors or violated some arcane Bureau regulations. And the agents I worked with in Cincinnati were some of the best teachers I ever had.

Hank Goodson and Dick Cleary were two of them. Hank was in his early forties, quick with a smile, a guy who specialized in confidence men, bad-check artists, forgers—crooks who lived by their wits, not by fists and guns. He loved the job. As Hank explained it to me, "It's a mental challenge, a game between me and them—and they play by the rules. When I catch them, they just shrug and say, 'You got me.' They're a better class of criminals, not like those violent dirtbags the rest of you guys have to mess with." On the other hand, Special Agent Dick Cleary, who usually worked fugitive cases, had no problem with violent dirtbags. A big guy and the second-youngest man on the squad next to me, Dick moonlighted as a semipro hockey player—under an assumed name, since the Bureau prohibited outside jobs. His nickname was High Sticker, which may give you an idea of how he dealt with violently resisting suspects. I never found out why Hank and Dick had been relegated to Cincinnati. It wasn't the sort of thing you asked about; if they wanted you to know, they'd tell you. But Cincinnati was lucky to have them.

With some of the others it was pretty clear how they'd wound up in Cincy. Bill Markham, a sharp-dressed man in his mid-forties, had been the one-man resident agent in Watertown, New York, near the Canadian border, until he somehow got crosswise with a Royal Canadian Mounted Police official, who complained to SOG—this to the "embarrassment" of the Bureau. Next stop, Cincinnati. Ken Kirwin's offense was more self-inflicted. A chunky, ruddy-faced man in his forties, he was New York City born and bred, and like a lot of NYC kids he'd never gotten a driver's license—and when he became an agent, no one thought to inquire whether he had one. He managed to get by through a succession of field offices without his lack of a license—or driving skills—posing a problem. But when he finally worked his way up to his "office of preference," the NYC Field Office, he got into a minor traffic accident in a Bureau car and the secret was revealed. It didn't help that in contravention of one of the most basic FBI regulations, he had his girlfriend in the BuCar with him at the time.

Then there was Bill Weatherwax, aka the Waxman or just Waxy. One look at Waxy and you knew exactly why he was a Cincinnati Field Office agent. An older guy, in his mid-forties—at the time that seemed old to me—Waxy's trousers were always baggy, his trench coat permanently stained, and despite its being 1970, he still wore a fedora, not in the classic low-over-the-eyes Bureau manner, but pushed way back and tilted to the side like some sort of snap-brimmed beret. His voice sounded like a load of bricks in a cement mixer, and he talked out of the side of his mouth like a character in a Damon Runyon story. He was exactly what a special agent was not supposed to look like in Mr. Hoover's FBI.

But Waxy was also one of the best criminal investigators in the entire Bureau, consistently way ahead in arrests and the value of recovered stolen goods—statistics that were the Bureau's mother's milk. His specialty was interstate transport of stolen property, not small stuff but big cases involving eighteen-wheeler-truck hijacking rings, major interstate fencing operations, multimillion-dollar thefts of heavy construction and farming equipment. His informants in the criminal world were legion, and he had kind of a sixth sense when it came to working investigations, as if he could see where a case was going even before he got there. His ability—and more important, his statistics on arrests and recoveries of stolen goods—had allowed him to survive in the FBI, even after a rogue informant had gotten him in trouble in his native Chicago's field office and he'd been exiled to Elba—Cincinnati, that is. Whenever a special agent in charge gave him trouble, all Waxy had to do was say, "Check the scoreboard!"

Waxy also had balls of brass. One hot summer day we were having lunch at a diner when Waxy got a call on the pay phone from one of his informants that a hijacking gang was unloading a truck full of stolen tires at a nearby warehouse. Unfortunately we didn't have our guns with us. We weren't required to always carry our guns, but when we did, Bureau regs said they had to be kept concealed under our suit jackets, and it was too steamy to keep our jackets on; our guns were back at the office. Nevertheless, we ran gunless out to our BuCar, Waxy called for backup, and we sped to the scene. The backup hadn't arrived yet, but five guys were outside the warehouse unloading the truck. Waxy walked up to them and pointed his index finger like it was a gun—his finger!—and said, "FBI. You're under arrest! Get against that wall!" When they were slow to comply, Waxy told them—I swear to God—"You better move fast! The smell of death is in the air!" The five guys, probably thinking this G-man was dangerously out of his mind, did as ordered, and Waxy got five more arrests on his stats—and I nearly died laughing.

As for the much-dreaded special agent in charge of the Cincinnati office—we'll call him SAC Smith—it was true that he could be a hardheaded jerk sometimes, as almost all SACs had to be. But his predecessor—we'll call him SAC Jones—had gone beyond being a jerk. He was a full-fledged, full-bore, no-holds-barred asshole, a screaming, desk-pounding martinet who seemed to take joy in making his agents' lives as unnecessarily miserable as possible. He was so personally despised that during the agents' bimonthly poker games his photo would be taped to the toilet so everybody could piss on him. Not long before I arrived, SAC Jones had been rewarded for his hard-assed behavior by being named SAC of the prestigious San Francisco Field Office, and he was replaced in Cincinnati by SAC Smith. SAC Smith was a rather mild-mannered man who tried his best to emulate his tough-acting predecessor, but somehow he just couldn't quite pull it off. For a while Cincinnati still maintained its reputation as Elba—but at least it wasn't hell.

It certainly wasn't hellish for me. On the contrary, I had a great time! Over the next year I got to work with my squadmates on all sorts of criminal cases: fraud, fugitives, bank robberies, interstate transport—you name it. Of all of them, I liked working with Waxy on interstate stolen-goods cases best.

There were plenty of those cases to be made. Directly across the Ohio River from Cincinnati were the "twin cities" of Newport and Covington, Kentucky. Newport in particular had long been known as Kentucky's Sin City, a haven for bootleggers and illegal gambling operators and prostitutes and thieves and all manner of other criminal elements. By 1969 the big-time bootlegging industry had disappeared, although more than a few backwoods moonshine stills were still operating in that part of Kentucky; sometimes when we were investigating cases, people would call us "revenuers," a reference to the Treasury agents who pursued bootleggers during Prohibition. But plenty of other criminal types still remained in Sin City. And when thieves hijacked a truck or stole some jewelry in Kentucky and took it across the bridge to market it in Cincinnati, that was interstate transport—which meant they belonged to us.

Sometimes a lot of money was involved—which also involved some nice fat stats for the Bureau. For example, one time Waxy and I, acting on a tip from one of his informants, bagged a hijacked truck packed with some one hundred thousand bottles of name-brand aspirin that the thieves planned to sell to crooked Cincinnati pharmacies for twenty cents on the dollar. The catch was that when reporting the value of the recovered stolen aspirin, following Bureau procedure, we used the retail per-bottle value of the aspirin, not the wholesale value—which meant that the aspirin was valued by us at about $150,000. (The same valuation policy applied to stolen cars. Even the most beat-up, derelict-looking recovered stolen Ford or Chevy was given an "excellent condition" Kelley Blue Book valuation.) That in turn meant that when the Director made his annual appearance before congressional appropriations committees, that one truckload of aspirin made a nice addition to his "value of recovered stolen goods" statistics. Coupled with the fines assessed against defendants in federal criminal cases—whether the fines were actually paid or not—nationally those numbers could amount to a couple hundred million dollars, more than the total annual budget for the entire Bureau!

Hoover was probably the only department head in the federal government who could claim that his organization provided a net profit for the taxpayers. I say "claim" because obviously the Bureau wasn't really turning a profit. But Hoover used statistics like a staggering drunk uses a streetlight pole—for support, not illumination—and seldom did Congress ever question his numbers. Not once since 1955 had Congress ever reduced the Bureau's annual appropriation; instead, Congress increased it every year. Some critics argue that Hoover ignored complicated organized crime investigations in favor of high stats from the low-lying fruit of car thefts and interstate transport of stolen goods. That's partly true, but it was largely because until the RICO Act the Bureau had little jurisdiction over many Mob crimes. Nevertheless, the Bureau made life miserable for any number of organized crime "top hoodlums," putting them under close surveillances, accosting them in public places, having the IRS audit their "legitimate" businesses. Just ask the aforementioned Joey Doves.

Interstate transport cases were not white-collar crimes; sometimes they could be dangerous. The receivers of stolen goods, the middlemen fences and their customers, weren't much of a problem. For the most part, they were businessmen—crooked businessmen, but businessmen nonetheless. But the criminal gangs that stole the stuff didn't hesitate to pistol-whip a truck driver or murder a snitch—or try to shoot an FBI agent with a hidden crossbow.

It happened like this. Waxy got a tip from a couple of his informants that a well-known Ohio hijacking gang was stashing stolen tractor trailers in an old barn in a rural area until the swag could be off-loaded and sold in the city—furs, electronics, untaxed cigarettes, you name it. Based on this information from two "consistently reliable sources"—Waxy's informants—we got a search warrant from a federal judge and drove out to serve it. After scoping out the nearby farmhouse—it was unoccupied—we walked up to the front of the barn. The swinging double doors were padlocked from the outside, but I had a crowbar, and I was just about to pop the padlock and open the doors when Waxy put his hand on my shoulder.

"Wait. Something's not right."

I wasn't sure what he was talking about, but I would never question Waxy's instincts. He led me around to the back of the barn, where I pried open a window and crawled in, and Waxy followed. A truck recently hijacked in Kentucky was parked there all right, but that wasn't what caught our attention when we looked around. What caught our attention was a large and fully cocked crossbow, aimed at the barn front doors, with a trip cord attached to the trigger and leading to the doors. It was a booby trap. If I'd broken the outside padlock and opened the doors, there was a good chance I would have taken an eight-inch steel crossbow bolt square in the chest.

"How'd you know?" I asked Waxy, hoping that my voice didn't sound shaky.

He shrugged. "Ahh, I've seen this before. And I had a feelin'."

Thank God for Waxy's experience—and his feelings.

As it turned out, the hijacked truck was chock-full of brand-new, still-in-the-box TV sets, and eventually we rolled up the gang members. Like a lot of stolen-goods rings in this part of the county, the gang was a family affair—a patriarchal father in command of sons, brothers, uncles, cousins. They all faced federal felony interstate-transport charges—and for the patriarch, who owned the barn, there was a sweetener. It's illegal to set booby traps in defense of property, so he was also charged with attempted assault on a federal officer.

Waxy and I got a sweetener as well. SAC Smith sent a memo to the Director describing our crossbow booby-trap encounter, which was the sort of thing the Director always got a kick out of. He loved hearing about devious and nefarious methods devised by criminals, only to see them be outsmarted by his alert special agents. As a result, Waxy and I both got "letters of commendation"—the polar opposite of "letters of censure"—in which the Director praised our "outstanding work." There was nothing personal in the Director's commendation letter to me; Waxy and I both got the exact same letter, signed in blue ink with the Director's name, and no doubt actually signed by Miss Gandy. Nor did we get the cash "incentive awards" of $250 or $500 that the Director handed out for particularly noteworthy accomplishments.

But I did get a note from Miss Gandy: "Dear Paul, I heard about your recent 'adventure.' Please be careful!" She signed it in her usual way, "hwg." Miss Gandy was and always would be Miss Gandy.

Being careful wasn't always easy, especially when it came to fugitives, most of whom were Unlawful Flight to Avoid Prosecution (UFAP) cases—that is, ordinary criminals who violated federal law by fleeing across state lines. (The US Marshals also pursued fugitives, especially prison escapees, bond defaulters, and parole violators; usually we'd leave those kinds of cases to them, but we'd pick up those guys, too, if they came our way.) Many of the UFAP fugitives were the "violent dirtbags" Hank Goodson spoke about—murderers, rapists, that sort of thing. Whenever we got information that a fugitive might be in our area of operation, we'd go through the usual drill: study his file to learn his habits and haunts, show his mug shot to bartenders and convenience store clerks and in other places where he might hang out, find out the addresses of known friends and family members, and make discreet inquiries of their neighbors. We'd ask them to call us if they spotted the guy, and often they did; it helped if a reward was pending.

Once we got a good location on the guy, we'd set up a stakeout, usually two of us, sometimes four, depending on the fugitive's known propensity for violence. Ideally, we'd nab him as he came out of his house or was walking down the street, rolling up on him from behind, shouting, "FBI, you're under arrest!," and getting him cuffed before he knew what hit him—and before he had a chance to resist or pull a weapon. But sometimes fugitives would fight, and sometimes they'd run. I tore out the knees of more than one set of suit trousers while wrestling with a fugitive on a grimy urban sidewalk or tackling a runner along some dusty road in Kentucky. Although I often had to draw my .38 revolver, like most agents I fortunately never had to shoot anyone during my FBI career—with one possible exception that I'll get into later. I say *fortunately* partly because I didn't want to kill anybody, and partly because any shooting of a suspect—even the most violent, depraved predator imaginable—would require an enormous amount of paperwork.

Fugitive apprehensions were a big part of a street agent's job, and they were a chance to shine. Nabbing a particularly dangerous fugitive almost always resulted in a commendation letter, and maybe a cash award; nabbing a Ten Most Wanted fugitive was a surefire ticket to a cash award and maybe even a promotion. (As we'll see, later I and some other agents came *this close* to bagging a Top Tenner.) Fugitive apprehensions were also an important statistic in the Director's annual reports to Congress, so the pressure to keep the numbers up was unrelenting. Since every fugitive apprehension carried the same weight in the stats, whether it was a vicious Top Tenner or some hapless mope who was wanted for hanging a couple of bad checks in Kansas City, SAC Smith insisted that we work as hard to catch the small fry as we did the bigger fish.

I did my best. But there was one category of federal fugitives I tried to avoid pursuing. And it was because of them that, for my first time as an FBI agent, I started wondering if I was doing the right thing.

Some 9 million Americans served on active duty during the Vietnam War, about 2 million of whom were drafted under the Selective Service Act. Draftees accounted for roughly one-third of the more than fifty-eight thousand Americans who died in the Vietnam conflict. (The remainder of the dead had voluntarily joined the military.)

Even at the time, most people recognized the inequities of the draft system. Out of 27 million young American males who were eligible for conscription during the Vietnam War, fewer than one in ten actually wound up in the army. (Females could enlist in the military but they were never drafted.) The others avoided being drafted through various means. Some had actual physical impairments that prevented them from serving, while others found friendly doctors who'd certify that they suffered from some disqualifying ailment. A lot of guys used connections or family influence to land coveted spots in the local National Guard, knowing that "weekend warriors" were almost never sent to Vietnam. Cops, clergymen, certain specialized workers—and FBI special agents—got "occupational deferments" that exempted them as long as they stayed on the job. And millions of college students got a class 2-S exemption, which allowed them to at least put off being drafted, ideally until the war was over.

So the draft burden fell most heavily on the poor, the uneducated, the kids with no connections—kids from the inner city in Cincinnati or the backwoods of Kentucky. Most of those draftees did their jobs well in the military, and many served with great distinction. But many tens of thousands of draftees (along with a number of voluntary enlistees) went AWOL—absent without leave—shedding their uniforms and heading for home. If that home was in southern Ohio or northern Kentucky, it was our job in the Cincinnati FBI Field Office to catch them and send them back.

Officially there were some fifty thousand "deserters" from the US military during the Vietnam War, and many times that number went AWOL. A service member was AWOL if he stayed absent for less than thirty days; upon his capture or voluntary return, he would face a reduction in rank, forfeiture of pay, and perhaps a short stay in the stockade. If he was gone longer than thirty days, he was classified as a deserter, with correspondingly harsher potential penalties, including lengthy prison terms and even the death penalty if it was in time of war. (Since Vietnam wasn't a declared war, the death penalty didn't apply.)

Unlike ordinary criminal fugitives, most of the military fugitives were relatively easy to find—and not just because their military-style haircuts made them stand out. The main reason they went AWOL in the first place was because they missed their mamas or their young wives or their girlfriends, so if you kept your eyes on the women, usually the men would show up. Sometimes neighbors, especially men who'd served in the military, were more than willing to drop a dime on an AWOL if they spotted him. And sometimes after a few weeks "vacation" the AWOL would decide to turn himself in and face the music with the military. Occasionally, an AWOL would try to fight to stay free, but most of the time they came along quietly. They weren't criminals at heart, and very few were anti-war radicals and firebrands; they were just scared, homesick kids.

Military fugitives were a boon to the Bureau's fugitives-apprehended statistics. Statistically, they counted the same as any criminal fugitive, and sometimes they counted even more: a lot of AWOLs were repeaters, guys who went AWOL two, three, or even four times before the military gave up on them and kicked them out. But every time we caught one, it was a separate checkmark on the fugitives-apprehended list. As a result, SAC Smith loved it when we caught AWOLs or deserters.

But I hated it.

I'd been troubled by the Vietnam War from the start, and the longer it went on, the more troubled I became. It seemed pointless and wasteful and just plain wrong that we were spending tens of thousands of American lives—and even more Vietnamese lives—to prop up a corrupt government in a small country thousands of miles away. I never participated in an anti-war demonstration, and obviously I didn't advertise my feelings within the Bureau, but that's the way I felt. I also felt a little guilty, since I'd done everything I legally could to avoid being drafted. I was willing to serve my country—in fact, I felt that I was serving my country as an FBI agent—but I didn't want to serve it by fighting in an unrighteous war in Vietnam. Yet here I was sending young draftees back to fight a war that I wasn't willing to fight in. It felt hypocritical—and the more I learned about the AWOLs I was catching, the worse the feeling got.

The kid with the thousand-yard stare was a case in point.

I was at my desk in the squad room at the office one day when the supervisor came over and handed me a slip of paper with a name and an address on it, and a copy of a military photo ID.

"Hey, Letersky, we just got an anonymous call about this guy, a deserter. Caller says he's at this address, his mother's house, right now. The rest of the squad is busy, so I want you and"—he named an agent from another squad; we'll call him Special Agent Miller— "to go out and pick him up."

Inwardly I groaned, but orders are orders. I hooked up with Agent Miller, a tough-looking guy in his late thirties who'd served in the marines in the Korean War, and we drove out to the address, a small wood-frame house in the Vine Street district, a mostly black working-class neighborhood on the north side of Cincinnati. We knocked on the front door, and when no one answered, we knocked a little harder and called out, "FBI!" The door cracked open a bit and a weary-looking middle-aged black woman wearing a waitress's uniform peered out.

"FBI, ma'am." I said, showing my credentials. "Is your son here?" I could tell from the look on her face that he was. "We need to talk to him. Do you mind if we come in?"

She didn't have to let us in. We didn't have a search warrant for the house, and aside from an anonymous tip we had no proof that the deserter was inside. But we were the FBI. Resignedly, with a sigh, she opened the door.

The house was small but well-kept, the sort of place a single-mother waitress could afford if she was working extra shifts. Two young children—a bright-eyed boy about ten, a pretty little girl a few years younger—were sitting on a couch, watching a cartoon show on a tiny black-and-white TV. When we walked in—two white men in coats and ties—they stared at us wide-eyed, but they didn't say anything. And there, sitting next to them on the couch, was our guy—a painfully thin, brown-skinned twenty-year-old dressed in jeans and a T-shirt. The strange thing was that he didn't seem to notice that we were there. He didn't even look up. He just kept staring at the TV—not really watching it, just staring at it, like his head was a million miles away.

Agent Miller quickly walked over and told him to stand up and turn around, then handcuffed his hands behind his back and patted him down. The guy didn't resist or say anything at all.

His mother started to cry. "Please, do you have to take him?" she sobbed. "Please don't. He's a good boy."

"He's a coward and a traitor!" Agent Miller snapped.

Even though I was still a green young agent, I shot him a look. There was no need for that.

At the same time, the mother stepped back as if she'd been slapped. "No, sir, he's not! He's not! Wait!"

She darted toward the bedroom, and Miller moved his hand toward his gun, not to draw it but just to be ready—and I did the same. You could never tell. In fugitive cases, sometimes the women would fight you harder than the fugitives themselves. I was about to follow her into the bedroom, just to make sure, but a second later she came back out holding an army-green dress uniform on a hanger. The coat jacket had two rows of ribbons over the left pocket; later Miller, the ex-marine, told me that one of the ribbons was a Purple Heart, meaning the kid had been wounded, and another was a Bronze Star, for valor in combat.

"See?" the mother said. "He's no coward! He's already been to the war!" She glanced at Miller. "He was a good boy, never caused no trouble. Never had no father to speak of, and he never could learn to read so well, didn't finish high school, but he had a good job at the plant. He was a happy boy, had friends, a girlfriend, too, but then they sent him his draft letter and sent him over there. And now . . ."

Her voice trailed off. She draped the uniform over a chair and looked at her son, and my gaze followed hers. The kid was still just standing there, staring off toward some distant place, as if he didn't know, or care, what was happening to him. Something was clearly wrong with this kid; it was like he was a zombie or something. I wondered if he was on drugs.

His mother read my expression. "No, he's not using, never did.

It's just . . ." She thought for a moment. "It wasn't so bad when he first come back. They sent him down to Fort Campbell"—that was in southern Kentucky—"to finish up his time, and he'd take the bus up here on a weekend sometimes. But they picked on him a lot down there, 'cause of the way he is, you know, and he just got quieter and quieter, didn't want to talk to nobody. And one day he just said, 'Mama, I ain't goin' back.' Since then he's hardly said a word to anybody, even me."

"You must have known somebody would come looking for him," I said. "Especially here."

"Wasn't no other place to send him. I was hopin' they'd just let him go. He already did what they wanted him to do."

"C'mon, we gotta get him out of here," Miller said to me quietly. That the kid had been in combat in Vietnam had softened the former marine, at least a little.

"No, wait, please, sir." She turned to me. "Please, he's only got another month till his two years is up. Can't they just mail him his discharge paper or whatever you call it?"

She must have known better than that. But she was desperate.

"I'm sorry, ma'am, but I'm afraid it doesn't work that way."

"Then please, can you take him to the veterans' hospital? He needs help!"

I shook my head. "I'm sorry, but there are rules. I'm sure the army will take care of him."

For the first time she looked angry. "The army?" she spat out. "I know how the army'll take care of him. They'll put him in jail, that's what the army'll do. Then in a few years what are they gonna do? Take my other boy?"

"We gotta go," Miller said. He started moving the handcuffed kid toward the front door, and I moved with them.

"No!" his mother shouted, jumping in front of us, blocking the way.

"Please, ma'am," I said.

Then she looked at me with pure hatred in her eyes. "You! They ever send you to the war?"

I shook my head no.

"No, course not. You're a college boy, right? They don't send no college boys to fight their damn war! They send him! They send us!"

It wasn't hard to figure out whom she meant by "us."

Finally we edged past her, and she limply stood aside, weeping. As the kid passed by his mother, he briefly seemed to come awake.

"It's all right, Mama, don't cry," he said in a soft, almost inaudible voice—which of course made her cry even harder. I could still hear her cries as we loaded the kid into the BuCar. I would hear them in my head for a long time.

We drove the kid down to the US Marshals lockup, where they'd hold him until the MPs from Fort Campbell came up to get him. Nobody said a word, certainly not the kid.

But after we signed him over and headed back to the office, Miller suddenly said to me, "McNamara's Morons."

"What?"

"McNamara's Morons," he said again. "He's one of them."

"Them what?"

Miller shook his head, seemingly in disgust. "McNamara? Johnson's defense secretary? It was his bright idea. Started a few years ago, when they couldn't get enough guys to enlist, and with all the goddamned draft dodgers out there they couldn't round up enough draftees, either. So they lowered the minimum standards, started taking the Cat Fours."

"What's that?"

"Category IVs, guys who scored in the lowest twenty-five percent of the IQ test. Guys who couldn't read or weren't too sharp in the first place, mostly ghetto kids and hillbillies. That's what everybody calls 'em, McNamara's Morons. They said they were gonna help them, teach them how to read, teach them a trade, but mostly they just stuck them in the infantry, the grunts. Doesn't look like they helped that kid much. Looks like he wasn't too bright to begin with, and now he's got some serious static in the attic."

Static in the attic. At the time no one had ever heard of PTSD—post-traumatic stress disorder. I wasn't sure if Miller was right about

"McNamara's Morons," but later I learned it was all true; the Pentagon program was officially called Project 100,000, and it was just as Miller described it.

"What'll happen to him?" I asked. Until then I hadn't given much thought to the fates of the military fugitives we picked up.

Miller shrugged. "Depends. With all the deserters out there, the military's trying to get tough, make an example out of 'em. This kid is being 'returned by apprehension,' he didn't voluntarily turn himself in, so they might give him a DD"—he meant a dishonorable discharge—"and send him to the military prison at Leavenworth. And I'm tellin' you, that's a hard place. But with his combat record, if he's lucky, they might give him a BCD"—bad conduct discharge—"and just kick him out. Either way he'll lose his veteran's benefits, and that bad paper will follow him around the rest of his life."

Miller didn't speak for a while. Then he said, "Look, don't tell anybody I said this. But I'm starting to hate that goddamn war."

I could tell how difficult it was for him to admit that. And I knew how he felt.

Bringing in that kid was the hardest military-fugitive case I had to handle—hardest emotionally anyway—but it wasn't the last. I had a job to do, and I had to do it. But it became increasingly difficult to square that portion of the job with my personal convictions.

Then I got drawn into another aspect of FBI work that conflicted with my personal beliefs.

And it was exactly what J. P. Mohr had warned me about.

A number of colleges and universities fell within the Cincinnati Field Office's jurisdiction. Three of the largest in the immediate area were the University of Cincinnati and Xavier University in the city, and Miami University in Oxford, about forty miles north.

None of those universities was exactly a hotbed of anti-war activism, at least not in 1969. Sure, some relatively small demonstrations took place on the campuses, with people holding signs saying STOP THE WAR! and THE DRAFT MAY BE HAZARDOUS TO YOUR HEALTH! But mostly the campuses were peaceful. Most students at UC and

Miami seemed more interested in their studies, and in the athletic exploits of the Bearcats and the RedHawks, than they were in protesting the war. Besides, most of the male students still had their 2-S student deferments. (Not until the very end of 1969 would the then-current draft system be replaced with a lottery system to determine who was called and who wasn't. It removed some of the inequities in the draft system, but not all.)

But peaceful protests weren't the rule on campuses elsewhere. Thousands of students clashed violently with police at the University of Wisconsin and the University of Michigan and UC Berkeley and across the nation. There was a rash of campus bombings and arsons—sixty-one of them in the 1968–69 academic year alone—as well as violent takeovers of college buildings, often with college administrators held as "hostages"; many Americans were outraged by a widely distributed photo of an arrogant-looking member of the Students for a Democratic Society (SDS) sitting at the commandeered desk of the president of Columbia University in New York City, casually smoking a cigar. Coupled with increasingly violent anti-war protests in the streets, the campus and civil unrest convinced J. Edgar Hoover, among others, that events were spinning out of control, that something had to be done. At the strong urging of Assistant Director William Sullivan of the Domestic Intelligence Division—actually it was Sullivan's idea in the first place—in mid-1968 Hoover approved a plan to combat the rising tide of anti-war violence and civil disobedience.

The plan was COINTELPRO—New Left. As J. P. Mohr had explained to me, it was basically the same sort of program the Bureau had used and was using against the Communist Party, the Klan, and the extremist black liberation movement. The Bureau would "expose, disrupt, misdirect, discredit and otherwise neutralize" the violent New Left groups that opposed the war and the US government, as well the people who supported those groups. Students, professors, anti-war clergymen—all were potential targets.

It was all Top Secret. As Hoover repeatedly stressed in memos to SACs, "Under no circumstances should the existence of the program be known outside the Bureau"—certainly not in Congress or the press. Even within the Bureau it was closely guarded. Most agents I knew had probably never even heard the word *COINTEL-PRO*, at least not then.

My involvement with COINTELPRO—New Left began casually enough. It started when my squad supervisor stopped by my desk and told me that SAC Smith had an assignment for me. All of the SACs at all the field offices were under enormous pressure from SOG to collect intelligence on campus protest activities, particularly those involving the SDS. So the SACs sent agents posing as students to hang around the campuses, just nosing around, and ideally they'd develop informants who could deeply penetrate the SDS and other potentially violent groups and report back to the Bureau. Since I was the youngest agent in the Cincinnati Field Office—and looked it—SAC Smith thought I'd be perfect for the job.

And my attitude was—Okay, no problem!

I want to make this clear. Although I had my own feelings about the war and had no objections to peaceful protests, I had no reservations about investigating the violent elements of the anti-war movement—the bomb makers, the Molotov cocktail throwers, the demagogues who actively encouraged others to "kill the pigs" and hurt innocent people. To me, killing people in America to stop the killing in Vietnam made as much sense as destroying that Vietnamese town "in order to save it." I could go after the malefactors with a clear conscience, just as I would have gone after the Klan if I'd been a Bureau agent in the Deep South in the early 1960s.

That was especially true of the SDS and their violent offshoot, the Weathermen. Originally formed in 1960 as the student arm of the socialist labor movement, the SDS was initially a pro-labor, pro–civil rights, "ban the bomb" activist organization that espoused nonviolent methods of protest. The group was Communist leaning, and a number of its leaders traveled to North Vietnam, Cuba, and other Communist nations—where I'm sure they were given tours of "model" collective farms and schools and hospitals, while being spared the unpleasantness of seeing political prisons and execution chambers. In my opinion they were gullible and misguided, but for the most part they weren't personally violent.

That began to change in the latter half of the 1960s. With anti-war protests increasing, the SDS grew to a claimed three hundred local chapters and thirty thousand "supporters"—the group wasn't big on formal membership rolls—and their tactics increasingly shifted away from nonviolent protest to "direct action." The only question was just how violent they wanted to be. In 1969 the most radical SDS faction broke with the main group and formed the Weatherman faction, named after the Bob Dylan song lyric "You don't need a weather man to know which way the wind blows." The Weathermen were led by such self-described "Communist revolutionaries" as Bernardine Dohrn, a former high school cheerleader and law school graduate, and Bill Ayers, the son of a wealthy business executive. They vowed to ally with violent black liberation groups and create a "white fighting force" that would "bring the war home" and violently overthrow the US government. The Weathermen set off their first bomb in Chicago in 1969—the first of many.

Those were the guys I wanted to go after.

So I went undercover—which sounds more exciting and dramatic than it actually was. I didn't get any special training, no instruction in spy "tradecraft," no elaborate background cover story complete with fake papers and identification; it wasn't like they were sending me into East Berlin. If anybody asked, I was just "Paul," a third-year political science student, and nobody ever asked to see a student ID card. As for my FBI-like appearance, that wasn't a problem, either. My hair was already a little longer than it had been at SOG, and besides, in Cincinnati in the late sixties a lot of college guys still had short hair, including a significant number of ROTC students; the hair wouldn't make me stand out. All I had to do was put on well-worn jeans, scuffed-up tennis shoes, and the appropriate college sweatshirt and I was set.

(As I mentioned earlier, Hoover generally frowned on using FBI agents as undercovers, preferring to develop civilian informants instead. He made an exception with some New Left investigations, although he stood firm in forbidding his agents to grow long hair or beards or mustaches, or to wear scruffy clothes on duty. Since obeying those orders would have defeated the purpose, Assistant Director Sullivan and some SACs secretly defied the instructions and allowed some of their agents to better look the part of radical student activists.)

Most of my time as an undercover agent on the various campuses wasn't spent on COINTELPRO activities; I wasn't trying to "disrupt or discredit or neutralize" anyone. Instead, I was doing basic intelligence gathering—keeping my ears open, chatting up students in the cafeterias or the student unions, checking the bulletin boards for planned demonstrations, trying to find out if anyone was planning to do anything stupid. I went to a few small anti-war demonstrations, just to observe, and although the Cincinnati campuses didn't have much in the way of active SDS chapters, occasionally an SDS organizer would be brought in to speak. They offered up the usual sophomoric, self-righteous rants about "US imperialism" and the "colonialist oppression of the people"—standard-issue Marxist ideology—but none specifically urged anyone to set off a bomb.

As for recruiting informants, that proved difficult—especially since Hoover had a firm rule prohibiting the recruitment of any informant under twenty-one. (In most states at the time anyone under twenty-one was still legally a minor.) Given that roughly three-quarters of all the students on a college campus were eighteen, nineteen, or twenty, that significantly reduced the potential informant pool. In fact, I only signed up one person as a formal FBI campus informant—and that was the athletic director at one of the campuses, an old-school type who had no patience with "hippies" and "troublemakers" and was happy to pass along anything he heard about subversive activities. His value as an informant was limited; I doubted there were many "subversives" on the football or basketball teams. But even if I'd recruited an army of informants, they probably wouldn't have had much to report. Again, this was Cincinnati, not Berkeley.

I should note that all the activities I've mentioned so far were perfectly legal. There's no law against an FBI agent attending a public event without first standing up and announcing, "I work for the FBI!" Nor is it illegal to recruit informants. Without informants, criminal investigations at every level—federal, state, and local—would grind to a halt. I suppose if I'd ever been publicly "made" (that is, identified) as an FBI undercover agent, it would have "embarrassed the Bureau" and I would have been in trouble at the office—but I wouldn't have gone to jail.

Still, there were some things that the Bureau, and I, did that fell into a gray area of the law—a pretty dark gray area.

I wasn't privy to all of what the Bureau was doing as part of COINTELPRO—New Left while I was in Cincinnati. Despite Hoover's earlier ban on illegal wiretaps and black bag jobs, I'm sure they were used in some of the hot spots of SDS and other anti-war group activity in other field office divisions, either with a wink from the Director or on the unauthorized orders of Assistant Director Sullivan. (Later, during the rash of Weathermen bombings, those illegal methods were definitely used in pursuit of Weathermen fugitives—and as we'll see, some FBI agents were indicted for them. Also, unbeknownst to me, the CIA and other US intelligence agencies were conducting similar intelligence and counterintelligence operations against the New Left and other alleged radical groups, both in the United States and abroad.)

For the most part, though, the Bureau's early COINTELPRO operations against the New Left consisted of harassment. Close surveillances of suspected "SDS communes." Anonymous letters sent to parents or employers of anti-war activists warning them of their children's or employees' "dangerous subversive activities," always being careful to ensure that the letters were sent on "locally purchased stationery" that couldn't be traced to the Bureau. Anonymous telephone calls to SDS members accusing other SDS members of being FBI informants. Infiltrating actual FBI informants into SDS' or other groups' leadership circles to monitor their plans. Secretly pressuring university administrators or boards of trustees to fire "radical" anti-war and anti-government professors. And so on.

Last official portrait of J. Edgar Hoover, 1972. He'd grown older since I'd first met him six years earlier, but to the end he was bulldog tough and defiant. *FBI photo*

Hoover was appointed director of what was then called the Bureau of Investigation in 1924, at the age of twenty-nine. *Library of Congress*

Tommy-gun-toting FBI agents and police in the 1930s Gangster Era. The killings or captures of gangsters like John Dillinger and Alvin "Creepy" Karpis made Hoover and the FBI household names. Hoover and his G-men inspired countless books, films, and TV and radio programs. *Oklahoma City Police Department/ Wikimedia Commons*

WANTED

JOHN HERBERT DILLINGER

On June 23, 1934, HOMER S. CUMMINGS, Attorney General of the United States, under the authority vested in him by an Act of Congress approved June 6, 1934, offered a reward of

$10,000.00

for the capture of John Herbert Dillinger or a reward of

$5,000.00

for information leading to the arrest of John Herbert Dillinger.

DESCRIPTION

Age, 32 years; Height, 5 feet 7-1/8 inches; Weight, 153 pounds; Build, medium; Hair, medium chestnut; Eyes, grey; Complexion, medium; Occupation, machinist; Marks and scars, 1/2 inch scar back left hand, scar middle upper lip, brown mole between eyebrows.

All claims to any of the aforesaid rewards and all questions and disputes that may arise as among claimants to the foregoing rewards shall be passed upon by the Attorney General and his decisions shall be final and conclusive. The right is reserved to divide and allocate portions of any of said rewards as between several claimants. No part of the aforesaid rewards shall be paid to any official or employee of the Department of Justice.

A wanted poster of John Dillinger. Although many Americans, including my grandfather, viewed Dillinger as a Robin Hood–like figure, Hoover reviled Dillinger and other gangsters as "rats," "cowards," and "scum." Hoover's view was closer to the truth. *Stocktrek Images, Inc. Alamy Stock Photo*

Clyde Tolson, left, and Hoover in 1936. Tolson was the FBI's number two man and Hoover's most trusted confidant. Unsubstantiated rumors about their relationship persist to this day. By the time I started working for the Director, Tolson was a sick and feeble old man but he was still feared within the Bureau. *FBI photo*

Miss Helen W. Gandy, circa 1950. Miss Gandy was Hoover's personal secretary for half a century, but her modest title and outwardly gentle demeanor belied her enormous power and influence. She guarded and protected Hoover from scheming politicians, ambitious bureaucrats, and, in at least one case I witnessed, a suspected assassin. She was one of the most formidable women I have ever met. *FBI photo*

Hoover and newsman Walter Winchell ring in the New Year. Winchell was one of America's most influential journalists from the 1930s through the 1950s, and an unabashed supporter of Hoover and the FBI, but the friendship between the two men faded as Winchell's career faded. Winchell called me many times trying to reach Hoover, but I was under standing orders to tell him the Director was out. *NY Daily News Archive via Getty Images*

As an international celebrity himself, Hoover enjoyed the company of numerous Hollywood celebrities. Here he's seen with two of the biggest stars of the 1950s—Marilyn Monroe and comedian Milton Berle. The FBI kept an extensive file on Monroe and her alleged associations with left-wing individuals; Hoover also kept a copy of Monroe's famous "nude calendar" photo on display at his home. *FBI photo*

Hoover greets Efrem Zimbalist Jr. who played the role of Inspector Lewis Erskine in the popular ABC TV series *The F.B.I.* from 1965 to 1974. Hoover thought Zimbalist—a World War II hero, political conservative, and happily married family man—represented the perfect FBI agent. The Bureau maintained control over all the scripts and casting for the show, and assigned a special agent to the set to keep an eye out for anything that might be embarrassing. The desk these two are standing in front of was Hoover's ceremonial desk that he used for photos. His actual working office was behind the double doors at the rear. Zimbalist's annual visits to the Director's office while shooting exteriors for the show were always a big event when I worked there. *FBI photo*

Julius and Ethel Rosenberg were arrested in 1950 for passing American nuclear weapons secrets to the Russians and executed by electric chair three years later. Throughout his long career Hoover was obsessed with the threat of Communist subversion. *Larry Higgins, New York World-Telegram and the Sun Newspaper Photographs Collection, Library of Congress/FBI*

Martin Luther King Jr., 1964. Hoover was convinced the black civil rights movement was infiltrated and controlled by Communists. With the approval of Attorney General Robert F. Kennedy, Hoover ordered Bureau agents to wiretap King's phones, and, later, to plant eavesdropping bugs in his hotel rooms. No evidence of direct Communist influence was discovered, but the bugs provided lurid details of the charismatic young civil rights leader's extramarital affairs. I broke the news to the Director that King had been shot in Memphis—and his reaction was shocking. *Dick DeMarsico, New York World-Telegram and the Sun Newspapers Collection, Library of Congress*

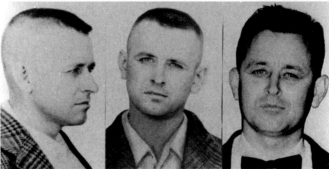

Despite the Director's long-running public feud with the charismatic civil rights leader, Hoove launched the biggest international manhunt in Bureau history to find King's killer. The FBI identified the assassin as James Earl Ray, a racist escaped convict who was eventually arrested England and returned to Tennessee to face trial. Ray died in prison in 1998.

Klux Klansmen burning a cross in 1958 in
rth Carolina. To battle the Klan the FBI
d the same counterintelligence program
)INTELPRO) tactics it had used against the
nmunist Party USA and other alleged subversive
ups—anonymous mailings and phone calls, close
/eillances of Klansmen and their families, and
ts of paid informants. Years later, Hoover and
Bureau were severely criticized when they used
ilar tactics against black nationalist groups and
ical "New Left" organizations. *State Archives of
th Carolina, Wikimedia Commons*

Hundreds of thousands of Americans
protested the war in Vietnam, including
this demonstration near the Pentagon
in 1967. Hoover, along with presidents
Johnson and Nixon, firmly believed
the demonstrations were organized by
Communists. Hoover and the Bureau
launched the COINTELPRO—NEW
LEFT operation in an attempt to
harass and discredit anti-war groups
and organizers. As a special agent I was
asked to play a small role in the effort
and I didn't like it. *Lyndon B. Johnson
Library, Wikimedia Commons*

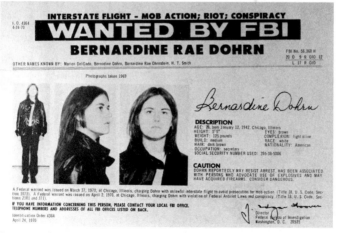

FBI wanted poster of Bernardine Dohrn, cofounder of the violent Weather Underground
;anization, which was responsible for a series of bombings nationwide. A self-described
/olutionary communist," Dohrn was on the FBI Ten Most Wanted list from 1970 to 1973,
·n most of the federal charges against her were dismissed. Based on information from a
fidential informant, my partner and I staked out a drag nightclub one night in a vain attempt
·apture her. *FBI photo*

Hoover served as FBI Director under eight presidents, from Calvin Coolidge to Richard Nixc with varying degrees of influence. John F. Kenne treated Hoover with deference, but his young brother, Attorney Genera Robert F. Kennedy, was openly contemptuous of aging FBI chief—and vic versa. *White House*

Hoover and LBJ were longtime friends and neighbors when Johnson was serving in Congress, and the Director wielded major influence during the Johnson Administration. However, I was under strict orders never to bother Hoover when he was at the track—even if the president was calling. *FBI photo*

Hoover at the White House with President Nixon, Attorney General John Mitchell, and Nixor aide John Ehrlichman, circa 1969. Hoover and Nixon had been friends and political allies sinc Nixon's Red-hunting days, but the relationship cooled when Hoover defeated a White House plan to dramatically increase domestic counterintelligence programs against New Left anti-wa activists and others. The Director's refusal prompted Nixon and his men to create their own domestic spying and dirty tricks operation—the infamous White House Plumbers. *White Hou*

That's me with the Director in 1968, when I was a civilian clerk on Hoover's personal staff prior to becoming an FBI special agent. When, years later, I looked at this photo I couldn't help noticing how wrinkled my slacks looked next to my boss's perfectly pressed pair. *FBI photo*

Picking up skills on the shooting range, which was located at the FBI Academy at Quantico. Despite never firing a gun prior to New Agents Training, I soon became expert in the use of a .38-caliber revolver (with either hand), a .30-caliber rifle, and, as seen here, a 12-gauge shotgun. Even though Tommy guns were no longer standard issue, we got to shoot those, too!

∨ Agents Training graduating class, December, 1968. I'm in the last row, fourth from the right.

Arthur Gates Barkley, at right, a Phoenix truck driver, pioneered the "hijacking for ransom" of U.S. airliners that was later made famous by D. B. Cooper. In 1970 Barkley used a pistol to commandeer a Trans World Airlines flight and demanded $100 million in ransom. After the plane landed at Dulles International Airport outside Washington, DC, Barkley engaged in a brief gun battle with several FBI agents, including me, before being subdued. Here he's being taken to jail by my partner FBI Special Agent Jim Siano. This was the first of many skyjackings in which I was involved. *Everett Collection Historical/Alamy Stock Photo*

Beset by enemies who wanted him out of the Director's office, but still defiant, J. Edgar Hoover died at age seventy-seven of a heart attack at his home on May 2, 1972. His body lay in state at the Capitol—an honor previously accorded to no other civil servant—and was then taken to National Presbyterian Church for the funeral service. *FBI photo*

President Richard Nixon delivers the eulogy for J. Edgar Hoover at the Natic Presbyterian Churc Nixon was secretly delighted that "the Hoover problem" h solved itself. I was sitting between Mis Gandy and Clyde Tolson in a special "friends and family" section of the churc (not shown). *Bettm Archive/Getty Imag*

It all must have seemed like a good idea at the time. Remember, this was a period when the nation was under increasingly violent assault from radical revolutionaries who proudly declared their intentions to destroy America—or "Amerika" or "Amerikkka" as they often spelled it in their literature. Even if their actions seldom equaled their rhetoric, J. Edgar Hoover believed them—and so did Richard Nixon's administration and most of the "silent majority" who elected him. They wanted the FBI to do something, even if they didn't know—or didn't want to know—what that was.

I wanted to do something about the threat to our national system and institutions as well, provided it was important and useful. But then one day I realized that what I was doing wasn't that important or useful at all.

The Cincinnati Field Office had a rather large resident agency in Columbus, Ohio, about a hundred miles away, which covered Ohio State University. Ohio State had a pretty active SDS presence, and the RA was aggressively building up its SDS files. So I was directed to have some posters printed up announcing an upcoming SDS rally and protest to be held on the Ohio State campus, with free bus transportation offered from the Cincinnati area to Columbus. The posters were the usual stuff—SDS! BRING THE WAR HOME!—and featured a picture of a bus painted in psychedelic colors like the one in Tom Wolfe's book *The Electric Kool-Aid Acid Test*.

Of course there was no such SDS rally planned at Ohio State; it was an FBI ruse. But I put up the posters on the Cincinnati campuses and rented a couple of old school buses, and on the appointed day maybe thirty or forty kids showed up and headed off to Columbus for the "rally." When they arrived, they were greeted by a half dozen agents from the Columbus RA, who told them that the SDS had canceled the rally. They also told them that they, the agents, were investigating a campus bombing, which they weren't, and that they were going to interview the kids as potential witnesses. Most of the college kids had probably just been curious or were looking for a little fun on another campus, a chance to meet some new girls or guys. But now they were thoroughly scared and intimidated—a bombing!

the FBI!—and they gave up their names and addresses and anything they knew about the SDS, which was pretty much nothing.

This was pure COINTELPRO stuff. And for the FBI it was a twofer. The Bureau discredited the SDS with the canceled "rally"— by the time the interviews had concluded the buses had disappeared and the kids had to make their own way back to Cincinnati—and the agents collected a few dozen new names to be added to the Bureau's "suspected SDS sympathizers" files.

It was just as Mr. Mohr had said. We couldn't tell who the enemy was, so now everyone was the enemy.

The whole thing bothered me. Even setting aside the civil liberties considerations, it seemed counterproductive, foolish, a waste of time. Give me a bombing or a campus arson and I'd be gung ho, I'd work it like a man possessed. But I didn't want to be part of this chickenshit harassment anymore. For that matter, I didn't want to chase military AWOLs anymore, either. I wanted to work on real crimes, against real criminals. Finally, I decided to tell my superiors exactly that.

I knew I'd be taking a big chance. Special agents, particularly brand-new special agents, simply didn't pick and choose which cases they'd work on. To refuse to work certain cases would almost certainly get them a disciplinary transfer to Butte, or even termination "with prejudice" for insubordination.

But I had an ace in the hole. A few weeks earlier I'd been at my desk in the bullpen when SAC Smith came up to me, looking puzzled—and a little worried.

"Letersky, there's a call for you, on my line. It's from the Director's office."

I was surprised, but tried not to show it. "Okay, sir, would you mind if I took it in your office?" I glanced around at the crowded bullpen, where the other agents were staring at us. "For privacy?"

SAC Smith grunted his assent, so I walked into his private office, closing the door behind me, while the SAC stood outside, cooling his heels and watching through the glass window. I picked up the phone and it wasn't the Director or Miss Gandy or Mr. Mohr calling. It was my old Director's office pal, John Cox, just calling to tell me he was starting New Agents Training the next week. I congratulated him and we spent a few minutes bantering back and forth, but all the while I kept a serious look on my face. After we hung up, I walked out of the office, said, "Thank you, sir," to SAC Smith, and kept walking. I knew he was dying to ask me what the Director had said, but I didn't say another word.

As I got back to my desk, I saw some of my squadmates smiling and giving me a thumbs-up. By that time they knew that despite my earlier work in the Director's office, I wasn't a rat or a snitch. I knew they knew that because they'd started teasing me about my alleged exalted status, calling me "the Polish Prince" or "Prince-ski." Waxy especially took delight in busting my chops about being the Director's fair-haired boy. Sometimes when he'd get into an argument with someone, Waxy would grab a phone, shout, "Get me the Director's office!," then hand the phone to me and say, "Here, Prince-ski, ask the Director about this!" The agents knew they didn't have to treat me differently than anybody else.

But supervisors and assistant special agents in charge and SAC Smith weren't so sure. They had to keep their noses to the wind, to pick up any whiff of special influence—and act accordingly to protect themselves.

So when I went to my supervisor and made my request—no more AWOLs or campus undercover work—he kind of gulped and went pale. He was a good enough guy, but a nervous sort, like many midlevel management types. He did what most midlevel management types do when confronted with a perplexing problem—he kicked it upstairs:

"Talk to the SAC," he said.

Which I did. I sat down in front of SAC Smith's desk and repeated my request, noting my work as a campus undercover and AWOL chaser and citing "personal reasons" for not wanting to do them anymore.

The SAC listened, trying to look stern, and when I finished he said, "What're you, Letersky, some kind of hippie?"

"No, sir."

"You sound like one. You think I can allow one of my agents, any agent, to march in here and start making demands about which cases he will and will not accept—for personal reasons?"

"It's not a demand, sir. It's a request." Actually it was a demand; I was ready to quit over it. But I didn't want to phrase it that way. "And it's for the good of the division. I just think I would be more . . . effective working criminal cases. And I think my stats have been pretty good in that area."

That seemed to brighten him. The SAC loved talking about good stats. "Yes," he said, smiling, "for a new agent they haven't been bad, not bad at all."

Then he grew stern again. "Look, Letersky, I want to make this clear. We don't play favorites here in the Cincinnati Division. Whatever influence or connections someone has within the Bureau is absolutely irrelevant. The job is the only thing we care about here."

I knew what he was talking about; he hadn't forgotten my call from "the Director's office." And what he was saying was bullshit. Influence and connections within the Bureau played a role in Cincinnati and every other field office, just as they did in every other human organization, government or private sector. But the truth was that I had no connections or influence, at least not in this situation. I knew damn well that if the SAC decided to put in a call or send a memo to the Director about my refusal to work AWOLs or campus undercover, Hoover would have seen it as gross insubordination and an alarming display of sympathy for traitors and subversives. He would have bounced me out of the Bureau in a heartbeat, without a second thought.

I knew that, but the SAC didn't—and I didn't tell him. One thing I'd learned from the Director was that if somebody wants to think you have more power than you actually have, by all means let him think it. J. Edgar Hoover had played that card a thousand times in his career. And I was playing the same card now.

I sat there quietly for a few moments while SAC Smith drummed his fingers on the desk, as if he were thinking it over. But I knew he'd already decided to take the easiest—and least risky—course of action.

"Okay, Letersky," he finally said, trying to sound like the hard-ass that he wasn't. "Just this once I'm going to make an exception. There are plenty of other cases to work, so go work 'em. Now get out of my office."

"Thank you, sir," I said. And I never arrested some hapless AWOL or put up a phony sign on a campus again.

Please don't get the wrong idea. I'm not putting myself up on some high moral pedestal here. I hadn't changed anything. Other agents still had to do COINTELPRO operations and chase military fugitives. The only difference was that I wasn't one of them.

But at least I felt better about myself. I was happy to be a bona fide crime-busting, brick-ass G-man again. I was happier still when, after a little over a year in Cincinnati, I was notified what my next field office assignment would be.

I hadn't asked for the assignment. But apparently, someone in the Seat of Government liked me.

CHAPTER 6

Streetwise

H ello, Miss Gandy!"
She was standing in front of a filing cabinet, her back to me,
when I popped my head into her office. As she turned around, she
was smiling and her brown eyes were bright.

"Paul! So good to see you!"

We didn't hug or anything; as I said, neither of us was a natural
hugger. But I could tell she was pleased that I'd stopped by. It was
a Saturday afternoon, and no one else was in the Director's suite.

I held up the brown paper bag I'd brought. "I thought you might
like a sandwich."

She laughed. "Just like old times! That's so nice." Her tone
changed to mock disapproval. "I was wondering when you would
finally come by."

It had been a month since I'd first reported to my new field office
in Alexandria, just across the Potomac River in Virginia. This former
resident agency had been expanded into a full-fledged field office to
take some of the pressure off the Washington, DC, Field Office—
and for me it was a dream assignment. The office was newly stocked
with aggressive young agents from across the country, and its prox-
imity to Washington ensured that we'd get a lot of interesting, high-
profile cases, while sparing us the brutal cross-bridge commute into
the city. And the Alexandria SAC was a respected straight shooter
named Jack McDermott, who would later be appointed SAC of the
Washington Field Office.

"Well, we've been settling in." I said. I haven't mentioned this before, but by this time I was married, with a young son and eventually two daughters—which is why I said "we." Sadly, the marriage wouldn't last, but my love for my children always would.

"Oh, I understand," Miss Gandy said. "Now, how about that sandwich?"

We sat down and started nibbling on our tuna sandwiches and getting caught up. I'd purposely come in on a Saturday when I knew Miss Gandy would have time to chat; I'd stop by and say hello to Nancy Mooney and Mr. Mohr and others another time, but first I wanted to talk to Miss Gandy. I hadn't tried to set up a meeting with the Director—and I didn't intend to. You've probably realized by now that Hoover wasn't big on small talk, and I didn't want to waste his time. Besides, I already knew the Director; if he ever wanted to see me, he'd let me know.

I asked Miss Gandy how my replacement in the office was working out—I'd never met him.

She shrugged. "Oh, he's a nice young man. But he's no Polish Prince."

I must have blushed a little because she added, laughing, "Yes, I heard that was what they called you in Cincinnati. We have our sources, you know."

I wondered if she had also heard about my little rebellion with SAC Smith—and if she'd told the Director. But I quickly dismissed the thought. She would have known what his reaction would be.

"Miss Gandy, that's something I've wanted to ask you about. Why did they send me to Cincinnati in the first place?" I said "they" but I meant her and Mr. Mohr.

"Oh, we just felt you would benefit from being with some . . . seasoned agents your first year. Were we right?"

I thought about Waxy and the others. "You're always right, Miss Gandy. I also want to thank you for what you did. Bringing me to Alexandria, I mean. I don't know what I would have done if you hadn't."

She waved the thanks away. "That was no problem. Mr. Mohr was very helpful—and he approved as well."

She meant Hoover. Again, in the Director's office you never had to ask who "he" was.

I have to back up a little bit here. When I first got my second-office assignment at the end of my tour in Cincinnati, I learned that the Bureau was going to send me to New York City. For a second-year agent it was a prestige assignment to a high-profile field office—but I was horrified. I was making about $20,000 a year, which was pretty good money at the time, but it wasn't New York–level good money, especially for a family man. My young son had some serious medical problems, and the Bureau's insurance plan didn't cover everything. And back then the Bureau didn't offer a cost-of-living differential to agents assigned to New York. So the only way I could afford to work in the most expensive city in America would be to get a place way out on Long Island or in New Jersey and commute sixty or seventy miles one-way every day—and even then it'd be a financial stretch. I'd thought about asking Miss Gandy or Mr. Mohr to intervene—but again, my pride wouldn't let me.

Fortunately, fate had intervened in the form of Nancy Mooney, my old office mate. We talked by phone a few times while I was in Cincinnati, just to stay in touch, and I mentioned my predicament to her, strictly as a friend. I didn't ask or expect her to, but she mentioned it to Miss Gandy. Later, Nancy told me Miss Gandy said, "Oh, we'll take care of that!"—and shortly thereafter I got a Bureau letter nixing New York and sending me to Alexandria. I suppose I'd taken advantage of a connection once removed, but my pride was still intact—and I found an affordable house just a five-minute drive from the Alexandria Field Office.

"Well, I appreciate it anyway," I said.

"I'm sure you'll enjoy it here. So, your family is well?"

"Getting better and better." We talked for a while about my son's medical condition, which was steadily improving. Then I looked around the office. "So, how are things around here? How's he doing?"

I meant physically. Hoover had recently turned seventy-five.

"Oh, he's a bit tired these days, I suppose. His 'no calls' times are getting a little longer." She meant the Director's postlunch naps. "Small wonder when you think about all the pressure he's under." She grimaced. "The White House has been . . . difficult."

"Nixon?" I said, surprised. I knew that Nixon and the Director had been longtime allies and even personal pals—again, it's hard to use the word *friends* in connection with the Director. Hoover had been close to Nixon in the young congressman's Red-hunting days, and when he was vice president. The Director kept up his personal contacts even when Nixon was in the political wilderness after his 1960 presidential loss and his humiliating defeat for the California governorship in 1962. Nixon had been to the Director's home for dinner a number of times, including once after Nixon became president—a rare social excursion for the famously antisocial president. Although they came from different generations, the two men had much in common: a sincere if overheated fear of Communist subversion, a public commitment to old values and law and order, and a passionate, lifelong belief that they were surrounded by political enemies. Some people called that paranoia, but I'm reminded of the old saying "You're not being paranoid if people really are out to get you"—and for both men that was certainly true.

(Strangely enough, as a twenty-four-year-old law school graduate in 1937 Nixon had applied to become an agent in Hoover's FBI. He was interviewed by the SAC in Los Angeles, who made the following notations in his report on the young applicant: "Personal Appearance—Good. Features—Ordinary. Personality—Good. Assurance—Self Confident." The SAC had rated Nixon "Qualified" and recommended that he be appointed as soon as there was an opening. But in the meantime Nixon found another job.)

"No, not President Nixon," Miss Gandy corrected me. "The others. Especially that awful Mr. Ehrlichman!"

She was referring to John Ehrlichman, the president's senior White House aide. The name didn't mean anything to me at the time, but soon enough everyone in America would know it—including Ehrlichman's fellow inmates at the minimum-security federal prison in Safford, Arizona. Later I learned that when Nixon took office, he'd promised that the Director would have "direct access" to the Oval Office at all times—a promise he had no intention of keeping. Instead, he made Ehrlichman his liaison with Hoover, meaning that when the Director wanted to talk to the president, he had to go through Ehrlichman—which pleased neither of them. Ehrlichman later made his feelings about Hoover plain when he wrote about their first meeting: "His big head rested on beefy, rounded shoulders, apparently without benefit of neck. He was florid and fat-faced, ears flat against his head, eyes protruding. He looked unwell to me." Ehrlichman's feelings about Hoover went downhill from there—and vice versa.

As for "the others" in the Nixon administration Miss Gandy referred to, I didn't know them, either, but before long everyone would learn their names: H. R. Haldeman, Charles Colson, John Dean, among others. Like Ehrlichman, eventually all would wind up serving time. But now they were all powers within the administration—and all thought that Nixon should fire Hoover. One newspaper had even cited an unnamed White House source as saying, "The old goat has got to go."

"Mr. Ehrlichman walked in here the first time with his nose in the air and he hasn't put it down since," Miss Gandy said contemptuously. "He thinks he's such a big shot. But we'll see about that!"

I wasn't sure how an executive assistant, even the executive assistant to the Director of the FBI, thought she could scuttle one of the closest associates of the president of the United States. But I did know that if I were Ehrlichman, I wouldn't want Miss Gandy on my case.

"How's the new AG?" I asked, meaning John Mitchell, Nixon's former law partner whom Nixon had appointed attorney general. Like so many others of "the president's men," Mitchell, too, would one day land another position within the federal government—as inmate No. 24171-157 at a federal minimum-security prison in Alabama.

"He's nice enough," Miss Gandy said, "except for that smelly pipe he's always smoking. They get along well. He generally leaves the

Director alone. Not like the others." She meant RFK and Ramsey Clark. "The Director is particularly fond of Mrs. Mitchell."

She meant Martha Mitchell, the fifty-eight-year-old daughter of an Arkansas cotton broker known for her biting wit and her late-night calls to Washington dignitaries and news media types, usually after more than a few drinks. The newspapers loved her, as did, presumably, John Mitchell, but the rest of the Nixon crowd viewed her as a political loose cannon—which she was. But the Director seemed genuinely amused by her. It was Martha Mitchell who, when introducing Hoover at a social function, famously said, "Take a good look at him, because when you've seen one FBI director, you've seen them all."

"And Mr. Tolson?" I said. "I heard he's been—ill."

"When hasn't he been?" Miss Gandy said unsympathetically. Over the past twenty years Tolson had been hospitalized at least a dozen times for strokes and heart problems. "Mrs. Skillman"—Dorothy Skillman, Tolson's executive assistant—"told me he's mostly blind in his right eye now. She says it comes and goes, but lately it's been more coming than going."

Tolson, like Hoover, was past the mandatory retirement age of seventy, but Hoover had declared him an "essential" employee and kept him on as an "annuitant," meaning Tolson collected his federal retirement benefits and the Bureau paid the remainder of his salary. He'd done the same thing for Miss Gandy, who was now seventy-three—although in her case, she actually was essential.

"You never liked him, did you?" I meant Tolson.

She sniffed. "I would say it was rather the other way around—from the very start."

"He never liked you? How could anyone not like Miss Helen Gandy?"

I was teasing, but with Tolson on her mind she wasn't in the mood for joking. "Not just me. He hates all women. He's a . . . a . . ."

"Misogynist?" I offered. The word wasn't as commonly used back then as it is now.

"Yes, he's a misogynist. Always has been. He thinks women are just poor dumb creatures, with no minds of our own. He's never given me—I mean, he's never given us any credit for all that we've done."

I didn't want to remind Miss Gandy that the Director had his own biases against women as well, firmly believing that they had no place in traditional male roles—including, for example, as special agents of the FBI. I guess the difference was that while the Director liked many women as individuals, Tolson did not. Even Mrs. Skillman seemed to find working for that cranky old man to be a trial.

Miss Gandy was still fuming, mostly to herself. "It's our Bureau just as much as it is the men's. Try running this place without us."

I couldn't resist. I was, after all, a man of the early 1970s, with at least some of the patronizing attitudes that implies. "Why, Miss Gandy, are you becoming a women's libber?"

She didn't smile. "Not in the way you men probably think of it." I think she meant the bra-burning thing, but I wasn't about to get into that. "Not in any radical way, of course. But, yes, in some ways I think I am. I think I always have been."

I mentioned earlier that Miss Gandy was the highest-grade-level and highest-paid female in the entire Justice Department. Today I wonder if, had Miss Gandy been born fifty or sixty years later, we could say the same thing about her—except without the "female" part.

There's an addendum to this, something I didn't know. Years later it would come out that even as Miss Gandy and I were speaking, the Bureau was conducting COINTELPRO operations directed at some members and groups of the women's liberation movement— WLM in Bureau-speak—using paid female civilian informants to infiltrate meetings and otherwise keep an eye on them. That was partly because many of the women's rights activists were also active in anti-war New Left circles. But it was also because the Director actually believed they were a potential threat to "national security." As he put it in a memo uncovered years later, "It is absolutely essential that we conduct sufficient investigation to clearly establish subversive ramifications of the WLM and to determine the potential for violence . . . as well as any possible threat they may represent to the internal security of the United States."

Obviously I didn't know about this at the time, but Miss Gandy almost certainly did. And how did that square with what she said to me?

I don't know. It was another mystery surrounding this mysterious woman.

Anyway, Miss Gandy and I chatted for a while longer about inconsequential things, until I sensed it was time for me to go. As I said goodbye, Miss Gandy said she hoped I'd continue to stop in from time to time, and I promised I would. Then, even though it was a Saturday afternoon, I headed back across the river to work—to do the real work of an FBI agent.

Almost all of the many books and articles about the FBI in the Hoover years concentrate on the political controversies—wiretaps and buggings, spying on Americans, Hoover's battles with various politicians and groups. And of course, those things were important. But most people tend to forget that while all the political stuff was going on, the vast majority of the Bureau's seventy-six hundred special agents were engaged in the actual business of the FBI—fighting crime. That included me. Sure, I had an interest in what was going on in the Director's office. But for most of my time in the Alexandria Field Office, even though Washington was just across the river, the capital and its intrigues might as well have been a million miles away. I had cases to work—everything from bank robberies to dangerous fugitives to bombings to aircraft hijackings to thefts committed on US government property.

A few of those cases attracted national interest, some garnered local press attention, and many were of little significance to anyone except me and the crooks I locked up. But they were all interesting cases to work, and as in Cincinnati, I had some great fellow agents to work them with. As I said, the expansion of the Alexandria office resulted in a lot of young, talented, and aggressive agents being brought in from around the country—and two of the most talented and aggressive were Jim Siano and Joe Pistone.

Jim, a tall, athletic Italian American guy, had already gained distinction in the Bureau for playing a key role in the sensational and horrific 1968 kidnapping of Barbara Jane Mackle, the twenty-year-old daughter of a wealthy Florida real estate developer who was a close personal friend of Richard Nixon's. Mackle had been abducted at gunpoint from a Georgia motel by a man and a woman who knocked her out with chloroform and buried her alive in a fiberglass box in a pinewood forest with only a pipe to breathe through and a small supply of food and water. Agents found her, still alive, three days later, and shortly thereafter Jim and others cornered the male kidnapper in a Florida swamp and arrested him. After a nationwide search for the female perp—she was the first women ever to make the Bureau's Ten Most Wanted list—agents captured her three months later. It was just this sort of brilliant investigative work that had made the Bureau famous since the 1930s, and Jim was rightly proud to have been a part of it.

As for Joe Pistone, he was a Sicilian-heritage guy from New Jersey who's now better known by another name—Donnie Brasco. In 1976, after the Bureau relaxed the Hoover-era rule against using agents as undercovers in criminal cases, Joe posed as a small-time jewel thief named Donnie Brasco and went undercover to penetrate the Bonanno and Colombo crime families in New York. Joe spent six years undercover, rising within the organized crime ranks and almost becoming a "made" member of the Mafia before the Bureau decided it was too dangerous and pulled him out; his exploits were later chronicled in a book and in an Al Pacino–Johnny Depp movie called *Donnie Brasco*. Joe's courageous work resulted in more than a hundred Mafia members being sent to jail, and in recognition the Bureau gave him a lousy $500 "incentive award"—which pissed everybody off, especially Joe's wife, Peggy. To this day Joe still has to live under an assumed name in an "undisclosed location."

So those were the kind of guys I got to work with—and live with, since Jim, Joe, and I all bought houses in the same neighborhood in a northern-Virginia suburb. It was a great time and place to be an FBI field agent, and a great learning experience as well.

One thing I learned about was the joys and sorrows of working with informants.

I mentioned earlier that any street agent was only as good as his sources; Waxy in Cincinnati proved that, and he had given me early instruction in the care and feeding of informants. Every agent was expected to have at least a half dozen informants in his stable. In my case, some of my "criminal informants" were more-or-less "straight" citizens who operated in criminal-rich environments—a bartender in an outlaw-biker bar, a stripper in a club frequented by street gangsters, that sort of thing. Those informants would be paid for good information, twenty bucks here, fifty bucks there. But some of my other informants were career criminals, usually small-timers, and those criminal informants could be compensated in two ways—with small cash payments and/or a "get out of jail free card" provided by me. If they got into a minor beef with local cops—and I emphasize that it had to be minor—I'd try to spring them. The problem with criminal informants was that they were just that—criminals—and so they were bound to get into serious trouble sooner or later, usually sooner. Consequently, the average shelf life of a criminal informant was only three or four months.

Still, sometimes before they got put on ice they provided good information on an important case. One informant I remember well was a guy I called Continental Slim.

I met Slim in connection with a fugitive case we were working on: a guy named Arthur Vincent Hall, aka Boss, a thirty-nine-year-old African American, was wanted for a series of bank robberies in New York and New Jersey and reportedly had ties to the DC area. This guy was a real sweetheart. Local cops had cornered him after one of the bank robberies, but Boss grabbed an eight-year-old boy, put a .357 Magnum to his head, and threatened to blow the kid's head off if the cops didn't back away. He got away and released the kid, physically unharmed, a few miles away, but legally it was still a kidnapping. Boss claimed to be a black liberation crusader, always bragging about "killin' the pigs" and so on, but it's hard to see how robbing banks and kidnapping a little boy added much to the cause of civil rights.

Anyway, one day we got a call from the Arlington, Virginia, police saying that a local Ford dealership had reported a "suspicious" sale—a guy who bought a candy-apple-red Thunderbird and a pastel-yellow Lincoln Continental, both brand-new, both for cash, both at full sticker price, and both at the same time. The buyer registered the sale in his own name—Arthur V. Hall—which for a guy on the run was either incredibly stupid or incredibly arrogant. Either way, shortly thereafter the cops got a tip that the Continental was parked in the driveway of a two-story brick house in Arlington, and that our guy was living there. So four agents, me included, and two Arlington cops went out to pick him up.

The front door was wide open when we got there, and we went in to look around. I found the keys to the Continental on the kitchen table—they were still on the dealer's key chain—and slipped them into my pocket. Then we heard a noise upstairs. I went up the stairs with a Bureau-issued 12-gauge shotgun in my hands, walked into a bedroom, and drew down my shotgun on a young black male who was holding a pair of alligator shoes in his hand.

"FBI! Drop the shoes and put your hands up!"

He did, and another agent turned him around and cuffed him and patted him down. No weapons. All the while the guy kept saying, "You got the wrong dude, man! The wrong dude!"

I already knew that. He didn't match the description or the mug shot. Apparently Boss had already fled, probably in the missing Thunderbird. The other agent left to search the other rooms while I kept my shotgun on this guy. "What's your name?"

"Robert Wagner," he said—too quickly.

"Yeah, right." These street guys never gave you their real name right out of the gate. Besides, Robert Wagner was a famous movie and TV star who had once been married to an equally famous Hollywood actress. "And I guess your ex-wife is Natalie Wood. Gimme your real name or you're going to be in trouble—big trouble."

He thought it over. "Carl Leroy Pitts."

That sounded better. "Street name?"

"They call me Slim." That fit, too. He was thin as a rail.

"Where's Boss? And what are you doing in his house?"

"I dunno know where he is, man. He's around, is all I know."

I finally got the story out of him. It seems he knew Boss from way back in the hood, and recently Slim had been to some parties here at Boss's house. As soon as Slim heard Boss was gone, Slim had hurried over to see what he could steal from the house—starting with the alligator shoes. He admitted to having served time, first in juvie, the juvenile detention center, and later short sentences in the local lockup for attempted burglary and petty theft. One of the Arlington cops called in his name and didn't come up with any outstanding warrants. So I didn't care about this guy—but I cared about catching Boss.

"Okay, Slim"—I uncuffed him—"I'm gonna let you go, and I'm gonna do you a favor." I took out the set of keys I'd found on the kitchen table and jingled them in front of him. "I'm going to look the other way while you get in that Lincoln in the driveway and get out of here."

Slim's eyes lit up. A Lincoln Continental! Of course, this wasn't proper Bureau procedure on my part, but technically the Lincoln wasn't a stolen car, even if it had been paid for with suspected stolen cash.

"But in return, you're going to give me Boss. If you don't give him up in a week, I'm going to take the car back and arrest you."

"Arrest me? For what?"

I looked at the pair of shoes on the floor. "Attempted interstate transport of stolen alligator shoes. And I'll tell the federal magistrate to set bail at a million dollars and to appoint you the dumbest public defender they've got and to slow up the paperwork. You'll be locked up till you're an old man before you even go to trial. And the magistrate will do it. He's my father-in-law."

This was all bullshit, of course, but sometimes you had to lay it on thick with these guys.

Slim was thinking. "I dunno, man. I could get killed doin' that."

"Maybe so, but at least you'll be driving a nice car."

The logic of that illogical statement appealed to him. "Can I keep the shoes?"

"Yes, you can keep the damn shoes. What's it going to be?"

Slim finally agreed, and I explained the situation to the other agents and the two cops. They understood perfectly. I gave Slim my number, and with a final warning from me—"Remember, Slim, one week"—he drove away with the Continental, and the alligator shoes.

Sure enough, six days later he called and gave me an address in Southeast Washington. I called it into the Washington Field Office—it was in their area of responsibility—and I went there to assist. With some other agents and some DC cops we quickly arrested Boss without any trouble, he being naked and asleep when we found him. Later a friend of mine in the Crime Records Division, which handled the Bureau's Ten Most Wanted list, told me that Boss had been next in line for the list as soon as one of the other fugitives got arrested and there was an opening. So I just barely missed getting a Top Tenner. Still, it was a solid arrest.

As for Continental Slim, he'd never been a particularly good criminal, but he turned out to be an excellent informant—for a while. Over the next couple of months he gave up two guys who'd been in a shots-fired bank robbery in DC, and he fingered two more from a surveillance photo of a northern-Virginia bank heist. All were arrested, some by me, some by others at my request, and my stats went up accordingly. Continental Slim was an asset to my career, and even though he was a criminal, I liked him. Not that I'd ever invite him to my home or anything, but he had a winning smile, and a sunny personality—and he produced.

And like most informants, he was also a huge pain in the ass. Sometimes he'd call me at home at 3:00 a.m., just to chat, and when I yelled at him about it, he'd say, "I just want you to know I'm out here circulatin', I'm circulatin'." Then one day I got a call from a detective with the Cook County Sheriff's Office in Chicago, saying they'd picked Slim up during a "routine traffic stop"—in Chicago that meant DWB, "driving while black," especially in a brand-new Lincoln—and found an unlicensed handgun in the car. Funny thing was, the detective said, the car came back registered to an apprehended fugitive named Arthur Vincent Hall, aka Boss, while Slim's fingerprints came back as Carl Leroy Pitts. Pitts had told them I was a friend of his, the detective said, and that I'd explain everything. I did, and the detective agreed to let Slim go, with the Lincoln but without the gun—and now I owed the Chicago detective a favor. When Slim got back, I chewed him out—I'd expressly ordered him not to leave the DC area—and I threatened to take the car away. But he hung his head and pleaded with me like a teenager being grounded by his dad. "Please don't take my car away, I'm sorry, man, it won't happen again."

But of course it did. A month later I got a call from a friend of mine, a special agent in the Baltimore Field Office, who had Slim in custody. He said that Slim had crashed the Continental into another car—a police car, for God's sake—and when the cops searched it, they found a sawed-off shotgun and a bag of cash from a bank up the street that had just been robbed. Apparently Slim had been trying to work his way up in the criminal world, and being Slim, he botched it. There was no way I could or would spring him on this one—not even a "get out of jail free" card from the Director himself could do that—and Slim knew it. My agent friend said Slim didn't want to talk to me directly, but he just wanted me to know he was "ashamed."

I'm sure he was ashamed—ashamed of being caught. I never saw him again.

As I said, informants could be important assets to an FBI agent's career. But they could also be a complete waste of time—like the informant who told us where we could find the aforementioned Bernardine Dohrn.

Since 1969 members of the Weatherman faction of the SDS—later renamed the Weather Underground Organization or WUO—had committed dozens of successful or attempted bombings, firebombings, and killings across the United States. They shot and killed a cop during a bank robbery in Massachusetts, put bombs in police cars in Chicago, firebombed the home of a New York judge, set off bombs in bathrooms in the Capitol and the Pentagon. They even managed to bomb themselves, accidentally setting off a bomb in an upscale Greenwich Village townhouse in 1970 that killed three

Weathermen. (It also damaged the home of actor Dustin Hoffman, who lived next door, but he was away when it happened.) Whether Dohrn was personally involved in those or any other WUO bombings isn't clear, but as the cofounder of the violent organization, she was certainly a suspect. In October 1970, after she skipped bail on federal anti-rioting charges, she was put on the Bureau's Ten Most Wanted list.

So when Jim Siano told me he had a lead on Dohrn that he wanted me to work with him, initially I was thrilled. But somehow Jim didn't seem that excited—and I soon found out why.

Jim explained that he had an informant named Billie who owned a nightclub in DC next to the main Greyhound bus terminal. Billie told him she'd seen a young woman "who looked a lot like Bernardine Dohrn" talking with one of Billie's customers, and after the young woman left, the drunken customer told Billie that the woman was indeed the Ten Most Wanted fugitive—and that she was coming back to the club to meet with him again sometime in the next couple of nights. Oh, and one other thing, Jim said. The nightspot Billie owned was a drag club.

Bernardine Dohrn. In a drag club. Next to the bus station.

Jim read my look. "I know, I know," he said. "But Billie's given me good information in the past. We've gotta follow up."

I wanted to ask him where he got this "we" stuff, but he was a friend. And he was right, he—we—had no choice. You have to understand that after Dohrn made the Ten Most Wanted list and her face was staring down from thousands of post office walls across the country, the Bureau got hundreds, even thousands, of calls from people who'd seen someone who "looked a lot like Bernardine Dohrn"—and if there was even the slimmest, most remote chance that it was true, the lead had to be followed up. Billie's "lead" on Dohrn may have been the slimmest ever, but Jim and I knew that if it ever came out that we'd passed up a lead that could conceivably have led to Dohrn's arrest, well, we might as well start packing and get driving directions to Butte.

So, posing as curious businessmen—Jim refused my suggestion

that he go undercover in one of his wife's dresses—we spent the next couple of evenings at Billie's place, watching the shows and chatting up some of the performers and patrons. Even though I had quite a bit of street experience under my belt by then, at heart I was still a small-town boy from western New York—so this was quite an education. One thing I learned was that many of the elaborately costumed performers weren't gay, but instead were guys who just liked dressing up in women's clothing—my attitude being, to each his own. And they seemed nice enough.

Of course, Bernardine Dohrn never showed up, nor did the young woman who "looked a lot like Bernardine Dohrn." Although at least a dozen wanted Weathermen would be captured in the next few years, Dohrn wasn't among them. Not until 1980 did she and her husband—and WUO cofounder—Bill Ayers give themselves up, and she pleaded guilty to misdemeanor bail jumping. She and Ayers both later became professors at universities in Chicago, institutions partially supported by taxpayer funds from the US government—the same "Amerikan" government against which Dohrn and her ilk had once declared war.

As far as I'm concerned, the Weathermen still have a lot to answer for—not just for their own crimes, but for the crimes they helped inspire. And I took one of the crimes they inspired personally.

One day another agent and I were on our way to serve an arrest warrant when we got a radio call: robbery in progress, shots fired, officer down at Arlington Trust Bank in Crystal City, a commercial section in Arlington. We were the first agents to arrive, and when I ran into the bank, gun drawn, I discovered that the robbers had fled and the shooting was over—but the horror was not. Sitting on the floor, his back against a wall, was the branch manager, Henry Candee, shot multiple times, his blood spreading in a large pool around him. Nearby was another body, also lying in a massive blood pool. He was an Arlington County Police Department cop—and he was a friend of mine.

As a field agent I often worked with local police, on everything from arrest warrants to stolen cars to bank robberies, so I got to know many of them. This officer was Israel Gonzalez, a twenty-five-year-old Cuban American motorcycle cop—everyone called him Speedy, after the cartoon character—and he was one of the nicest guys you'd ever want to meet. Although I could hear the siren wails of ambulances in the distance, I knew it was too late for Speedy and the bank manager. There was too much blood. They were both dead.

More agents and local police quickly arrived, and we were able to piece the story together from some of the traumatized and blood-spattered bank employees and customers. Two men dressed as telephone company workers and driving a stolen telephone repair truck had opened a manhole cover outside and cut the alarm wires from the bank. They walked into the bank, took the bank manager back to the vault area, drew handguns, and demanded he open the vault. There was a struggle, and one of the men shot the bank manager.

Meanwhile, a customer flagged down Officer Gonzalez and said something strange was going on in the bank. Today the protocol would be to call for backup, secure the bank's perimeter, and summon hostage negotiators. But it was different back then. Gonzalez bravely rushed into the bank, heard the shots, and exchanged fire with the bandits, wounding one in the hand. At that moment the two bandits' secret lookout man, a bespectacled forty-eight-year-old dressed in a business suit and wing tips, walked up behind Gonzalez and shot him three times in the back. The two robbers and the lookout man fled without any money, but one of the bank employees recognized them as members of the Tuller family, a father and his two teenaged sons, who lived in a nearby apartment building. And that was when the story got strange.

Until shortly before the robbery, the father and lookout man, Charles Tuller, had been a GS-15 executive with the US Department of Commerce's Office of Minority Business Enterprises. Although he was white, he'd developed a fixation with the black liberation movement and was an ardent admirer of "Communist revolutionaries" such as the Weather Underground, an admiration he passed on to his sons; they'd caused a stir when they set up an SDS chapter at the local high school in Arlington. Eventually the Tullers hatched an insane scheme to set up a compound in Canada, a sort of revolutionary redoubt that would attract like-minded militants and from which they'd launch cross-border attacks that would bring down the US government. Why they thought the Canadian government and the Royal Canadian Mounted Police would welcome this effort is unclear. But to finance the Communist compound they needed capitalist money—hence the attempted bank robbery.

Unfortunately, by the time we identified them and rushed to their apartment, the Tullers were in the wind. Four days later the Tullers and another accomplice shot and killed an Eastern Airlines ticket agent named Stanley Hubbard at the Houston airport and stormed onto a plane. They forced the pilot to fly them to Cuba, while the Tullers repeatedly shouted, "The revolution has begun!"— and threatened to kill several of the passengers. Once in Havana the passengers and crew were released unharmed, but the Tullers were thrown into jail by their hero, Fidel Castro; the last thing a revolutionary turned dictator wants is a bunch of actual revolutionists walking around. After a few months Castro released them to work in the sugarcane fields, where the Tullers quickly realized that the Communist life wasn't all it was cracked up to be. Three years later Castro gave them $1,400 and some phony IDs and they made their way back to the United States. But after one of the boys was captured during another botched robbery in North Carolina, Charles Tuller and his other son surrendered to the FBI at the Washington Field Office. I only wish I could have been there to see it—and to watch as the Tullers were sentenced to spend the rest of their miserable lives in prison for the murder of Officer Israel Gonzalez and their many other crimes.

The Tuller case was a very strange story. But one part of it wasn't so unusual—the hijacking of the airplane. Because at the time, airplane hijackings—officially known as aircraft piracy and popularly known as skyjackings—were almost routine. And it was my experience in dealing with those federal crimes that would eventually send my career in a new direction.

• • •

As I write this, in the autumn of 2020, in the nineteen years since the tragic terrorist attacks of September 11, 2001, no successful hijackings of a US commercial airliner have occurred anywhere in the world. But between 1961 and January 1973, there were 159 such hijackings, with the majority occurring between 1968 and the end of 1972. Like the Tullers, most of the US airline hijackers demanded to go to Cuba, either because they were revolutionary enthusiasts or just nuts. Others wanted to go to Italy, Sweden, the Bahamas, even North Korea and North Vietnam. The policy of US airlines when confronted by skyjackers was simple—absolute compliance. If it was at all feasible, wherever the skyjacker wanted to go, that was where they'd point the plane, on the assumption that once the skyjacker was delivered to his destination, the passengers and crew would be safely released and the plane eventually returned to its owner.

At first that was a generally sound assumption. In the 1960s, very few US passengers or crew were killed or injured in skyjackings, so for the airlines the rash of skyjackings was more of an inconvenience than a threat. As a result, the airlines bitterly resisted any calls for increased security measures, arguing that it would "alarm" passengers and conflict with the "fly the friendly skies" image the airlines were trying to project. So at the time no US airline passengers or their baggage were sent through a magnetometer or an X-ray machine, much less sniffed by a dog or body searched. As noted earlier, I know it's hard for people in this post-9/11 world to believe, but back then you went to the airport, bought your ticket, boarded the plane, and if you had a bomb in your suitcase or a gun in your pocket, no one knew it—until you decided to use it.

The Bureau wasn't pleased with the airlines' compliance policy on skyjackings. To us they weren't merely inconveniences. They were crimes, and if we didn't try to stop them and punish the perpetrators, it would only lead to more skyjackings—and given the mental state of many of the skyjackers, sooner or later a lot of people were going to be hurt or killed. But the airlines continued to resist.

Then in the early 1970s skyjackings took a new turn. Suddenly it was no longer just a case of radicals and nutjobs wanting a free flight somewhere. US aircraft and their passengers and crews began to be used as hostages in extortion cases, in which a skyjacker would demand huge sums of money for the safe return of the planes and the people. The most famous of these airborne extortionists was the guy known as D. B. Cooper, who in 1971 skyjacked a Northwest Orient airlines Boeing 727 near Seattle. He demanded—and received—some parachutes and $200,000 in cash (about $1.3 million today) from the airline, after which he bailed out somewhere over the Pacific Northwest and was never seen again.

But while Mr. Cooper was the most well-known example of the extortion-skyjacker genre, he wasn't the first. That distinction belonged to a forty-nine-year-old unemployed Phoenix bread-truck driver named Arthur Gates Barkley. He also had the lesser distinction of being my first—but not last—skyjacking case.

On June 4, 1970, Barkley boarded Trans World Airlines (TWA) flight 486 from Phoenix to National Airport in Washington, DC. He carried on board with him a .22-caliber pistol, a straight razor, a small steel can of gasoline, and a grudge against the Internal Revenue Service, which he claimed owed him $471.78. Somewhere over New Mexico, Barkley, who stood six-four and weighed about 240 pounds, calmly walked into the unlocked cockpit, waved the gun, and ordered the pilot to land at Dulles International Airport in northern Virginia. En route he demanded $100 million in cash from the US government or else he'd set the plane on fire and kill all sixty-five passengers and crew, himself included.

In keeping with the airlines' compliance policy, TWA officials agreed to the payoff scheme, rounding up a little over $100,000, which was put in a bag and delivered to the plane on the runway at Dulles. Maybe they thought that a hundred grand would satisfy Barkley, or that he wouldn't bother to count it. Either way, they were wrong. With all the passengers and crew still on board, the Boeing 727 began a long, aimless, circuitous flight around the northeastern United States.

By now a dozen agents from the Alexandria Field Office, whose territory included Dulles Airport, were at the scene, me included.

And what we were learning was scary. Barkley had given his real name to the pilot—he wanted the world to know how the US government had screwed him—and the pilot relayed it to ground control. When we contacted Barkley's Veterans Administration psychiatrist in Phoenix (Barkley was a World War II veteran), the shrink told us that not only was Barkley capable of destroying the plane and everyone aboard, but that he almost certainly wanted to do so. Destroying the $100 million would just be part of his revenge.

We had to get that plane back on the ground—and as it turned out, Barkley wanted the same thing. He'd finally counted the $100,000 and realized it was a little bit short. (One look at the money bag should have told Barkley it wasn't even close to the $100 million he'd demanded. Even in hundred-dollar bills, $100 million would have weighed just over two thousand pounds; it literally would have been a ton of money.) Somewhere over Ohio, Barkley called over the radio, "Nixon can't count! I said I wanted one hundred million dollars! I'm coming back for it!" We quickly had Dulles Airport employees line the runway with a hundred US mail sacks, which we told Barkley contained a million bucks each; he'd be able to see them as the plane came in for a landing. Of course, the "money" in the sacks was just wadded-up papers, but it didn't matter. Barkley wasn't going to get his hands on any of them. And no way were we going to let that plane take off again. The moment the plane landed and came to a stop, our snipers shot out the tires.

(This did not please Charles Tillinghast, the chairman and CEO of TWA, who, despite Barkley's obvious suicidal intentions, was still in a "full compliance" frame of mind. When Jack McDermott, the Alexandria SAC, informed him by phone from the control tower of our plan to disable the plane, Tillinghast vehemently objected and threatened McDermott with all manner of dire consequences if we damaged his valuable airplane. This went on for a few minutes—I was standing next to McDermott during the conversation—until finally the SAC said, "Mr. Tillinghast, I'm far more concerned about the passengers than about your airplane, and if you don't like it, you can shove that plane up your ass!" Hoover, who'd had a long-standing public beef with Tillinghast over TWA's earlier refusal to allow armed FBI agents on TWA flights, approved the SAC's response.)

Once the plane landed, it got hectic. A half dozen of us ran up to the plane and crouched beneath the fuselage, guns drawn. With Barkley occupied in the cockpit, two passengers popped the emergency exit and started bailing out onto the wing. Barkley opened the forward fuselage door and fired off a couple of shots at them, and the pilot, a scrappy former marine named Dale Hupe, tried to grab the gun. Barkley shot him in the stomach and he fell back into the cockpit.

At the sound of the first shots several of us ran out and started firing at Barkley as he popped in and out of the doorway and fired back at us. It was the first and only time I fired my service revolver in the line of duty. One of our shots hit Barkley in the hand—it was impossible to say whose—which caused him to drop the gun. That gave us an opportunity to boost my partner Jim Siano up into the open fuselage door, and he tackled Barkley. But Barkley had recovered his gun, and during the struggle Barkley jammed the gun into Jim's stomach and pulled the trigger—twice. Miraculously both were misfires. Finally Jim got Barkley handcuffed.

Pilot Hupe recovered from his wound, and Barkley eventually was sent to an institution for the criminally insane for the rest of his life. Meanwhile, the nation's first-ever skyjacking-for-ransom attempt made front-page headlines across the country. It was followed by a rash of other skyjackings, some of them by the usual nutcases and some for financial gain, including D. B. Cooper's. And a few of them came my way.

In one case a fifty-eight-year-old coal miner with black lung disease was on a plane on the ground at Dulles, holding a gun and demanding to be taken to Israel. When the pilot radioed that the skyjacker wanted to give himself up, with another agent I stormed onto the plane and grabbed his gun, after which he looked at me and said pitifully, "Can I go home now?" No, he couldn't go home— he got twenty years. In another case a fifty-year-old engineer from Pennsylvania hijacked an Eastern Airlines jet, demanding and receiving six parachutes and $350,000 and ordering the pilot to fly to

Honduras. Having learned something from the D. B. Cooper case, I with other agents was in a smaller DC-9 chase plane that followed the hijacked flight, the idea being that if we saw him bail out in US airspace, we could land at the nearest airport and start the manhunt. Instead he bailed out over Honduras, out of our jurisdiction, but he eventually surrendered and was extradited and sentenced to twenty years.

As traumatic as skyjackings were for airline crews and passengers, for a young special agent of the FBI they were exciting. And, frankly, my experience with skyjackings and general airline operations—I'd worked a number of stolen-goods cases at Dulles Airport—eventually led me to a new assignment.

I was at home one evening a few months after the Barkley skyjacking when Jack McDermott called me. "Hey, Polack, I got something for you."

That was what everybody called me at the Alexandria office—Polack. That wouldn't be socially acceptable today, but I didn't mind. At the time it was just part of the rough humor that was common in a man's world—and I gave back as good as I got. Besides, it was better than Prince-ski.

Anyway, McDermott filled me in. The Popular Front for the Liberation of Palestine had recently skyjacked four planes simultaneously in Europe, all bound for New York City, two of them US planes that were spectacularly blown up in the Jordanian desert after the passengers and crew were taken off. Alarmed, the Nixon administration was launching a new, experimental "sky marshals" program to place armed undercover agents aboard selected US carrier flights in Europe, the Mediterranean, and the Middle East. (The FAA already had a limited sky marshals program in place, but Nixon wanted FBI agents involved, which Hoover reluctantly agreed to; other government agencies such as the US Marshals and Customs also participated.) The idea was to assess the feasibility of the sky marshals' effort. McDermott had chosen me to be one of the first FBI agents in the program. It sounded good to me, and I quickly agreed.

(There was one glitch. Still continuing his feud with TWA's Tillinghast, Hoover prohibited any of his agents from flying on TWA flights during the program. It caused some hard feelings—but that was the Director.)

So I spent the next two months flying undercover on Pan Am flights from New York to Paris, London, Rome, Tehran, Pakistan, the Middle East, and back. Usually I sat in first class—certainly not for my personal comfort, you understand, but simply to be near the cockpit in case of trouble. (Let me tell you, once you've flown first class a few times—especially back then, when first class really was first class—you'll never be happy in coach again.) There were no incidents on any of the flights, and when I wrote up my final report, I recommended that armed federal agents not be placed aboard US aircraft in the future.

My reasoning was simple. There were more than 5 million flights in the United States alone in 1970, and to put two or three sky marshals aboard even 1 percent of those flights would require an army of tens of thousands of sky marshals, which was impossible; the US government simply didn't have the resources. So even the dumbest or most crazed skyjacker would have to know that the chances of having a sky marshal aboard his particular flight would be minuscule. And even if one was aboard, what's the sky marshal going to do? Have a shoot-out at thirty-five thousand feet with a guy who's holding a bomb? No, the only effective way to reduce hijackings was on the ground, by imposing mandatory preboarding individual and baggage screenings—"friendly skies" be damned.

Somebody must have been listening because in 1973 the FAA finally required all persons and luggage to be individually screened, although those regulations didn't prevent hijackers from carrying box cutters onto four planes on September 11, 2001— with terrible results. Meanwhile, the Nixon administration went ahead with the sky marshals program, hiring hundreds of relatively low-paid—and in my opinion, inadequately trained—men and women to police the skies. But at least the FBI wasn't part of it. I went back to Alexandria.

Which led to a somewhat unsettling conversation with my SAC,

Jack McDermott. On my first day back he called me into his office. "Welcome back. You ready to start doing some real work again?"

I told him I was—and I meant it.

"You know, I've been meaning to tell you," McDermott said, "that's some rabbi you've got."

He must have thought I looked confused.

"Hoover." He explained. He added unnecessarily, "The Director." You'll recall that in law enforcement circles, a rabbi was a high-ranking official who guided and protected a junior man's career—and in the FBI, obviously there was no higher-ranking official than J. Edgar Hoover. "A few days after you left for the airlines program I was talking to the Director on the phone, and I mentioned that I'd picked Special Agent Letersky for the assignment. And Hoover said—I'm quoting here—he said, 'Yes, Letersky, he was involved in that hijacking at Dulles last summer. He's a good man, he'll do well.' End of quote."

I'll admit I was pleased that the Director had noticed me—but I didn't want to admit it to Jack McDermott. "So what'd you say?"

"Oh, I agreed with him, of course. I told him I was confident you wouldn't crash more than one or two planes, tops."

We both laughed. I was a seasoned enough agent by now to be able to share jokes with the SAC—and as I said, McDermott was a good guy and a straight shooter.

"Thanks a lot," I said.

"Yes, quite a rabbi," McDermott repeated. "With the Director on your side you'll be bounced up to SOG before you know it. Of course, that's assuming Hoover lasts that long."

That last part was unsettling—for two reasons.

One reason was the reference to my going back to SOG. It reminded me of my last conversation with the Director before I went to New Agents Training. Back then I hadn't been at all sure that I wanted to go back to SOG and start climbing up the bureaucratic ladder; now, after several years on the street, I was pretty certain that was the last thing I ever wanted to do. It would mean a couple years as a supervisory agent at headquarters, then two tours with the goons in Inspection Division, traveling to far-flung field offices and resident agencies for weeks at a time, then back to SOG as a senior supervisory agent, then a couple tours as an assistant special agent in charge at different field offices, then an appointment as the SAC in a small field office, then maybe being moved up to a larger field office, then maybe, just maybe, a boost up to a division head at SOG again. It would mean at least a half dozen moves for my family over twenty years, and even then I'd know all the while that at any time I could get crosswise with somebody at SOG and be bounced back down to the bricks, making it all for naught. I loved being an FBI agent, but I knew that someday I'd have to decide if I loved it that much.

Fortunately, that someday was still in the future. But the other unsettling thing that McDermott had referenced—J. Edgar Hoover's likely being near the end of his reign—wasn't.

I said earlier that for most agents, most of the time, the Byzantine machinations of Washington, DC, were a million miles away. Still, gossip and rumors and vague reports from the Seat of Government inevitably trickled down through the ranks—and because I knew some of the people involved, I was more attuned to it than most. Some of what I knew came from my periodic conversations with Miss Gandy and J. P. Mohr, and some of it came from the newspapers. Much of what was happening I wouldn't know about until much later.

But by the end of 1971 I knew full well that J. Edgar Hoover was battling two implacable foes. One was his political enemies, both in and outside the Bureau. And the other was time.

And I knew that sooner or later, one of those foes was bound to win.

CHAPTER 7

A Lion and a Tigress in Winter

Well, Paul, we finally nailed that traitorous bastard," J. P. Mohr said. "It shoulda happened a long time ago."

It was late 1971, and I was sitting in Mr. Mohr's office on the fifth floor of the Justice Department building, just down the hall from the Director's office. I'd stopped in to say hello to him a couple of times since I'd been assigned to Alexandria, and each time he was cordial and welcoming, but I could tell he was pressed for time. Today, though, he seemed relaxed, leaning back in the chair at his desk and smiling. As for the "traitorous bastard" they'd "nailed," Mohr wasn't referring to one of the Weathermen, or to some spy caught selling secrets to the Russians. He was talking about now-former assistant to the director William C. Sullivan—Crazy Billy.

"Yes, I saw something about it in the newspaper," I said. The headline in the *Washington Post* had said, "Top FBI Official Forced Out in Feud with Hoover."

"Oh, it was a row, all right. They had a big argument—Sullivan was shouting at the Director, if you can believe that—and the Director ordered him to take annual leave, and when he came back, we'd changed the locks in his office and the Director made him turn in his resignation. Boy, was Crazy Billy pissed! He and Felt"—Deputy Associate Director Mark Felt—"started screaming at each other, right out there in the hallway. Felt called him a Judas, and Crazy Billy said he was going to kick Felt's ass!"

Mr. Mohr grinned at the image of the short, rumpled, fifty-eight-year-old Sullivan engaging in geriatric fisticuffs with the tall, slim, fifty-seven-year-old Felt. Mr. Mohr didn't like either man but he actively despised Sullivan—all the more so because he and Sullivan had been fraternity brothers at American University back in the late 1930s and had once been close friends.

"That little son of a bitch!" Mr. Mohr said. "Felt would have killed him!"

I'd heard through the Bureau grapevine about the Director's feud with Sullivan, and the Sullivan/Felt confrontation in the hallway had been the talk of the Bureau. But I didn't know all the details. "So what happened?" I asked. "With Sullivan and the Director?"

As I've mentioned, Mr. Mohr was an inveterate gossip, always ready to tell tales of Bureau intrigue. He didn't tell me everything. Some of it was still too secret and closely held even for him to talk about and would only come out in public later. But what happened was this:

The year before, Deke DeLoach, the former number three man, retired to take a high-paying job with the PepsiCo company—this to Miss Gandy's enormous satisfaction. ("I told you he'd never be director," she'd said to me, smiling.) To replace DeLoach, the Director promoted Sullivan, then head of the Domestic Intelligence Division, to the number three position—which, given Tolson's incapacity, actually made Sullivan second-in-command of the Bureau. Sullivan, you'll recall, was the one who wrote the so-called suicide letter to Martin Luther King and who masterminded the COINTELPRO operations against the Klan, the black liberation movement, and the New Left. As you might guess from his Crazy Billy nickname, Sullivan was a mercurial man, brilliant in his own way but unpredictable. He was also arrogant and argumentative and thoroughly unpopular among the other assistant directors, especially J. P. Mohr. Nevertheless, Hoover initially favored Sullivan to an almost-unprecedented degree, even going so far as to call him Bill.

Then things began to go sour. As noted, beginning in 1965 Hoover severely reduced the number of Bureau wiretaps and buggings and officially banned illegal black bag jobs altogether—investigative techniques that Sullivan argued were vital for the Bureau to combat the dark forces arrayed against the US government. To the Director's mounting annoyance, Sullivan consistently asked Hoover to authorize expanded "special investigative techniques" against the New Left and other groups, and the Director consistently refused. As Hoover put it in a 1967 memo, such techniques "will not meet with my approval in the future." It wasn't so much the civil liberties aspects that worried the Director; he'd authorized plenty of taps and bag jobs in his day. Instead, Hoover was worried that the FBI might get caught—and given the prevailing political winds, that would "embarrass the Bureau."

The whole thing made Crazy Billy even crazier. Eventually he began privately sanctioning out-of-channels buggings and bag jobs without Hoover's approval. Sullivan also started cultivating some of the more radically conservative members of the White House staff, including a twenty-nine-year-old former army intelligence officer and current national security aide named Tom Charles Huston. Through them, Sullivan spread the word to the White House that Hoover was "getting soft" and should be replaced. Sullivan also let it be known that if Hoover was ever forced out, he, Sullivan, would be happy to take the director's job.

"That backstabbing son of a bitch." Mr. Mohr shook his head in disgust. "Can you believe that? After all the Director did for him?"

But it wasn't just Sullivan and some White House aides who were unhappy with the Director's reluctance to wage a tougher war against the nation's real or perceived domestic enemies. So was Richard Nixon himself.

Given their long association, Nixon expected Hoover to protect him—and often Hoover did. For example, at Nixon's request the Director called off the Bureau's customary full-field background investigation of one of the president's high-level appointees, attorney general–designate John Mitchell, apparently because it would have brought out embarrassing information about Martha Mitchell's growing drinking problem, and that she and John weren't quite married yet when their first child was conceived. (That wouldn't be a big deal today, but in the late 1960s it was still considered an embarrassment.) In another case, when a Washington reporter threatened to run a story that several high-level White House aides were gay—they included Ehrlichman and Haldeman—Nixon asked Hoover to discreetly check out the rumors. Hoover assigned Mark Felt, then head of the Inspection Division, to personally conduct an investigation, and he quickly determined that the rumors were completely baseless—much to Nixon's relief.

But other tasks the Director performed for Nixon were far more significant. For example, in 1969, after the *New York Times* broke the story that the United States was secretly bombing North Vietnamese staging areas in Cambodia, Nixon's national security adviser, Henry Kissinger, called Hoover and demanded in the president's name that the FBI find out by any means necessary who'd leaked the information—including wiretaps on the homes of some of Kissinger's own subordinates and personal friends. Somewhat reluctantly, Hoover ordered wiretaps on seventeen people—National Security Council staffers, news reporters, a general in the Pentagon, and others—but only on condition that the taps be approved in writing by the attorney general. If news of the wiretaps ever got out, Hoover didn't want to be left holding the bag. To Nixon's displeasure, neither the Kissinger wiretaps nor the FBI's related investigation of the secret-bombing leak ever turned up the leaker.

(Hoover was right to be worried that the story of the "Kissinger wiretaps" eventually would come out. It did—during the Watergate hearings—and the wiretaps issue was included in one of the articles of impeachment against Richard Nixon.)

You could argue, as Nixon later did, that the Kissinger wiretaps had at least a semilegitimate national security basis. But Nixon and his men wanted more. Nixon was well aware that Hoover had done blatantly political favors for Nixon's predecessors, including Johnson's use of the FBI to spy on potential opponents at the 1964 Democratic National Convention. Nixon's attitude was that if Hoover had helped other presidents against their enemies, why couldn't Hoover do more to help him, Dick Nixon, against his enemies—

specifically those hippies and college professors and radical priests and other activists who were now blaming Nixon for the damned Vietnam War? But Hoover still resisted expanding the use of taps and bugs and bag jobs.

Frustrated, in the summer of 1970 Nixon ordered the aforementioned Tom Charles Huston to come up with a plan to "improve" the intelligence provided by the nation's various intelligence agencies—the CIA, the National Security Agency, the Defense Intelligence Agency, and most especially Hoover's FBI. The proposal he came up with would later infamously be known as the Huston Plan, but although it bore Huston's name, Bill Sullivan's fingerprints were all over it. Working closely with Sullivan, Huston called for a massive expansion of domestic intelligence and counterintelligence operations against the New Left and other groups. The plan envisioned virtually unlimited wiretaps and bugs and illegal break-ins; increased surveillance of US citizen "subversives" at home and abroad; illegal mail openings; monitoring of international phone calls from the United States; and greatly expanding the number of college campus informants, which would require lowering the Bureau's minimum informant age from twenty-one to eighteen.

The Huston Plan was everything Sullivan wanted but had failed to get from Hoover. Not surprisingly, Hoover hated it. That was partly because he despised the youthful and arrogant Huston, referring to him as "that damn hippie" and intentionally calling him by the wrong name in face-to-face meetings—"Mr. Hoffman," "Mr. Hutchinson," and so on. And it was partly because the plan threatened to force the Bureau into closer cooperation with the CIA and the other intelligence agencies, with whom the Director had long been feuding.

But Hoover primarily objected to the Huston Plan for the same reason he had resisted Sullivan's and Nixon's earlier demands for enhanced intelligence gathering: Hoover was afraid the details of the plan would leak—a demonstrably good possibility in the leak-prone Nixon administration. Since the plan called for Hoover to serve as the point man for all of the domestic intelligence activities performed by the other agencies, he knew that if the details of the proposal ever got out, he and he alone would have to face the howls of outrage that would surely follow in Congress and in the press and from the public.

The Director was far too skilled a political poker player to let that happen. So Hoover killed the Huston/Sullivan plan—but carefully. He let the White House know that he'd go along with the proposal, but only if he had written authorization by the attorney general and the president himself. Hoover knew Nixon would never affix his signature to a document allowing the virtually unlimited use of patently illegal activities against political dissidents; even Nixon couldn't do that. So the Huston plan died, Tom Charles Huston went back to Indiana to practice law—and Bill Sullivan seethed.

"The Old Man outfoxed 'em," Mr. Mohr told me with obvious satisfaction. "That snot-nosed punk Huston thought he could come in here and get the best of J. Edgar Hoover? Not a chance."

Hoover's subtle murder of the Huston Plan didn't completely end warrantless wiretaps and black bag jobs and surveillances of dissidents by the Bureau or by the CIA or other agencies. But the Director's intransigence at least kept those domestic intelligence activities from spinning totally out of control. I know it's hard for his critics to accept that the hated J. Edgar Hoover, whatever his motivations, managed to ward off the most massive abuse of American civil liberties in the modern era. But it happens to be true.

Nixon, though, was still frustrated with Hoover's caution in domestic intelligence gathering, and Nixon's aides were pressing him to do something about "the Hoover problem"—specifically, to fire the Director. But Nixon was notoriously reluctant to fire anyone, especially when it was face-to-face, and Nixon knew that only he, the president, could fire the still-popular J. Edgar Hoover. He wanted to do it, but he didn't know how.

Outwardly, Nixon and Hoover maintained their show of friendship. For example, after Nixon defended the aging Director's performance at a press conference, Hoover called to thank him—a call that was recorded by the White House taping system:

"Mr. President," the Director said, "I want to thank you for what you did."

"Well, Edgar, I always stick with my friends," Nixon lied.

"Yes, Mr. President, you always do," Hoover responded, knowing better.

But then came the last straw for Nixon—the so-called *Pentagon Papers* case.

In June 1971 the *New York Times* published the first in a series of articles on the *Pentagon Papers*, a massive study of US involvement in Vietnam from World War II to 1967. Commissioned by then–defense secretary Robert McNamara, the supposedly Top Secret study revealed that presidents Truman, Eisenhower, Kennedy, and Johnson had all lied to the American people about the US involvement in that small, faraway country, with historically tragic results.

The leaked documents had nothing directly to do with Nixon. Nevertheless, the president was furious, convinced that the leak was part of a conspiracy among members of the remaining "Kennedy crowd" within his own administration—what might today be called the deep state—to sabotage his handling of the war. He demanded that Hoover and the FBI find the leaker and uncover the conspiracy.

Finding the leaker wasn't hard. He was Daniel Ellsberg, a former marine officer and Defense Department civilian analyst who openly admitted he'd purloined the documents and given them to the *New York Times* and other papers. As for the vast conspiracy within the administration, despite an extensive investigation the Bureau never found it, because it didn't exist. The *Pentagon Papers* leak only involved Ellsberg and a few other people who simply wanted to help stop the war—and as Hoover informed the president, it was even doubtful that Ellsberg could successfully be prosecuted for stealing the documents.

That was it. Convinced that Hoover was "dragging his feet" on the Ellsberg investigation and other domestic intelligence operations, Nixon made a fateful decision. "If the FBI was not going to pursue the investigation," Nixon later wrote, "then we would have to do it ourselves." He ordered his aides to create the White House's own domestic intelligence unit—the Special Investigations Unit, nicknamed the Plumbers because their initial purpose was to plug "leaks." The Plumbers were an amorphous group, with members constantly moving in and out, but two key figures were involved. One was G. Gordon Liddy, ironically a former FBI man who'd served in the Bureau from 1957 to 1962, where he earned a reputation for strange and reckless behavior. One Bureau story about him was that he once got caught doing a black bag job in Kansas City and had to be bailed out by the chief of police—a demonstration of burglary bumbling that would be repeated years later, with historic results. The other major plumber was E. Howard Hunt, a former CIA man and a prolific author of fanciful spy novels. Those were the guys to whom Nixon and his men entrusted the Nixon presidency.

Meanwhile, Nixon's dissatisfaction with Hoover was continuing. The president began telling aides, "He [Hoover] should get the hell out of there, he ought to resign while he's on top." There were mutterings that the Director was "erratic," "unable to do the job," even "senile." Finally, in the fall of 1971, after careful planning with his aides, Nixon invited Hoover to a private breakfast at the White House, during which he planned to strongly suggest that the Director resign—and if he didn't, to demand his resignation. It was an open secret among Washington insiders that J. Edgar Hoover was on his way out.

But for reasons never fully explained, Nixon backed off. The joke that was soon going around had it that Nixon said, "Now, Edgar, we need to discuss this issue of retirement." And Hoover responded, "Retirement? That's ridiculous, Mr. President. You're still a young man!" I wouldn't put it past the Director to have said something like that.

Nixon later said that after Hoover indicated he wouldn't offer his resignation voluntarily, he decided not to demand it. That was partly because of his "personal feelings" about the Director, Nixon said, and also because "Hoover's resignation before the [1972] election would raise more political problems than it would solve."

Maybe so. Whatever the reason, Hoover kept his job—but Crazy Billy Sullivan lost his.

Sullivan's scheming to replace the Director had continued—he was the likely source of the White House belief that the Director was "senile"—and his clashes with Hoover intensified. In the summer of 1971 Hoover demoted Sullivan and promoted Felt over him. Sullivan was furious and finally wrote the Director a twelve-page, single-spaced letter—the sort of letter you might write when you sit up all night, fuming and drinking—rehashing his conflicts with the Director and noting, "My wife and three children regard you, to put it mildly, as a very strange man." Sullivan quickly followed that one up with another letter in which he hinted darkly that he knew all of the Bureau's secrets and would reveal them if the Director didn't resign. Hoover promptly fired him, leading to the near fistfight in the hallway that so amused Mr. Mohr.

"Yep, Felt would have torn him apart." Mohr said, still smiling. Then his face darkened. "You know, Paul, I don't think I've ever seen the Director as hurt as he was by Sullivan turning on him that way. I didn't like the son of a bitch, but to the Director he was almost like a son."

It was hard for me to imagine the Director with hurt feelings; I wasn't sure he had any feelings. But Mr. Mohr knew him better than I did.

"Now that bastard is out there telling tales to the damn press."

"Sullivan?"

"Yeah. The *Post*, the *New York Times*, *Time*, you name it, he's talking to all of them. It's all the same bullshit. The Bureau can't do its job. Morale is rotten. The Director should be fired. Of course, they never quote Billy by name. He's too smart for that. But it's him. Every time I read what the papers are saying, I hear his whiny little voice."

I'd read some of the stories, and they weren't necessarily all bullshit. For the first time in memory, even publications that had long supported the Director were openly questioning his performance—and publications that had in the past mildly opposed him were becoming more and more vociferous. "Deterioration of the FBI," the headlines said, "Congress Urged to Investigate the FBI," and so on. Apparently Sullivan, who still hoped to force the Director out and take his job, had become a "deep throat" even before Mark Felt became the Deep Throat.

"That sorry little bastard." Mr. Mohr continued fulminating about the sorry little bastard for a while, and when he finally wound down, I decided to change the subject.

"Anything new on the Media case?"

Mr. Mohr grimaced and put his hand to his forehead as if he were in physical pain. "Oh, Lord! What a damned nightmare! It's costing me a fortune!"

The Media I was referring to wasn't the news media, which at the time was usually called the press. Instead, Media was a small town in Pennsylvania—and even more than Sullivan, what had happened there would come closest to bringing the Director down.

It had been all over the newspapers and still was. On the night of March 8, 1971, eight members of a group calling itself the Citizens' Commission to Investigate the FBI broke into the Bureau's small, two-agent resident agency in Media, a Philadelphia suburb. It was easy enough to do since the agency office was located in an unguarded county office building. The agency office was equipped with an almost impregnable safe-like locking cabinet, but the safe was being used to secure Bureau gear that might have been attractive to ordinary burglars—guns, ballistic vests, radios. What the resident agents hadn't realized was that the truly most valuable items in the office weren't the guns or the radios, but the secrets—the FBI secrets that were locked in the filing cabinets lining the walls. Using crowbars, the burglars easily broke into the filing cabinets and made off with almost a thousand FBI *serials*—Bureau-speak for file documents.

The Director was predictably apoplectic. The story goes that when the resident agent came in the next morning and realized what had happened, he made two calls—one to Bureau headquarters to report the break-in, and the other to his wife to tell her to start packing. (The story may have been true. The resident agent was suspended without pay for a month and transferred to Atlanta.) Desperate to retrieve the documents and arrest the burglars, Hoover sent in the legendary FBI inspector Roy Moore, the man who'd led the Klan investigations, to handle the MEDBURG (short for "Media burglary") investigation, along with at least two hundred FBI agents. It was the biggest Bureau investigation in years.

Meanwhile, the burglars were busily making copies of the stolen FBI documents and mailing selected portions to various news media, some of whom happily published them. For the first time ever, the Bureau's secret documents were exposed to public view.

There weren't any major individual bombshells; it was more of a drip-drip-drip of information that was disturbing to the public and embarrassing to the Bureau. Some of the documents identified by name a local college campus police chief, a switchboard operator, and a secretary as FBI "informants"—the same sort of informants I'd tried to recruit in Cincinnati, ordinary people who just wanted to help the FBI. Other documents revealed FBI plans to infiltrate black student groups at nearby campuses, while another discussed the Bureau's brief investigation of an anti-war congressman's daughter who was enrolled at a local college. In one document Hoover urged Bureau supervisors in the Philadelphia area to step up interrogations of anti-war dissidents to "enhance the paranoia endemic in these circles and . . . get the point across there is an FBI agent behind every mailbox." One memo from FBIHQ even discussed the Director's aforementioned odd standards for Bureau job applicants, warning supervisors to beware of "long hairs, beards, pear-shaped heads, truck drivers," and adding, "We aren't that hard up yet."

The Media break-in didn't reveal all of the Bureau's secrets, not even close, but it was enough. Many of the things the FBI had long been accused of and had always denied were right there in black and white, in the Bureau's own words: Surveillance and harassment of peaceful anti-war groups, planting informants on campuses, investigating anti-war politicians and their families, targeting minorities. The disclosures led a still small but growing number of congressmen to demand a full-scale investigation of the FBI, and to use words like "Gestapo" and "an American KGB." No one mentioned that those "domestic intelligence" activities occupied only a small portion of the Bureau's time and manpower. No one cared about that.

But as harmful as the stolen files were to the Bureau's reputation, one phrase on a routine mail-routing slip would cause the greatest long-term damage to the FBI, and to Hoover. The phrase said simply, "COINTELPRO—New Left," with no explanation. The word *COINTELPRO* had never been seen by anyone outside the Bureau, and at the time none of the burglars or the reporters covering the story knew what it meant. But Hoover feared that eventually someone would figure it out. Shortly after the break-in, he ordered Sullivan to discontinue all COINTELPRO activities.

For Hoover the entire affair was humiliating. As months went by without any arrests, the Director had to grapple with how his vaunted FBI, the world's premier law enforcement agency, couldn't even solve a simple burglary—of one of its own offices! (The Bureau never would solve the case. Decades later, long after the statute of limitations had run out, some of the burglars finally came forward and proudly admitted their involvement.) It didn't help that even as hordes of FBI agents were frantically pursuing them, the burglars and those who supported them in the Philadelphia area were taunting the Director and the Bureau. They slapped THIS IS AN FBI CAR bumper stickers on Bureau cars while agents were at lunch and publicly invited Hoover and his agents to attend a mocking "This Is Your FBI at Work" street fair—provided the agents didn't bring their guns. People were laughing at the FBI.

"A nightmare," Mr. Mohr repeated. "You know what he wanted me to do?" "He" meant the Director. "He wanted me to close all of our resident agencies—all five hundred and thirty-eight of them! Can you imagine? I managed to talk him out of that, but he still ordered me to close a hundred, and to beef up security at the rest. So I've been getting calls from every congressman from Podunk to Palookaville, screaming at me not to take their FBI agents away.

And I'm having to buy new locks and alarms and safes for most of the other RAs. You know how much a safe costs these days? It's costing me hundreds of thousands of dollars!"

I understood how Mr. Mohr felt. Most people in small towns liked having FBI agents in their communities. As for the money, Mr. Mohr was the assistant to the director for administration, which meant he was responsible for every dime the Bureau spent—and sometimes he acted as if it were his own money. I felt a little sorry for him.

But people weren't just stealing the Bureau's secret documents—they were also stealing J. Edgar Hoover's trash. In March 1971, a reporter in the employ of Washington muckraker Jack Anderson, a longtime Hoover foe, stole the trash from the garbage can in the alley behind Hoover's house—which says something about the FBI Director's lack of personal security. After sifting through the contents, including the droppings contributed by G-Boy and Cindy, Anderson wrote a mocking column revealing that Hoover "brushes his teeth with Ultra Brite, washes with Palmolive soap, shaves with Noxzema shaving cream," and "takes Gelusil antacid pills."

"It's unsettling to think of a living legend like the great Hoover having gas pains," Anderson wrote, but added that it shows he "is as human as the rest of us." (Hoover, furious, said that Anderson "would literally go lower than dog shit for a story," and although the Director had earlier discouraged senior Bureau executives from giving him annual gifts, that year he asked them to give him a trash compactor.)

Other reporters were also nosing around, asking questions about the cost of the Director's bulletproof cars—$30,000 each, compared with the president's $5,000-per-year leased armored limousine—about his free annual trips to plush resorts in California and Florida, courtesy of Texas oil millionaires and other wealthy men, about his free meals at the Mayflower Hotel, about the royalties from his books, mostly ghostwritten by Crime Records employees on government time, about the use of Bureau employees to make repairs to his house. The reporters were circling like sharks—or, to use Hoover's favorite word for overly inquisitive members of the press, "jackals."

Hoover's age was also becoming more and more of an issue. A 1971 Gallup poll found that while 81 percent of those polled had a favorable view of Hoover and the Bureau—with only 4 percent unfavorable—a slim majority, 51 percent, thought the seventy-six-year-old Director should honorably retire. The theme was taken up by the press. For example, *Life* magazine, a longtime Hoover supporter, ran an editorial noting the Director's age and suggesting that he "honorably stand down." The *Los Angeles Times* said the best solution to the Hoover issue would be to "honor him, reward him, revere him and replace him."

To those and other calls for him to step down, the Director stubbornly replied, "I have many plans and aspirations for the future. None includes retirement." He added, "I don't consider my age a valid factor in assessing my ability to continue as Director of the FBI, any more than it was when, at the youthful age of twenty-nine, I was appointed to this position. I was criticized then as 'the Boy Scout.' Now I'm called 'that senile old man.'"

But despite his defiance, the attacks on Hoover only increased as 1971 ended and the last year of his life began. Even within the FBI, particularly among the younger agents, the feeling was growing that the Bureau under Hoover's continued reign had grown sclerotic, that SOG was increasingly disconnected from the agents in the field, that the old rules and regulations were more relevant to the Gangster Era than to the realities of the dawning decade of the 1970s. Many of the older agents still idolized the Director, and I think it's fair to say most of the younger ones still respected him for building the Bureau and protecting it for so long. But even so, they felt that it was finally time for the Old Man to go.

And I was one of them.

"Miss Gandy, why doesn't he just retire?" I asked.

It was early spring in 1972 and I was making another of my Saturday-afternoon visits to Miss Gandy's office. I knew the retirement issue would be sensitive. Although it was doubtful that Nixon would try to force the Director out in an election year—he was still popular with the public and still had some strong support in Congress—the calls for his ouster from politicians and the press had only grown since the year before. But even though it was a touchy subject, when Miss Gandy didn't answer, I asked again.

"Why doesn't he retire and tend to his rosebushes and go to the track every day and not have to deal with all this aggravation?"

I knew I was pressing her, but I did it anyway. I still respected the Director and cared about him personally, but I couldn't understand why he was so stubbornly hanging on past his time—long past his time. Here he was, seventy-seven years old, surrounded by a growing army of enemies, betrayed by his friends, his only companion, Tolson, so sick he could hardly get out of bed most days—and yet the Director still held on. I wanted to know why.

"I just don't get it. Do you?"

When Miss Gandy finally spoke, her voice was the angriest I'd ever heard it. "Don't you understand?" she almost shouted. "Doesn't anyone understand? He can't leave. If he did, he'd have to hand the Bureau over to them—to Nixon and those others."

I noticed she'd dropped the *president* from Nixon's name.

"If he left, he knows what that bunch would do. They'd replace him with some politician"—Miss Gandy said the word like a curse—"who'd do whatever they told him to do. It would ruin the Bureau. They've already tried that, you know, with Mr. Sullivan and that annoying young friend of his, Mr. Huston. But the Director wouldn't let them." She lowered her voice. "The Director said to me, 'I will never allow the FBI to become Nixon's personal Stasi.' And he didn't. He won't."

The Stasi was the East German Ministry for State Security, the equivalent of the Soviet KGB. Of course, some people thought—wrongly—that the FBI already was an American version of the Stasi or the KGB or the Gestapo. I didn't mention that to Miss Gandy, but I did have to wonder: Did she really believe—and did the Director really believe—that he was desperately hanging on to his job not for reasons of power or prestige or personal vanity, but instead to protect the Bureau, and thus the nation, from the Nixon administration?

I didn't know the answer. I still don't. But I realized then that any talk of a voluntary retirement for Hoover was wasted breath. He'd never walk away from the Bureau. It was all he'd ever had, and all he would ever have.

"Okay, I understand. He won't leave. But how about you?"

"What about me?" Her anger seemed to be subsiding.

"Why don't you retire, Miss Gandy? I mean, you're almost—" I was going to mention her age, but it seemed impolite.

She said it for me. "Yes, I'm almost seventy-five years old." She shook her head. "It's hard to believe."

"And you've been working six days a week for more than fifty years. Isn't it time for you to relax a little?"

She smiled at the thought. "Sometimes I wish I could. But, no, not now. I could never leave him."

I didn't say anything. But there was something about the way she said it, the finality of it, that struck me. Whether they liked it or not, they were both trapped, she and Hoover, he by his love of the Bureau, and she by her loyalty to—the Bureau? The man? Then I remembered what she'd said to me that time after she threw herself in front of the window to take a bullet for the Director. To her, and to him, the Bureau and the man were the same thing.

We chatted about other things for a while, and as always she asked about my growing family and wanted to see baby pictures. Maybe that was why I brought up the subject—and later wished I hadn't.

"Miss Gandy, do you ever wish that you'd gotten married, had a family?"

"Why, Paul," she said in a joking tone, "I thought you knew. I am married, to the—"

"I know, I know, married to the FBI. I used to do the tours, remember? But seriously."

She paused for a moment, thinking. "There just wasn't time," she said with a soft sigh. "You don't know what it was like back then, Paul, when the Bureau was young—when we were young. We were building something, something we all believed so much in. Then there were all the big cases, all the stories in the newspapers and on the radio—about us! It was so exciting, so . . . so . . . exhilarating. There were just never enough hours in the day."

"So no time for fun?"

She shook her head. "You're missing the point, Paul. The work was the fun. Oh, I suppose if you mean the usual kinds of fun, we had that, too. Remember, the Bureau was so small back then, only a few hundred agents, a few hundred support people. We actually were a family, everybody knew everybody else. We had baseball games and parties and dances." She gave me a reproving look. "You young people think we were always the stodgy old folks we are now, but we were young once, too."

"You're anything but stodgy, Miss Gandy. But there was no one you . . . never anyone that was . . ."

I was flailing, but she knew what I meant. "No, no." But then she appeared to be remembering, wistfully it seemed. "Well," she said, "there was one nice gentleman. . . ."

I had to ask. "Him?"

Of course I meant the Director. She seemed more surprised than shocked that I'd said such a thing.

"Oh, no, Paul, no," she said quickly. "No, of course not. It was never . . . it was not like . . ." She paused for a moment. "He had his lady friends, and they were all very nice."

I remembered the rumors about Dorothy Lamour and Lela Rogers. And then there were those other rumors—but again, I would never have asked her about that.

"Besides," she went on, "in those days it would have been most improper for a man and his executive assistant to . . . to . . ."

I could see I had made her uncomfortable. Then, without meaning to, I made her even more so. "Someone else then?" And then it just popped out: "Melvin Purvis?"

Miss Gandy reacted as if to an electric shock. Her eyes flashed and her face flushed. "That's not true! Certainly not! Who told you that?"

No one had really told me anything. It was just a nugget of Bureau corporate memory that had been passed down from the 1930s to the 1940s to the 1960s, and thus to me. I'd heard it from an agent in Cincinnati, an older guy who'd been with the Bureau since the 1940s. We'd been sitting around with some of the other agents, just bullshitting, and while they were talking about some of the legendary figures of the Gangster Era, this agent mentioned that Hoover's secretary—Miss Gandy—had once had a "thing" for Melvin Purvis. That was the word the agent used, a "thing," nothing more salacious than that. At the time I didn't give it much thought, and the conversation moved on, but now it was clear that the name had struck a nerve.

Some background is required. Purvis, a South Carolina–born lawyer, had joined the Bureau in 1927, when he was twenty-four years old. Hoover took a shine to "Little Mel"—Purvis stood less than five and a half feet tall—and rapidly promoted him through the ranks, culminating in his appointment as special agent in charge of the high-profile Chicago Field Office. In some ways Hoover was closer to Purvis than even to Clyde Tolson. Tolson was more of a kid brother to Hoover, or a junior member of a two-man business partnership, someone who followed the Director around and took orders. Purvis, on the other hand, was more of an actual friend to Hoover; their interactions were full of jokes, gossip, philosophical discussions, the sort of thing you'd see between two equals, or almost equals. Hoover called Purvis "Melvin," and he in turn addressed the Director as "J.E."

But the friendship quickly soured after Purvis led the manhunts that ended in the 1934 killings of Pretty Boy Floyd, Baby Face Nelson, and most of all John Dillinger. Purvis never claimed to have personally shot Dillinger, but that was a detail the newspapers generally ignored. Despite warnings from Hoover to keep his name out of the headlines, Purvis, "The Man Who Shot Dillinger," was soon the most famous G-man in America, surpassing even the Director. Furious, Hoover eventually drove Purvis to resign in 1935, and he became persona non grata in the FBI, his name never to be mentioned. Purvis went on to host the wildly popular *Junior G-Men* radio show, but his later business ventures met with only mixed success—the result, Purvis believed, of a decades-long smear campaign against him by Hoover and the Bureau. In 1960, ill and beset by alcoholism and dependence on prescription painkillers, Purvis shot himself in the head.

So what did this have to do with Miss Gandy? In 1972, I didn't know; all I had was that vague nugget of Bureau gossip. Then, decades later, in 2005, Purvis's son Alston Purvis published his nonfiction book *The Vendetta*, which contained portions of the correspondence between his father and Hoover. Suddenly it was clear that Miss Gandy had been the subject of frequent discussions between the two men—and they weren't talking business.

What you have to know about Purvis is that despite his diminutive stature, or maybe because of it, women adored him. More than just handsome, he had the sort of soulful, dreamy eyes that women fell for. The Director constantly teased him about his attractive power over "the ladies"—including Miss Gandy.

Once, in 1932, after Purvis sent a photograph of himself attending an official function to Hoover, he jokingly wrote back, "Your picture has disrupted my office this morning. My secretary"—that is, Miss Gandy—"has been floating around in the air and saying how 'SWEET' you look. I don't expect to get any work out of her today. It is a crime what effect you have on the fair sex."

There was more. Later Hoover wrote Purvis, "I don't see how my secretary and you can help but embark on the matrimonial sea," but he advised Purvis that he'd better hurry because he had competition. Hoover claimed that Miss Gandy had been spotted riding in a car while sitting on the lap of another Bureau agent—information that Purvis said he had "read with much interest and mixed feelings."

The bantering went on and on. Referring to an upcoming Halloween ball to be held at the Willard Hotel in Washington, Hoover wrote, "My secretary has indicated to me that she will not attend that festivity unless she can go in your company. So you may make your plans accordingly." After Purvis said he would attend, Hoover responded, "Miss Gandy has promised she will wear a cellophane gown. You can look forward to seeing all of Miss Gandy." To which Purvis responded, "Miss Gandy would look extremely well in a cellophane gown." (Need I explain that cellophane was a clear, transparent wrapping material made of cellulose, similar to today's plastic wrap? You can understand the implications of a "cellophane gown.")

Well, there was still more, but that's enough. For me, reading all this so many years later was more than a little discomforting, like reading about your grandmother's sex life—before she married Grandpa. And I had to wonder, Was it all just a joke on Hoover's and Purvis's parts, the sort of juvenile bantering about a woman that men frequently engage in? Surely Miss Gandy must have known about these letters, since she handled all of the Director's correspondence. Was she humiliated by them? Or was she in on it, perhaps coquettishly pleased for Purvis to know of her affections? Was Melvin Purvis the "nice gentleman" she mentioned to me? Or was it someone else—perhaps the man in the car with Miss Gandy on his lap?

I don't know. But if she did have affection for Purvis, it didn't outlast the Director's break with his former favorite G-man. There was never any question where Miss Gandy's loyalties lay. When Purvis tried to see Hoover in the 1940s and '50s, apparently to try to patch up the feud, Miss Gandy gave him the cold shoulder, telling him the Director was out somewhere and she didn't know when he'd return—which obviously was a lie. Miss Gandy always knew where the Director was, and when he'd be back.

Of course, I didn't know any of this when I sat in Miss Gandy's office in the spring of 1972. Even if I had, I wouldn't have believed it. Miss Gandy was right. It's impossible for young people to believe that old people were ever young, possessing the same wants and dreams and desires all young people have. I simply wouldn't have been able to process the concept of Miss Gandy riding around in a 1932 coupe while sitting on a man's lap, much less her wearing a cellophane gown.

"I'm sorry," I said to Miss Gandy, "I didn't mean to pry."

"All these ridiculous stories! The way men talk!" I wasn't sure if the sound in her voice was anger or pain. Maybe both.

She didn't speak for a moment. Then she said, "Even if I'd ever wanted to marry, he wouldn't have allowed it."

"The Director?" I remembered the story about when Miss Gandy first went to work for Hoover in the Justice Department in 1918, before he became Director, and she'd assured him she had "no immediate plans" to marry. "Even he couldn't have stopped you if you wanted—"

"You don't understand, Paul," she interrupted. "I would have had to choose. Just like he had to choose between the Bureau and . . . another kind of life. It's not just a joke, Paul. He—I—we are married to the FBI."

"Yes, but—"

She looked at me, fiercely. "I don't regret my life, Paul."

"Nor should you, Miss Gandy. I'm sorry, I—"

"We all make our decisions, and then we live with them. I don't regret mine." She waved away any further discussion. "Some things in the past are better left there," she said.

We talked a while longer, just about ordinary things, and she was almost her usual cheerful self again. Then it was time for me to go.

"Paul, please be careful out there," she said as I stood up. "All those bank robberies and hijackings and things."

"I will, Miss Gandy." I wanted to leave on an upbeat note. "Just one more thing. I'm curious. If you ever do retire, is there anything special you'd like to do? Travel, see Paris, something like that?"

She thought for a moment. "Well—now don't laugh, Paul. Promise? . . . All right. I've always wanted to take up fishing."

I laughed. "Fishing? You're kidding."

"Yes, fishing—and stop smiling! My father used to take me fishing when I was a girl in New Jersey and I always enjoyed it so. But I've always been too busy."

I wasn't sure if she was joking. But I knew that if this redoubtable woman ever did take up fishing, the fish had better watch out.

"Well, Miss Gandy, I certainly hope you'll get to go fishing someday."

She smiled, but when she spoke, there was a weariness in her voice. "Yes, maybe someday. Not now, but . . . it won't be long."

Miss Gandy was right. It wouldn't be long.

And when the time came, the politicians would do exactly what the Director and Miss Gandy feared they would.

I saw J. Edgar Hoover one more time.

It was mid-April 1972, and I had some business to take care of at the FBI Washington Field Office in the Old Post Office Building. I had plans to meet a friend for lunch at a restaurant on Pennsylvania Avenue, and since it was only a few blocks away I decided to leave my car and walk. It was one of those beautiful Washington spring days, with the sun shining warmly and the air balmy and fresh; a rainstorm the night before had washed away the city's dust and grime, if not its many generations of sins.

As I was walking past the Justice Department building, I glanced up at the fifth floor, just out of habit, the way you usually do when you pass by someplace where you used to live or work. The doors to the balcony of the Director's office were open, and there, standing back from the doors, in the shadows, was the Director.

I couldn't really see his face, I was too far away and the office interior was too dim, but I knew it was him. The square-shouldered, bull-necked form was unmistakable. He was standing the way I'd often seen him when I'd come into his office with a document or a phone message—silent, motionless, staring out at the city where he'd lived his entire life, the city he probably knew as well or better than anyone else, the city of weak men against whom he'd fought so many battles, and against whom there were so many more battles still to fight.

I don't think he saw me, and even if he had, he certainly wouldn't have waved or anything. The Director wasn't a waver. Then, in an instant, he turned away and was gone.

I stood there for a moment, looking up, thinking about the time I'd spent with that strange and perplexing man, a man of towering strengths and staggering weaknesses, a man of many monumental accomplishments and some disastrous failures, a man who shaped the course of history. I remembered what Miss Gandy had said to me, and I wondered:

Did J. Edgar Hoover ever regret his life?

• • •

A few weeks later, shortly after 10:00 a.m. on Tuesday, May 2, 1972, I was at my desk in the bullpen at the Alexandria Field Office when SAC Jack McDermott came up to me.

"Hey, Paul."

Paul? It sounded serious—and Jack looked serious.

"I know you were one of his guys, so I wanted to tell you myself. He's dead."

"What?"

"Hoover. I just got the call. They found him at home this morning. Looks like a heart attack. They're going to make a formal announcement later this morning, but the word's getting around and I wanted you to know. Sorry."

"Yeah, thanks."

I watched as Jack McDermott circulated through the office, spreading the word. A few of the older secretaries were crying, but in general there was no great outpouring of anguish. People clustered in small groups, talking in hushed tones, while others rushed to their phones to call wives, colleagues, friends.

Most of the agents looked stunned, disbelieving, while even the younger agents who'd chaffed under the Director's recent leadership showed no expression of satisfaction, much less joy. The news was far too momentous for that.

As for me, I guess you'll expect me to say that I was shocked, dazed, overcome with grief, but I was none of those things. It was more a sense of finality, of a door closing, a long chapter ended. It would take a while to completely grasp it, to fully understand the implications. But at that moment I knew this much:

The Director was dead. And for good or ill, the Bureau, and the nation—and in many ways my own life—would never be the same.

CHAPTER 8

Three Days in May

It was Jimmy Crawford who found him, lying on the floor of the master bedroom in Hoover's home. One touch of his cold hand told Jimmy that there was no need to call an ambulance. The spirit had long since flown.

The Director's last day on earth had been largely unexceptional. He arrived alone at the Justice Department building just after 9:00 a.m.—Tolson, as usual, was ill—then went over the morning paperwork before a 10:00 a.m. handshake-and-photo session with two special agents who were getting their twenty-year service awards and their wives and kids. He went out for lunch at noon at the Carvery—formerly the Rib Room—in the Mayflower Hotel, came back to the office at 1:15 p.m., enjoyed his customary "No calls" time, then did more paperwork and had a meeting with the Knoxville, Tennessee, director of public safety. The Director left the building just before 6:00 p.m., had dinner at Tolson's apartment, and returned home sometime around 10:00 p.m.

Only one aspect of his last day may have raised the Director's blood pressure. That morning, Hoover's journalist bête noire, Jack Anderson, ran the first of a planned weeklong series of columns about the Director, starting with one headlined "Hoover the Snoop Watches Private Lives." In the column the journalist reported that Hoover's FBI maintained files on the "sex habits, business affairs and political pursuits" of a host of famous people—not only Martin Luther King (that had long been public knowledge) but also such luminaries as Marlon Brando, black singer Harry Belafonte, civil rights leader Ralph Abernathy, and others. The column also referred to the FBI file on a Hollywood leading man who was reported to be homosexual; Anderson didn't name him, but it was Rock Hudson.

"Hoover appears to have a hang-up on sex," Anderson wrote. "He has assumed federal jurisdiction over sex."

What the Director must have found particularly disturbing was that the "lower than dog shit" columnist's story apparently wasn't based on Hoover's trash, or the usual "sources tell us" attribution, but on actual FBI files to which the reporter had apparently been given access. This wasn't Media, Pennsylvania, break-in material; it had to be coming out of the central files. If someone within the Bureau—possibly one of William Sullivan's remaining loyalists—was leaking documents to the hated Jack Anderson, that could spell no end of trouble.

(The files Anderson referred to weren't quite as sinister as they sounded. Most of the FBI "file" on Rock Hudson, for example, was the result of a 1966 "name check" request from the Johnson White House; the Bureau reported that it had no "derogatory" information on the actor, and that it hadn't conducted an investigation of him, but that it was "common knowledge" within the motion picture industry that he had "homosexual tendencies." More on those and other "celebrity files" later.)

Aside from the pesky Anderson, though, the Director's last day seemed routine. But it was the lack of routine the next morning, May 2, 1972, that frightened Jimmy Crawford.

Jimmy had officially retired a few years earlier after undergoing brain surgery—Hoover visited him several times while he was in the hospital—and he had passed the driver's job to his brother-in-law, Tom Moton. Hoover kept Jimmy on as a part-time caretaker for his house, a job that Jimmy enjoyed. That was why he was at the house on Thirtieth Place this morning, a Tuesday, to plant some roses in the backyard. But as Jimmy was unpacking the rosebushes, inside the house something was wrong.

Ordinarily Hoover came down the stairs at precisely 7:30 a.m.—

you could set your watch by it—when Annie Fields would have his breakfast of soft-boiled eggs and toast ready for him. But on this day seven thirty came and went, then eight, then eight fifteen. Annie began to get concerned. As she sat in the kitchen having coffee with Tom Moton, there'd been no sound of movement from Hoover's bedroom, and Cindy and G-Boy were yipping and yapping impatiently, waiting for their master to come down and give them the remains of his breakfast. Finally Annie called Jimmy in from the yard, and together they decided that he'd better check things out. Jimmy started maneuvering his way through the crowded living room and toward the stairs.

As he made his way up the stairs, past the large oil painting of Hoover at the first landing and the bronze bust of Hoover mounted on a pedestal at the top of the stairs, Jimmy felt a sense of foreboding. In all the years that he'd worked for the Boss, he'd never been in a situation like this. J. Edgar Hoover just didn't oversleep. Jimmy knocked on the master bedroom door, twice, and when there was no answer, he gently opened it. In the gloom—Hoover always slept with the heavy curtains tightly closed—Jimmy saw him, clad in pajama bottoms and lying motionless on the floor next to the four-poster maplewood bed. When Jimmy grabbed Hoover's hand, the flesh was cold, and rigor mortis was already setting in.

Half in shock, Jimmy called out to Annie and Tom, who were anxiously waiting in the kitchen. They rushed upstairs, and after Jimmy and Tom lifted Hoover's body off the floor and into a more dignified position on the bed, they started making calls—to Hoover's personal physician, Dr. Robert Choisser, who would arrive within the hour, to Tolson at his apartment on Massachusetts Avenue, to Miss Gandy, already at work. J. P. Mohr notified the other assistant directors and sent an urgent teletype to all the field SACs—including Jack McDermott at the Alexandria Field Office—so they could tell the troops before the news hit the press.

As soon as I heard the news, I thought about calling Miss Gandy, then decided not to, not yet. I knew how busy she'd be. Instead I called my friend Nancy Mooney.

"Oh, Paul, isn't it just awful?" Nancy said.

I agreed that it was. Nancy wasn't crying; she sounded more as if she couldn't quite believe it. I asked about Miss Gandy, how she was taking it.

"She's Miss Gandy. You know, calm and everything. And busy. She and Mr. Mohr are already planning for the funeral. It's just all so fast. Oh, Paul, what's going to happen?"

I assured her, without really believing it, that everything would be all right. I asked her to let Miss Gandy know that I'd called, and that I'd call her in a day or two. Nancy said she would.

Later I'd put together the story of what happened in the next hours and days. It's a story replete with duplicity, hypocrisy—and fear.

Just before noon, in the White House press briefing room, Acting Attorney General Richard Kleindienst made the official announcement. Kleindienst, a Nixon appointee who'd long been telling associates that Hoover was "out of his mind," said it was "with profound personal grief" that he was announcing Hoover's death, adding, "The nation has lost a giant among its patriots." Moments later Nixon himself walked in and said that he, too, deeply mourned the loss of one of his "closest friends and advisers." It must have been difficult for him not to smile now that the "Hoover problem" was over.

The Director's death was now official, but it wasn't exactly breaking news by that point. The word had already quickly spread through the Washington, DC, bureaucracy via the secretaries' grapevine, which in its scope and speed of transmission rivaled today's social media. A swarm of reporters and photographers and TV news crews were already assembled in front of the Hoover residence, now guarded by a squad of FBI agents dispatched to the scene. The newsmen were disappointed when undertakers from Joseph Gawler's Sons funeral home managed to spirit the body out of the house through the back door and into the back of a nondescript sedan, depriving the newsmen of the hoped-for film of a dead J. Edgar Hoover being hauled out on a gurney. Gawler's Sons had embalmed and casketed no end of powerful government figures over the past century, including presidents Eisenhower and Kennedy, and were wise to the ways of the vulture press.

Later, after consulting with Dr. Choisser, the Washington, DC, coroner ruled that Hoover died as a result of "hypertensive cardiovascular disease"—in other words, a heart attack. An autopsy was not legally required, and no autopsy was performed, which struck some people as mysterious. Already the rumors were circulating that Hoover had not died a natural death, that he had been murdered by one or more of the usual conspiracy suspects—the CIA, the Mafia, the White House, high-level cabals of the political far right and left, perhaps even rogue elements within the FBI itself. Over time the rumors of murder would take on a life of their own, and they still persist. But as with so many conspiracy theories, they tend to overlook one rather significant and undeniable fact: J. Edgar Hoover was an old man, and every old man dies sooner or later.

Not surprisingly, the death of J. Edgar Hoover was front-page news in every newspaper in the country, often accompanied by a 1930s photo of Hoover holding a Thompson submachine gun. "Mr. FBI Dies." "America Mourns #1 G-Man: Ruled FBI With An Iron Fist." "Federal Bureau His Monument." "Death At Home Climaxes Long, Devoted Career." Editorials extolled his virtues and generally downplayed his controversies; papers that had opposed him, such as the *New York Times*, nevertheless praised his "unique service to his country in the field of law enforcement for nearly five decades."

Even the hated Jack Anderson had some kind things to say. Although noting the FBI's "excesses" under Hoover and its use as a "political police force" by some presidents, Anderson wrote, "For his great accomplishments, the nation should pay homage to the Old Bulldog whose grim visage, gruff manner, and steel trap mind won't soon be forgotten."

In the halls of Congress there was a flood of memorial tributes to the late FBI Director. Senator after senator and congressman after congressman rose to praise Hoover's "patriotism," "incorruptibility," "genius"; a collection of the congressional tributes to the late Director runs to some 160 pages. Democratic representative

Edmond Edmondson of Oklahoma, himself a former FBI agent, described Hoover as "our first line of defense against the enemies of the Republic—both foreign and domestic." Representative Spark Masayuki Matsunaga (D-Hawaii) reminded fellow House members of an often-overlooked aspect of Hoover's legacy—that is, his strong but unsuccessful opposition to the "relocation" of hundreds of thousands of Japanese Americans from the US West Coast. One congressman, apparently unable to grasp the reality of it, praised the dead Director as the nation's "greatest living American."

Even Hoover's congressional enemies thought it proper—or at least expedient—to laud the old man. House majority leader Hale Boggs, who had a year earlier accused Hoover of tapping his phone and demanded that he resign—many of Boggs's colleagues thought the hard-drinking congressman must have been drunk—declared, "There is no man who has served this country with greater dedication, with greater love, and with greater productivity." Massachusetts senator Edward "Ted" Kennedy, a bitter Hoover foe and the subject of an extensive FBI file, praised Hoover's "honesty, integrity, and desire to do what he thought best for the country." Congress quickly voted to name the new FBI headquarters building on Pennsylvania Avenue, then under construction, the J. Edgar Hoover FBI Building.

Meanwhile, with Hoover conveniently dead, Richard Nixon was planning to politically milk the popular FBI Director's death for all it was worth.

Hoover had left Miss Gandy and Mr. Mohr explicit instructions about his funeral: he wanted a small, private Masonic ceremony at the National Presbyterian Church—he'd been a Mason all his life—followed by burial at Congressional Cemetery, where his parents and infant sister were buried. But Nixon had other ideas. Within minutes after the formal announcement of Hoover's death, Nixon talked with his square-jawed, crew-cutted chief of staff, H. R. "Bob" Haldeman about Hoover—a discussion that was picked up by the secret taping system installed in the Oval Office.

"Oh, he died at the right time, didn't he?" Nixon said. "It would have killed him to lose that office. . . . Thank God we didn't go with that ploy late last year of pushing him out. It wouldn't have worked."

Told by Haldeman that Hoover had specified a modest funeral ceremony, Nixon scoffed, "Nobody ever says he wants a big ceremony, but you gotta have one for Hoover. . . . We're gonna have a hell of a ceremony for him. . . . I have strong ideas about this damn funeral. I want it to be big."

The president initially wanted the funeral held in the forty-five-hundred-seat outdoor amphitheater at Arlington National Cemetery, with Nixon himself delivering the eulogy—he and Haldeman agreed it would make for great political TV—followed by a military-style burial there, preferably with Hoover's grave placed as far away as possible from the graves of the hated (by Nixon and Hoover) John F. and Robert F. Kennedy. But there were concerns about rain which could potentially turn Nixon's Hoover extravaganza into a soggy PR disaster. They considered the four-thousand-person-capacity National Cathedral as an alternative, but Nixon vetoed it when reminded that the dean of the National Cathedral was Francis Sayre, an anti-war activist whom Nixon described as a "left-wing son of a bitch."

Eventually the plans settled into place. At Nixon's suggestion and with Congress's enthusiastic approval, Hoover's body would lie in state in the Capitol Rotunda the next day, Wednesday, followed by the funeral at the smaller National Presbyterian Church on Thursday, with Nixon delivering the eulogy. It wasn't exactly what Nixon wanted, or what Hoover had requested, but knowing Hoover, I suspect that Nixon was probably right. Regardless of his stated wishes, I think the Director would have welcomed the pomp and circumstance.

But the president had more on his mind than just Hoover's funeral. There was also the matter of the Director's files—the so-called secret files that all of Washington knew Hoover kept in his office. Even before the official death announcement, on orders from the White House, Acting AG Kleindienst told J. P. Mohr to "secure" the Director's private office—and presumably the secret files. Mohr followed those instructions to the letter. He had the locks to the Director's personal inner office changed, not mentioning to the acting AG that, as we've seen, the files the White House was worried about were actually in Miss Gandy's office.

That night, Tuesday, there was a small private viewing at Gawler's Sons funeral home, where Hoover's body lay in a $3,000 bronze casket ordered by Miss Gandy. Preparing the body had been a rush job, and the undertakers hadn't had time to replace the black dye they'd washed out of the Director's hair and eyebrows. People who saw him in the open casket said that he looked much older and more frail and smaller than he had in life. But as one of his nieces said later, "I guess death does that to you." After the viewing, Miss Gandy directed the coffin to be closed.

I couldn't make it to the viewing, but the next morning I went to the Capitol to watch the lying-in-state ceremony. I was on my own time, not in any official Bureau capacity, but my FBI credentials got me to the top of the Capitol steps. At the time I didn't know I'd be attending the funeral service the next day, and somehow I felt drawn to pay my respects to the man whose life and career had profoundly affected my own. I have to say, I still didn't feel any overwhelming sense of grief. The death of a seventy-seven-year-old man, apparently without any extended suffering, is simply an ending, not a tragedy.

At eleven thirty, amid a light but steady rain, a Gawler's Sons' hearse delivered the bronze casket to the bottom of the main steps of the Capitol. The hearse was thirty minutes behind schedule, which I knew would have enraged the Director. I half expected him to burst out of his coffin and start ordering punitive transfers to Butte. The image made me smile.

Eight ramrod-straight, immaculately uniformed young members of the army, navy, marines, and air force—what the military called a "joint body-bearing detail"—met the hearse and began carrying the casket up the thirty-five steps to the bronze doors that opened onto the Rotunda. The Alexandria Field Office's territory included Arlington National Cemetery, so I'd often watched—and admired—the precision and military bearing of the young men assigned as pallbearers at military funerals.

But on this day I could see that the eight young military men carrying the coffin were struggling and straining with their burden—which led to another of the wild posthumous rumors about J. Edgar Hoover. Miss Gandy had ordered a casket lined with lead, which of course added to its weight; the thing weighed some twelve hundred pounds, not including the body inside it. At the time she hadn't known that the casket would have to be carried up thirty-five wet, slippery steps at the Capitol. Later some writers would suggest that Hoover's casket had the special lead lining to protect Hoover's corpse from vandals, or even from radiation in the event of a nuclear war; when it comes to J. Edgar Hoover, some people will believe anything. But the truth is much simpler. A sealed lead lining was common in high-end burial caskets, designed to protect against moisture seepage and preserve the body for a longer time—although why that should matter to anyone, much less the deceased, I can't say.

Eventually the sweating, straining joint body-bearing detail managed to bring the casket up the steps, past two rows of a military honor guard with their rifles in the present arms position. They carried the casket through the great bronze doors and into the Rotunda, then placed it on the catafalque on which the body of Abraham Lincoln had once lain in state. For J. Edgar Hoover it was a singular honor. Up to that time, only twenty-one Americans had lain in state in the Capitol Rotunda, most of them presidents or military heroes—Lincoln, Eisenhower, General Douglas MacArthur, Admiral George "the Hero of Manila" Dewey, JFK. Hoover was the only civil servant to share that sacred space.

The Rotunda, which soared 160 feet from the floor to the top of the Capitol dome, was packed with much of official Washington: senators and congressmen, all nine members of the Supreme Court, foreign ambassadors. Richard Nixon skipped the Rotunda ceremony, suggesting on the secret Oval Office tapes that he didn't want to share the spotlight with "those shit asses" on Capitol Hill.

Chief Justice Warren Burger, a longtime friend and ally of Hoover's, offered up a brief eulogy to what he called "this splendid man," a "great American who served his country so well and earned the admiration of all who believe in ordered liberty"—emphasis on the "ordered" part.

Then the dignitaries dispersed and the general public began filing past the catafalque, the first of more than twenty-five thousand people who'd pass through the Rotunda to honor J. Edgar Hoover over the next twenty-four hours.

Some who'd waited in line for the viewing were merely curious, drawn to the historic spectacle. But for the most part the mourners passing by the catafalque seemed sincerely moved by Hoover's death and the ending of an era. For some, Hoover was the tommygun-packing crime fighter of the 1930s, or the Nazi-saboteur hunter of World War II. For others he was the relentless foe of the godless Communists of the 1950s. Still others saw him as the last bulwark of American values, the one man in public life who refused to compromise with the unwelcome forces of change—the dope smokers and the anti-war demonstrators and the free-love advocates and the people who called police officers pigs. He was, simply, J. Edgar Hoover—and so by the thousands they waited for hours, in the rain, to pay tribute.

(Meanwhile, on the other side of the Capitol, on the West Steps, a bizarre scene was unfolding—one that I only heard about later. A group of about five hundred anti-war protesters were holding a long-scheduled demonstration on the steps at which the names of American war dead were read aloud, with one of the featured speakers being the aforementioned Daniel Ellsberg of the *Pentagon Papers* case. Enraged at this perceived insult to the state ceremony that he'd arranged for Hoover, Nixon ordered a counterdemonstration to be staged, a task that eventually fell to a young Republican operative named Roger Stone—yes, that Roger Stone, future pal of Donald Trump's. At the same time, acting on false reports that the anti-war protesters planned to swarm into the Rotunda and assault Hoover's coffin, G. Gordon Liddy and Howard Hunt called in some anti-Castro Cubans and ordered them to attack the protesters and "incapacitate" Ellsberg—or worse. Both efforts failed. Stone rounded up two dozen members of a group called College Republicans of DC to shout insults and slogans at the protesters—"Tell it to Hanoi!"—but they were outnumbered and ignored. The Cubans slugged a few protesters but couldn't get to Ellsberg. Six weeks later Liddy, Hunt, and some of those same Cubans would be caught in another, far more momentous, failure.)

After the Rotunda ceremony I went back to the Alexandria Field Office where SAC Jack McDermott had some news for me.

"Hey, Polack." I was Polack again. "I got a call from J. P. Mohr about you. He says Miss Gandy wants you to accompany her to the funeral tomorrow. They'll send the car to pick you up here at nine a.m." He smiled. "Don't be late. And wear a dark suit."

I was surprised, but not too much. I assumed Miss Gandy had a reason for wanting me there.

"So what's happening over there?" I asked. I meant FBIHQ.

McDermott rolled his eyes. "Oh, it's a circus. Mohr told me everyone's running around in a panic. Tolson resigned, and Nixon just appointed an acting director."

"That was quick. Who is it? Felt? Mr. Mohr?"

McDermott shook his head. "Not even close. An outsider. Some Justice Department guy named Pat Gray—L. Patrick Gray III, if you can believe that. Used to be a navy officer, submarine commander, then went to law school. He's one of Nixon's guys, worked for him in the '68 campaign, then Nixon made him deputy attorney general on the civil side. Never handled a criminal case in his life, Mohr says."

"Holy shit." Later I learned that Nixon had briefly considered keeping Tolson on as acting director, on the theory that his physical incapacity might make him easy to control. Tolson scotched that ludicrous idea by resigning, so Nixon and his men finally settled on Pat Gray—and in time it would become clear why. It was said that as a former navy officer, Gray's automatic response to an order from a superior was to salute, say, "Aye, aye, sir!," and do exactly what he was told. By making Gray acting director it would forestall the need for Senate confirmation. Again, I didn't know all this at the time, but I did know that having an outsider come in and start running the Bureau would be—well, I wasn't exactly sure what it would be, but I knew it would shake things up.

"Yeah," McDermott said, reading my thoughts. "Everyone's pissed, especially Felt. And Mohr has already tangled with this new guy. Had a real shouting match, I heard. Something about the damned 'secret files.'"

I heard about it later. On the morning of Hoover's death, Gray appeared in Mohr's office, asking where the "secret files" were kept. Mohr told him there were no special secret files since all FBI files were secret, in the sense they were not open to the public. Gray left, but then the next day, apparently under pressure from the White House, he showed up again in Mohr's office, this time demanding to see the secret files. When Mohr again told him there were no such files, tempers flared.

"Gray was spooked," Mohr said much later. "He said, 'Look, Mr. Mohr, I'm a hardheaded Irishman and nobody pushes me around.' And I said, 'Look, Mr. Gray, I'm a hardheaded Dutchman and no-body pushes me around.' I think I did cuss at him a little bit. Gray's problem was he didn't ask the right questions."

What Mohr meant was that if Gray had specifically asked to see the Personal/Confidential files or the Official/Confidential files, or if he'd asked if the Bureau had any files on presidents, politicians, movie stars, or other celebrities, then he, Mohr, would have had to tell him. But he didn't ask, and Mohr was in no mood to enlighten him. Judging by this and his later actions, L. Patrick Gray was not exactly the sharpest tool in the shed.

Anyway, the next morning at 9:00 a.m. sharp, Tom Moton arrived at the Alexandria office in the shiny black armored Cadillac to pick me up—which naturally prompted no end of mostly good-natured but pointed comments from my fellow agents about me being some kind of Bureau big shot. I laughed and told them they were all terminated—with prejudice.

Tom explained that at Mr. Mohr's direction we'd first pick up

Miss Gandy at her Connecticut Avenue apartment, then swing by Mr. Tolson's apartment on Massachusetts Avenue to pick him up. The funeral didn't start until 11:00 a.m., but Tom said Mr. Mohr wanted us there early because Tolson would have to enter the church in a wheelchair, and Mr. Mohr, who was always protective of Tolson, didn't want people to see that. I was just glad we were picking up Miss Gandy first. It would give me a chance to speak with her, and besides, I wasn't sure I would have liked being alone in the same back seat with Clyde Tolson.

It was the first—and the last—time I ever rode in the Director's car, and now I understood why Jimmy Crawford had always cursed it. An ordinary Cadillac of that model weighed two and a half tons, but with the armor and the bulletproof windows this one must have weighed close to twice that. Tom had to start hitting the brakes a half block before the car came to a stoplight, and then it struggled to gain speed afterward. The extra weight was too much for the springs and suspension, so every small pothole sent tremors up your spine. As I said earlier, the Director was personally fearless, so I wondered why, even with the prestige factor of having an armored car, he bothered with this monster. It was a mystery.

Another mystery was waiting for me when we got to Miss Gandy's apartment building and Tom went up to escort her to the car. As she walked out the front door, I noticed it immediately.

Miss Gandy was smiling.

"I'm sorry, Miss Gandy," I said as Tom held the door open and she climbed into the car. I said it automatically, without thinking. But my words didn't quite fit her smile. It wasn't a big grin or anything, more of a *Mona Lisa* kind of expression, but it was a smile nonetheless.

"Oh, I know, Paul, that's nice of you to say, but it's not necessary. It was time."

"And at least he didn't suffer."

"Suffer? No, not physically. Dr. Choisser said it would have been over in a few seconds."

When she said "not physically," I wondered if she meant he'd suffered in some other way. I wondered if she meant he'd suffered emotionally, but the word hardly seemed to apply to the most seemingly unemotional man I'd ever met. Even if he'd experienced emotional turmoil in his last days, Miss Gandy and Tolson would probably have been the only people in the world who noticed.

"Was he"—I searched for the right word, but couldn't find it— "depressed toward the end? With everything that was going on?" I was thinking of Nixon and his men.

"He was . . . *resigned* I think is a better word. He knew that after the election . . ." Her voice trailed off.

I knew what she meant. While Nixon would not likely have humiliatingly forced the Old Man out before the election, afterward it would have been a different story. That was assuming Nixon won, but that seemed more than likely given the disarray in the Democratic Party. Segregationist George Wallace was splitting the party— he'd be shot and paralyzed two weeks after Hoover's death—and the liberal anti-war candidate George McGovern was leading in the primaries. Nixon's groundbreaking trip to China earlier in the year had been popular, and although anti-war protests continued, America's involvement on the ground in Vietnam was dwindling, with just sixty thousand troops left from the high of more than half a million when Nixon took office. Nixon looked like a shoo-in. And even if he somehow lost, all of the Democratic candidates had promised to find a new FBI director. So no matter what happened, professionally Hoover was doomed. Unless . . .

"But couldn't he have done something?" I asked. I was thinking of the much-speculated-upon notion that the Director had something on Nixon that would save his job. Blackmail, in other words. "Everybody thinks—"

"I know what everybody thinks," Miss Gandy interrupted. "But people who think that don't know Mr. Hoover. Didn't know him," she corrected herself. Obviously she was having trouble getting used to the past tense. "He never would have revealed . . . certain things to destroy Mr. Nixon, because that would have destroyed the Bureau as well. He couldn't have, wouldn't have, ever done that."

"But Nixon didn't know that. The Director could have bluffed him."

"No, you don't understand, Paul. Mr. Nixon knew exactly how the Director felt about the Bureau. He would have removed him, but in a subtle way. And the Director knew it."

I understood. There'd been speculation that instead of firing Hoover, Nixon would simply announce out of the blue that he was promoting him, naming him FBI director emeritus or some such thing, letting him keep his office and his car and all his perks while giving all of his authority to another, more malleable man. And as Miss Gandy said, the Director would probably have taken it. He wouldn't have brought down the Bureau simply to exact his revenge. Still . . .

"But couldn't he have—"

She waved the conversation away. "It doesn't matter now, Paul. It's all for the best. I know this may sound odd, but I'm actually happy it ended this way."

That explained the smile—and she was right. The Director was dead, and all the talk and speculation in the world couldn't change that. And I realized that I'd been arguing against myself. I, too, had wanted the Director to leave, as long as it was done honorably and with dignity—and death was an honorable and dignified way out. It had indeed been all for the best.

I changed the subject. "I heard Mr. Mohr and Mr. Gray had a run-in."

Miss Gandy laughed. "Yes, they had a somewhat . . . heated conversation as I understand it. Later Mr. Felt brought Mr. Gray around to look at the Director's office—I mean his new office, Mr. Gray's."

"And?"

"Oh, he was nice enough, I suppose. He told me to take my time moving Mr. Hoover's things out, he didn't want to rush me, which was kind of him. He kept asking about 'the files,' as he put it. I showed him the file cabinets in my office and explained that according to the Director's instructions—Mr. Hoover's instructions—I would give all the official Bureau files, the Official and Confidential files, to Mr. Felt for safekeeping."

"And the others?" I meant Hoover's Personal/Confidential files.

"I told him I'm going to destroy them. Mr. Mohr and I."

The boldness of it surprised me. "Really? A lot of people are going to wonder what—"

She cut me off. "There is nothing in those files that is or was of concern to anyone but Mr. Hoover," she said evenly. "It's all just his personal correspondence that accumulated over the years, letters to friends, that sort of thing. None of it has anything to do with official Bureau business."

I wondered about that. If J. Edgar Hoover and the FBI were the same thing, as most people, including Miss Gandy, seemed to believe, then everything connected to him was official Bureau business. I knew the destruction of those "personal" files was bound to raise some serious questions.

Miss Gandy sensed what I was thinking. "Listen to me, Paul. Nothing in those files has anything to do with the Bureau. Do you understand?"

I knew she was lying to me, probably to protect me if anyone started asking questions—just as, several years later, she would lie under oath to a congressional committee to protect the Director's legacy. But I didn't say so.

"And what did Gray say about that? Destroying the personal files?"

She smiled again. "Oh, he seemed a bit . . . bewildered by it all. As I said, he seems nice enough, but I'm sure Mr. Nixon won't have any trouble with him."

Miss Gandy would prove to be both right and wrong on that score. Nixon and his men would have no trouble getting Gray to do exactly what they wanted. But what they didn't anticipate was that Gray was too dim or too naive to understand that he wasn't supposed to get caught.

"So what now, Miss Gandy? For you, I mean."

"Well, I've already put in my retirement papers. I'll spend a few weeks clearing up the files and then I'll—"

"Go fishing?"

She laughed. "Maybe. One thing for certain, I'll get my Christmas cards out on time this year."

We both laughed at that. Ever since I'd known her, and long before that, Miss Gandy had spent so much time signing and mailing the Director's hundreds of Christmas cards that her own Christmas cards never arrived before January. They always began with some variation of "Here I am, late as usual . . ."

"And what about you, Paul? Have you given any thought to what you'll do—after the Bureau?"

I was surprised by the question. Yes, I'd given it a lot of thought, but I'd never discussed my reservations about climbing up the FBI bureaucratic ranks with Miss Gandy.

"Why? Do you think I should leave?"

"Oh, that's entirely up to you, Paul. I'm sure you'll do well whatever you decide to do. It's just that with Mr. Hoover gone, nothing will be the same. I'm afraid the Bureau will be like it was in '24—much larger, of course, but the same. Mr. Gray seems to be the first step in that direction."

By "'24" she meant 1924, when Hoover had first taken over as director and the Bureau was a haven for incompetents and political hacks, a dumping ground for politicians who had patronage favors to pay off. Somehow the way she said it made me realize how long ago it had been, and how much had changed.

"Well, I'll stick around for a while at least, see what happens." I smiled. "Besides, right now I'm having too much fun."

It was true. Hoover or no Hoover, I still loved being a special agent of the FBI.

Miss Gandy shook her head. "Yes, I know about you young agents and your fun. Just be careful, Paul."

I promised her I would.

By this time we'd arrived at Tolson's apartment building on Massachusetts Avenue, and Tom went to get him.

"I wanted to ask, Miss Gandy, why did you invite me today? I mean, I appreciate it, but—"

She thought for a moment. "Well, I suppose I've always thought of you as the son—the grandson anyway—that I never had." Somehow I'd always sensed that, but she'd never said it before. It pleased me more than I'd imagined. Smiling, she added, "Besides, I didn't want to have to sit next to him in the church. You're going to sit between us."

At that moment the "him" she was referring to appeared, with Tom wheeling him toward the car. I got out to help load Tolson into the car, but he waved me away and struggled out of the wheelchair and into the back seat. He was ambulatory, but just barely. Typical for him, he offered no greeting, to Miss Gandy or to me. I sat in the front seat—I figured the back seat was wide enough for Miss Gandy not to get too close—and for the ten-minute drive to the church no one spoke a word.

We were ushered to our places in the small "friends and family" section—again, aside from a few of Hoover's nieces and nephews, there was no family—with me, as ordered, sitting between Tolson and Miss Gandy. We watched as the pews slowly filled with guests. The president's men were all there—Mitchell, Haldeman, Ehrlichman, and a smiling Acting Attorney General Kleindienst, who appeared to have somehow overcome the "profound personal grief" he'd described when announcing the Director's death. All the Bureau assistant directors were there, Mark Felt and Mr. Mohr among them, and most of the special agents in charge from around the country. Sitting with them, looking more like the stereotypical FBI agent than anyone else around him, was Efrem Zimbalist Jr. When she saw him, Miss Gandy quietly said to me, "Handsome as ever!" The president and his wife arrived last and sat in front of the TV cameras, next to Acting FBI director Gray. Although I'd never seen him before, to me Gray looked, as Miss Gandy had said, bewildered by his sudden elevation to the national stage.

Meanwhile, at the Capitol, after the last of the long line of mourners had passed by the catafalque in the Rotunda, and with the skies finally clearing, the military joint body-bearing detail loaded Hoover's casket into a hearse and brought it to the National Presbyterian Church, along a route lined with hundreds of saluting cops.

Again the uniformed service members strained under the casket's weight as they carried it into the nave and onto the chancel, but at least this time they didn't have to wrestle it up thirty-five steps.

And so the Army Chorus sang and the congregants prayed and the Reverend Elson read from Second Timothy. As the reverend was reading, Miss Gandy squeezed my arm and leaned over and whispered in my ear, "Is the reverend wearing cuff links?" We sat there like two kids trying not to giggle in church, remembering the time when I'd almost committed career suicide by "regifting" to Elson the set of gold cuff links he'd given the Director for Christmas.

Then Richard Nixon strode to the lectern and began to speak. "Today is a day of sadness for the American people, but it is also a day of pride. America's pride has always been in its people, a people of good men and women by the millions, of great men and women in remarkable numbers, and, once in a long while, of giants who stand head and shoulders above their countrymen, setting a high and noble standard for us all. J. Edgar Hoover was one of those giants."

Nixon went on in that vein for a while, at one point curiously and somewhat prematurely noting that "while eight presidents came and went . . . the Director stayed at his post." Actually only seven presidents had "went" while Hoover was director; the eighth, Nixon, was still in office, although not for as long as he thought he would be. But Nixon hit the other points: "He personified integrity," "honor," "principle," "courage," "discipline," and "patriotism." Nixon predicted that in the future "the memory of this great man . . . will be accorded even more honor than it is today." (As it turned out, he was completely wrong on that score.) Finally he quoted a passage from Psalms—"Great peace have they which love thy law"—and closed by saying, "J. Edgar Hoover loved the law of his God, he loved the law of his country. And he richly earned peace through all eternity."

It wasn't the words Nixon spoke that bothered me—I agreed with most of what he said—but instead the Nixonian insincerity of it all. The part about the Director having "richly earned peace through all eternity" struck a particularly false note. I was pretty sure that the Director would much prefer to spend eternity battling his enemies in hell rather than peacefully embracing them in heaven—and I bet Richard Nixon thought that, too. But I suppose insincerity and posturing are standard elements of political funerals, where the mighty and the powerful gather and pretend to mourn. I remembered what the Director had so often said about being "distinguished by his enemies"—and on this day J. Edgar Hoover was the most distinguished of men.

Then it was over. The organist struck up the recessional, and the guests streamed out of the church. Miss Gandy planned to ride to the cemetery with Mr. Mohr, and I had to get back to work. We said a brief goodbye, neither of us realizing that we'd never see each other again.

Everything was ending.

As J. Edgar Hoover had requested, they buried him in the Hoover family plot in Congressional Cemetery, a century-old, thirty-five-acre, privately owned tract on the Anacostia River, which was home to the graves of a host of long-forgotten congressmen and various other minor Washington notables. It had once been a stately place in which to spend eternity, and eventually it would be renovated and would become so again. But in 1972 the cemetery was in decline, with headstones left untended and weeds beginning to sprout—and soon it would only get worse. Within a few years, amid the general urban decay in the surrounding area, the cemetery became a certified eyesore, and a nighttime haven for thieves and prostitutes and drug dealers and their customers.

The Director would have hated that, to have what he called "the criminal element" walking on his grave. He would have hated it even more had he known that they'd be joined by legions of others who were only too happy to walk—or, rather, dance—on his grave, at least figuratively.

Because even as the last shovelful of dirt fell with a soft thud atop his coffin, the destruction of J. Edgar Hoover—both the man and his legacy—had already begun.

CHAPTER 9

Aftermath

Perhaps never before in American history has a public figure been so widely admired and lauded in life and so widely condemned and vilified in death.

It didn't happen overnight. The assault on the reputation and legacy of J. Edgar Hoover, and on the Federal Bureau of Investigation he created, started slowly, like a boulder breaking off from a mountainside and then quickly gaining speed, moving faster and faster and faster until it crashes at the bottom. It was unstoppable.

For the Bureau itself, the assault began with L. Patrick Gray III.

Gray quickly let it be known that it was no longer Mr. Hoover's FBI. Some of the changes he instituted were minor, and some merely cosmetic, but they were initially welcomed, especially by the younger Bureau agents. Sideburns got longer, shoes were less carefully shined, and the relaxation of Mr. Hoover's strict weight guidelines for agents meant that more than a few belts had to be loosened a notch or two. One change that pleased almost everyone was Gray's new directive allowing agents to take their Bureau cars home, which meant that if you got called out on a case in the middle of the night, you didn't have to drive all the way to the office to check out a BuCar.

Other changes were more significant. Within days after taking over, Gray announced that the FBI would begin accepting applications from women to become special agents, a move that sent shock waves through the Bureau ranks. The Bureau under Hoover had always styled itself as a quasi-military organization that was often called upon to perform tasks that were physically demanding and sometimes dangerous—in other words, it was no place for a woman. Obviously, many women strongly disagreed. Even before Hoover's death two women had sued to break the gender barrier, and it seemed likely they'd win in court. Although Gray liked to take credit, his announcement was largely a case of accepting the inevitable. In July 1972 two women began New Agents Training at Quantico, and since then thousands of women have served honorably in the Bureau ranks.

But despite those positive changes, unfortunately Patrick Gray had a problem. Strangely enough for a former military man, Gray didn't seem to understand that while it's fine for a commander to be liked, it's far more important that he be respected or even feared—and unlike Hoover, the affable Gray was neither. Early on he launched what might be called a charm offensive, promising to personally visit every Bureau field office to glad-hand with the troops and listen to their concerns. It may have sounded like a good idea, but when you calculate all the travel time involved, it clearly was a mistake. Gray was in his office so seldom that he quickly became derisively known throughout the Bureau and even in the press as Three Day Gray and then Two Day Gray. In Gray's absence, Associate Director Mark Felt was running the show—and because of a botched bag job, the Bureau was becoming an increasingly difficult and perilous show to run.

In the early-morning hours of June 17, 1972, Washington, DC, cops caught five men burglarizing the Democratic National Committee headquarters in the Watergate hotel/residential/office complex. In addition to burglary tools, the five men—four anti-Castro Cuban exiles and a former CIA agent—had in their possession various pieces of electronic surveillance equipment. Actually it was the second time the group had burglarized the DNC. In May, just weeks after Hoover's death, they'd slipped in and planted listening devices in two phones, but the devices weren't working properly, and in any case they'd bugged the wrong phones. This latest effort was designed to install better surveillance equipment, but the burglary was discovered by a security guard, who called the cops. Because the crime involved interception of communications, a federal offense, the Washington FBI Field Office was assigned to investigate.

And who were these bumblers? You already know. They were part of the White House Plumbers unit led by G. Gordon Liddy and E. Howard Hunt.

It's not my purpose here to go over the long, sordid story of the Watergate scandal, which eventually led to the resignation of Richard Nixon and the imprisonment of many of the president's men. But the Watergate burglary does raise some interesting historical questions.

For example, what if J. Edgar Hoover had been more cooperative with Nixon's ambitious surveillance schemes as laid out in the Huston Plan, or if he hadn't "dragged his feet" on the pointless Ellsberg "conspiracy" investigation? If Hoover had been more accommodating, maybe Nixon wouldn't have felt the need to create the White House Special Investigations Unit—the Plumbers—in the first place. And what if, lacking the Plumbers to do the dirty work, Nixon and his men had asked Hoover to bug the DNC—on "national security" grounds? Hoover would almost certainly have refused such a harebrained and nakedly political proposal, just as he had refused so many of Bill Sullivan's recent requests for bag jobs and other electronic surveillances; the risks of "embarrassing the Bureau" were far too great. But what if he hadn't refused? Liddy and Hunt may have been former FBI and CIA agents, respectively, but they obviously didn't know how to pull off a bag job; in fact, they'd already managed to bungle an earlier break-in at the office of Ellsberg's psychiatrist. But what if some of the Bureau's experienced "soundmen" had been called in to do the Watergate bugging instead of those White House bumblers? Our guys probably wouldn't have been caught, and even if they had been, as FBI special agents they might have been able to badge their way out of the situation with the cops. Either way, there never would have been a Watergate scandal, and Nixon would have finished out his second term.

But it didn't happen that way. And sadly, even though the Bureau wasn't involved in the break-in, it was still badly damaged by it.

The FBI's initial investigation of the break-in was complete and thorough—at least insofar as Patrick Gray and the White House allowed it to be. Gray was exactly what Hoover had feared his successor would be—a political hack who was working for the White House, and who was seemingly unconcerned about the Bureau's reputation and integrity. Throughout the investigation Gray fed White House counsel John Dean reports on who was talking to the FBI and what they were saying—it was like giving your team's playbook to the coach of the other team—and Gray actively tried to limit the Bureau's inquiry on alleged "national security" grounds. On John Dean's orders, Gray even went so far as to destroy relevant documents found in E. Howard Hunt's White House safe.

At the same time, Mark Felt, Gray's number two man, was also leaking information about the Watergate investigation—not to the White House but to *Washington Post* reporter Bob Woodward and other journalists. Felt's motives in becoming the famous Deep Throat are unclear. Felt later claimed he was trying to keep the Watergate story alive to protect the Bureau from Nixon's henchmen. Others speculate he was trying to destroy Gray in the hopes that he, Felt, would finally become director—a vain hope, since the White House already suspected him of being Woodward's source. But either way, the *Post* stories gave the impression that the White House and the FBI were engaged in a cover-up. In the Bureau's case that wasn't true—despite Gray's efforts, the Bureau was doing its best—but that was the public impression.

Gray's collusion with the White House eventually came out. In February 1973, Nixon formally nominated Gray to be the permanent FBI director, a nomination that had to be confirmed by the US Senate. It turned out to be more of an execution than a confirmation hearing, as hostile senators repeatedly caught the hapless Gray in misstatements and obfuscations and outright lies about his handling of the Watergate probe. After the White House, in John Ehrlichman's famous phrase, let Gray "twist slowly, slowly in the wind,"

Gray finally withdrew his name from consideration and ultimately resigned in disgrace. He'd only been in the job for just under a year, but the damage to the Bureau was done. Not only had the director of the FBI—albeit the acting director—participated in a cover-up, but he was also a fool. Even those of us who worked at the bricks level of the Bureau felt it: people didn't look at us quite the same way anymore.

The chaos continued. To replace Gray, Nixon named William Ruckelshaus, then the head of the Environmental Protection Agency, as a kind of temporary acting FBI director; he lasted just over two months before Nixon kicked him up to deputy attorney general and replaced him with Clarence Kelley, a retired FBI agent and current chief of the Kansas City Police Department. So in just a little over a year, the FBI had had four directors or acting directors—Hoover, Gray, Ruckelshaus, and Kelley. The Bureau was in turmoil.

But it wasn't just revolving-door directors and the Watergate scandal that were ruining the FBI's public image and morale. Just as Hoover had long feared, his secrets, the Bureau's secrets, were coming out.

Remember the phrase on the routing slip taken during the Media, Pennsylvania, resident agency burglary in early 1971? The one that simply said "COINTELPRO—New Left" with no further explanation? That single phrase sparked the interest of an NBC News reporter named Carl Stern. It didn't take a genius to figure out that *COINTELPRO* was Bureau-speak for "counterintelligence program," but what did that actually involve? After FBI officials refused to even discuss it, Stern filed a lawsuit to obtain COINTEL-PRO documents under the Freedom of Information Act. In late 1973 a court ordered the Bureau to turn over the requested documents—the first in a steady dribble of Bureau secrets that eventually became a deluge.

It was like the Media break-in magnified a hundred times. Every aspect of the COINTELPRO operations was revealed: The black bag jobs, the wiretaps and bugs, the anonymous phone calls to wives or employers, the Bureau-requested IRS audits, the secret smear campaigns, the informants, the "snitch jackets" put on dissident-group leaders, the dirty tricks, all designed to "expose, disrupt, misdirect, discredit and otherwise neutralize" Communists and Klansmen and civil rights leaders and anti-war groups and others.

As the revelations poured out, naturally the politicians got involved. In 1975 both houses of Congress held hearings on "domestic spying" by the FBI, the CIA, and other agencies, with one of their scathing reports likening the Bureau's efforts to "the tactics of totalitarian regimes." The nation in general was appalled by many of the revelations, so much so that in 1976 Director Clarence Kelley felt compelled to publicly apologize, saying, "Some of these activities were clearly wrong and quite indefensible."

Beyond the COINTELPRO activities, many people also thought other aspects of Bureau business were "clearly wrong and quite indefensible"—especially "the files," the dreaded FBI files on individual Americans.

The Bureau *did* have "files" on millions of citizens—just as your state Department of Motor Vehicles has "files" on millions of citizens. And yes, the Bureau files did contain the names collected over the years of hundreds of thousands of suspected "subversives," including members of the SDS, the KKK, the American Nazi Party, the Communist Party USA, and a number of anti-war and civil rights groups, along with files on thousands upon thousands of actual criminals. But as discussed in a previous chapter, the vast majority of the FBI files were mundane collections of background information on federal-job applicants and employees and others who had contact with the US government. There were files on politicians and congressmen as well, but there, too, the files were mostly just publicly available biographical material and legislative voting records, the same sort of files maintained by any federal agency with a congressional liaison function. Unless a congressman had a criminal arrest record or was the subject of a federal corruption probe or had been a "walk-on" in a Mann Act investigation of a DC brothel, or some such thing, chances were his FBI file was pretty tame stuff.

It's probably fair to say that most Americans didn't much care that the FBI had a file on some guy who applied for a job with the Department of Agriculture, or on some obscure congressman from Des Moines. But what astonished—and titillated—the public most was the breadth of FBI interest in famous people: movie stars, rock and roll singers, artists, writers, scientists. As the FOIA revelations came out over the ensuing years, Americans learned that Mr. Hoover's FBI had files on such diverse personalities as Marilyn Monroe and Albert Einstein, Steve McQueen and Charlie Chaplin, Lucille Ball and Norman Mailer and Ernest Hemingway, Frank Sinatra and Sammy Davis Jr., Mike Wallace and Walter Cronkite, Dr. Benjamin "America's Baby Doctor" Spock, the Beatles and Elvis Presley and Jimi Hendrix, and even, believe it or not, a file on the pure-vanilla, parent-friendly, manufactured-for-TV band the Monkees. And those were just a few.

It was shocking—and also more than a little misleading. The Bureau did have extensive files on such celebrities as Eleanor Roosevelt, whose association with left-wing causes before and during World War II prompted Bureau surveillance that was approved by her husband, the president. To cite another example, the famous symphony conductor Leonard Bernstein had more than eight hundred pages of documents in his file due to his dedication to leftist causes, including a report on the celebrity-rich 1970 fundraising party he held for the Black Panthers at his lavish Manhattan apartment, the party so skillfully skewered in Tom Wolfe's essay "Radical Chic"—although in fairness to the Bureau, there would almost certainly have been a similar FBI report in the unlikely event that Mr. Bernstein had held a fundraiser for the Ku Klux Klan. Numerous other celebrities had for one reason or another attracted the Bureau's attention.

But in many cases the files on celebrities consisted of little more than newspaper clippings, or they were created during legitimate Bureau investigations of murder threats or extortion schemes directed at the celebrities in question. And many of the celebrity files were pathetically thin. For example, the seven-page file on the Monkees concerned an absurd report by a Hollywood civilian FBI informant that the group was broadcasting subliminal anti-war messages during live concerts—and no action on that allegation was recommended or taken by the Bureau. So if someone says, "Hoover had an FBI file on the Monkees," it's one of those things that's accurate without quite being true. (It's a measure of how disconnected with 1960s popular culture some Bureau men were that the four Monkees were described in the file as "beatnik types.")

But it wasn't the FBI files on ordinary Americans, or even celebrities, that stirred the most heated passions of politicians and the press in the wake of the Director's death. No, what they wanted to see were the really secret "secret files," the shocking, salacious, lubricious, explosive files that everybody knew Hoover kept in his offices but nobody could find.

And in the middle of their desperate search for those files was Miss Helen W. Gandy.

She'd been busy in the days and weeks after I'd spoken with her on the way to the funeral. Working with Mr. Mohr, who retired soon after Hoover's death, she did exactly what she'd told me she was going to do. First she gave the Official/Confidential files—some seventeen thousand pages worth—to Mark Felt, who locked them away in his office. Eventually many of those files would surface under FOIA requests and would reveal details of wiretaps and buggings and COINTELPRO operations.

Then Miss Gandy took the Director's Personal/Confidential files and destroyed them. Working first in her office and later in the basement of Hoover's home, Miss Gandy destroyed every single file, thousands upon thousands of pages, ripping each page in half and then having them fed into an industrial-strength shredding machine. Half a century of history, half a century of J. Edgar Hoover's secrets, was turned into confetti.

Word of the destruction of the files eventually got out, and naturally Congress was outraged. Their attitude seemed to be "We are shocked—shocked!—that Hoover kept secret and no doubt salacious files on American citizens. Now we want to know what was in them." In an effort to find out, in 1975 a subcommittee of the House Committee on Government Operations conducted what was called an "Inquiry into the Destruction of Former FBI Director J. Edgar Hoover's Files"—and the star witness was Miss Gandy.

Perhaps the subcommittee members, headed by combative New York City Democrat Bella Abzug, thought they'd make short work of her, that this little old lady, this secretary, would be so intimidated by the awesome majesty of a House committee room that she would quickly fold and reveal all. If so, they obviously didn't know Miss Gandy.

You destroyed all of the Personal/Confidential files? the subcommittee members asked her.

Oh, yes, every one, Miss Gandy said, some thirty file drawers' worth, as Mr. Hoover had directed.

And what was in those Personal/Confidential files? they wanted to know.

Oh, just the Director's personal correspondence, Miss Gandy said, letters from friends, birthday cards, things like that, nothing pertaining to official Bureau business.

Nothing at all? the subcommittee members demanded. In all of those thousands and thousands of pages there were no derogatory documents on presidents? Members of Congress? Celebrities? Prominent people? Nothing on bag jobs and wiretaps and buggings and COINTELPRO?

No, no, no, absolutely not, Miss Gandy testified under oath.

The committee members went around and around, asking the same questions six different ways, hoping to trip her up, but they couldn't shake her. Finally one member said incredulously, "I find your testimony very difficult to believe, Miss Gandy."

"That is your privilege," Miss Gandy said sweetly. "I have told the truth."

But she hadn't told the truth. Based on references to the Personal/Confidential files found in other Bureau documents, the subcommittee members knew she was lying. But what could they do about it? The evidence was long gone, and in any case, were they going to prosecute a seventy-eight-year-old woman for perjury? Not likely.

So what was in the Personal/Confidential files that Miss Gandy destroyed? I don't know specifically what was in them, but I know damn well that at least some of the documents were official Bureau business that Hoover didn't want anybody to know about. And I also wonder what truly "personal" documents were in the Personal/Confidential files that Miss Gandy so efficiently destroyed. Copies of the aforementioned letters to Melvin Purvis? Love letters to Dorothy Lamour or someone else? Letters in which this most reserved and secretive of men poured out his deeply felt hopes and fears and aspirations?

I don't know, and neither does anyone else. Only one person in all the world knew what was in those files, and she wasn't talking—and she never would.

After half a century of keeping secrets for J. Edgar Hoover, Miss Gandy kept those secrets to the end.

It wasn't just Congress that was investigating Mr. Hoover's FBI. In the wave of anti-FBI sentiment that followed Hoover's death, the Bureau was also investigating itself.

Under pressure from Congress and the Justice Department, FBI director Clarence Kelley ordered an investigation into allegations that Hoover and other top FBI officials had routinely misused Bureau employees, equipment, and funds for their personal benefit. That was certainly true in Hoover's case. It was common knowledge that FBI employees built a porch addition to his home, that they filled out his tax returns, that they fixed his home refrigerator and his TV when they went on the fritz, among other benefits. I arranged some of those things myself, and at the time it didn't seem like any big deal, just part of the perks that came with being director, just like the free meals at Harvey's Restaurant and the comped vacation travel to California and Florida. But it looked different when viewed through the post-Watergate prism, and the Director's reputation for personal integrity suffered a blow.

Other senior Bureau officials suffered similarly. J. P. Mohr, for example, was cited by investigators for having Bureau employees wash and service his personal car and for his too-close association with a contractor who supplied the Bureau with electronic equipment. Others were tagged for accepting gifts made by the Lab's Exhibits Section or for improperly using small amounts of Bureau funds for entertaining visitors. It was all pretty picayune stuff, but they were things that an ordinary street agent would have been fired or punitively transferred for doing, so the hypocrisy element was there. In the end none of those senior officials, all of whom had retired, were indicted and tried in court for those minor irregularities, although one former senior Bureau official pleaded guilty to a misdemeanor and was fined $100.

Those senior Bureau officials were lucky. Because while they were being investigated for relatively minor offenses, scores of lower-level Bureau officials and agents were facing serious criminal charges—with some of their alleged "victims" being members and enablers of the violent Weather Underground Organization.

Despite the turmoil in the upper echelons, Hoover's death hadn't caused Bureau business to grind to a halt. An important part of that business was pursuing the fugitive members of the Weather Underground, who were continuing their campaign of bombings and assaults on police officers, including a bomb set off in the Pentagon two weeks after Hoover's death. (I was one of the agents who responded to that bombing, and while miraculously no one was killed, the damage was extensive.)

For the Bureau, the hunt for Weathermen like Bernardine Dohrn and Bill Ayers and others was far different and more difficult than chasing down common criminals. For one thing, ordinary criminals were usually stupid—that was why they were criminals in the first place—and they associated with people who were more than happy to give them up for money or to get out from under their own pending criminal charges. The Weathermen, on the other hand, were generally intelligent and well educated, and some had been trained in anti-surveillance tradecraft in Cuba and other countries friendly to their revolutionary cause. While the number of hard-core Weather Underground fugitives was small, a few dozen at most, they were supported by a much larger network of friends and family members, believers in the cause who wouldn't turn in the fugitives for cash rewards, people who were willing to go to jail for contempt rather than provide information on the fugitives when called before grand juries.

Frustrated by the lack of success in catching the fugitives, after Hoover's death Mark Felt ordered agents to conduct black bag jobs on five residences of Weather Underground family members and supporters in an unsuccessful effort to learn the fugitives' whereabouts. In an unrelated investigation, after the Palestinian terrorist attacks at the Munich Olympic Games in the summer of 1972, Felt also ordered "surreptitious entries" at the US offices of a suspected Palestinian terrorist organization, an action that apparently prevented several similar attacks in the United States.

No one ever seemed to care about the black bag jobs against the suspected Palestinian terrorists; there was never any official complaint that I'm aware of. But after the COINTELPRO revelations and the congressional hearings of the mid-1970s, some people cared a lot about the black bag jobs against the Weathermen and their supporters. To the dismay of some congressmen and officials in the Justice Department, Hoover was dead and unable to answer for the Bureau's many alleged abuses—which was lucky for the Director. If he hadn't been dead, if he'd survived into the white-hot anti-Bureau fervor of the post-Watergate era, he might have spent his last days in prison.

But there were plenty of other targets. At one point more than fifty Bureau agents and supervisors were the subjects of criminal investigations for various alleged civil rights violations, including the Weather Underground bag jobs. The Justice Department eventually decided not to prosecute the lower-level agents, but they charged Patrick Gray, Mark Felt, and former FBI Domestic Intelligence Division head Edward Miller with conspiracy to deprive American citizens of their civil rights in connection with the

Weathermen break-ins—the same felony charge the Bureau had used against Ku Klux Klan church bombers in the 1960s. Charges against Gray were later dropped, but Felt and Miller were found guilty, and while they weren't sent to prison, they were fined and became convicted felons. President Ronald Reagan later pardoned them, citing their "good-faith belief that their actions were necessary to preserve the security interests of our country"—a statement that might also be applied to J. Edgar Hoover. The ultimate irony is that because of the black bag jobs, the cases against many of the fugitive Weathermen were considered legally tainted, and most of the charges against them were dropped.

So it all added up, bit by bit—the files, the bag jobs and bugs, the petty corruptions. The damage to the reputation and prestige of J. Edgar Hoover's FBI was profound and long-lasting. By 1975, only 37 percent of Americans polled had a "very favorable" opinion of the Bureau, less than half as many as a decade previously. To many Americans, the FBI was no longer a defender against the nation's enemies; the FBI was the enemy. That was reflected in popular culture. Faced with its declining ratings, in 1974 ABC canceled *The F.B.I.* TV series. Inspector Erskine had cracked his last case, and the FBI that he—and J. Edgar Hoover—had represented no longer existed. In fact, the very name J. Edgar Hoover was becoming politically toxic. When the new FBI headquarters building—the J. Edgar Hoover FBI Building—was finally dedicated in 1975, President Gerald Ford praised the men and women of the Bureau but barely mentioned the man whose name was on the building. And ever since then there have been persistent calls in Congress and the news media to remove Hoover's name.

True, much of the damage to the Bureau's reputation and image was self-inflicted—primarily Hoover inflicted. Certainly many of the things the Director did were "clearly wrong and quite indefensible." And yet, some perspective is required.

Obviously the Bureau sometimes went too far in collecting information on law-abiding Americans. What business was it of the FBI's if Rock Hudson was gay, or if Paul Newman was seen at an anti-war rally? And sometimes Hoover did misuse the information the Bureau collected. It wouldn't surprise me at all if some congressman who was publicly denouncing the Bureau got a visit from an FBI agent bearing a faded copy of a police report showing that the congressman had been convicted of soliciting a prostitute in 1956. Hoover always played hardball in defense of the FBI, and in defense of himself.

But the notion that Mr. Hoover's Bureau was some sort of Orwellian monster probing into every aspect of everyone's life, that it amassed "an enormous amount of information on virtually every American," as one congresswoman claimed, simply isn't true. Compared with the personal information on individuals that's available today, Hoover's paper files on a small percentage of Americans seem hopelessly old-fashioned, even quaint. In a few seconds at a keyboard, a government agency or private entity of today can easily collect more personal information about you than a dozen of Hoover's agents could have discovered in a year. Somehow the American concepts of individual freedom and personal privacy managed to survive the FBI files of the Hoover era; whether those concepts will survive the excesses of the Information Age and social media remains to be seen.

As for Hoover's tactics against dissident groups, many of those also went too far. In a free and democratic society, no law enforcement agency should conduct warrantless searches of law-abiding people's homes or launch anonymous smear campaigns against peaceful political opponents of the government. But the efforts of Hoover's FBI should also be considered in the context of the times. Some—not all, but some—of the people and groups targeted by COINTELPRO and other Bureau attacks on civil liberties were themselves actively attempting to deprive other Americans of their civil liberties. The Weathermen, for example, had openly declared war on the American government, and they were setting off bombs to make their point—and the Bureau was trying to make them stop. Maybe the ends didn't justify the Bureau's means, but they may explain the Bureau's means.

Another point bears repeating. Many of the people who were

and are outraged by the Bureau's use of shady tactics against college professors and students and black leaders—even the most extreme ones—seem noticeably less outraged that those same methods were used against Klansmen and Nazis and other right-wingers. Maybe they're correct to call Hoover an abuser of civil liberties, but at least he was an equal opportunity abuser.

One more thing. I said at the very beginning of this book that I hoped there'd never be another J. Edgar Hoover—and I meant it. He stayed too long, past his prime, to his own detriment and in some ways to the detriment of the nation. It would have been better for all concerned, Hoover included, if Lyndon Johnson hadn't waived Hoover's mandatory retirement in 1965, if Hoover had honorably faded from the public scene before the bitter divisiveness and turmoil of the late sixties and early seventies.

But here's another one of those what-if scenarios. What if there'd never been a J. Edgar Hoover? What if there'd never been an FBI director who was as popular and politically influential as Hoover was and thus was unable to stay in office as long as Hoover did? What if every president since FDR had appointed his own FBI director, someone who might have been even more willing than Hoover to follow the president's commands, no matter how politically motivated? In other words, what if every president since FDR had had his own L. Patrick Gray III? How would our national story have been changed, and would it have been for the better or for the worse? Especially now, when despite our best efforts the FBI has so often found itself being politicized, it's something to think about.

But despite all the blows to J. Edgar Hoover's professional reputation, his legacy as a public figure might have survived, intact if not unscathed. Perhaps in time he would have been forgiven for his excesses and been remembered for his accomplishments. After all, John Kennedy was forgiven for his reckless philandering and his decisions that left us inextricably committed in Vietnam. Lyndon Johnson, while not forgiven for expanding the war, has deservedly been credited for his landmark civil rights legislation. Even Richard

Nixon eventually rose beyond Watergate to become a kind of honored elder statesman, especially in foreign affairs.

Could the same thing have happened to J. Edgar Hoover?
Might he be remembered today as a flawed but still-worthy figure
in American history?

It could have happened that way. Except that as the years passed,
the attacks on J. Edgar Hoover got personal.

Even today, a half century after his death, when people happen to
find out that I once worked for J. Edgar Hoover, they almost always
ask me two things. The first is some variation of "Oh, yeah, Hoover.
He was gay, right?"

I don't get angry at the people who ask me that. They're just
repeating what they've heard. People have heard it so many times
they just assume it must be fact. So if they ask if Hoover was gay,
I just say, "I don't know," and then I try to steer the conversation
in another direction.

And that is absolutely true. I don't think J. Edgar Hoover was gay,
but I don't know if he was gay or wasn't gay. None of us can really
know what thoughts and desires live in the minds and hearts of others.

But I do know that there hasn't been a single piece of credible
evidence—emphasis on *credible*—to show that Hoover ever actively engaged in homosexual practices. Unfortunately, that hasn't
stopped any number of journalists and authors and Hoover haters
from stating authoritatively that he was indeed gay.

Rumors about Hoover's sexual orientation—and specifically
about his relationship with Clyde Tolson—circulated throughout
his career. The subject first came up publicly, in a snide and oblique
way, in the 1930s, when a national magazine ran a profile of him
that said Hoover "walks with a mincing step" and favored dandi-
fied clothing accessories in the color called Eleanor Blue—a reference to Eleanor Roosevelt's first inaugural gown. (Hoover did have
an odd walking style, short of a rapid short-step—but then,, John
Wayne walked funny, too.) Later, if Hoover heard that someone was
spreading the rumor that he was homosexual, he'd dispatch agents

to interview the accuser and demand to know what evidence he had—to "put up or shut up" as Hoover phrased it. In almost every case they decided to shut up. It was an intimidating and grossly improper tactic, of course, so you can add that to the list of Hoover abuses—but it doesn't prove that Hoover was gay.

During my time in the Bureau I occasionally heard other agents joke about it—in whispers—referring to Hoover and Tolson as "J. Edna and Clyde" and so on. But those were insults, not accusations. I certainly never had any reason to believe Hoover was gay when I worked for him. Even Hoover's worst enemy within the Bureau, William C. Sullivan, never so much as hinted that Hoover was gay, not in interviews nor in a scathing book he published after Hoover's death. Sullivan called the Director everything else—evil, corrupt, insane, a blackmailer, and so on—but he never called him gay.

The fact is that the only proven "evidence" anyone has of Hoover's alleged homosexuality was completely circumstantial and would today be considered homophobic stereotyping—that he lived with his mother until he was in his early forties, that he never married, that he liked flowers, that he was seldom seen in the company of a woman (Dorothy Lamour and Lela Rogers notwithstanding), and that his best friend and constant companion, Tolson, was a man who also never married. But if never being married is evidence of homosexuality, I guess you could argue that Miss Gandy was a lesbian.

As for the "evidence" produced by various writers, it is easily dismissed. Someone "heard" that Hoover was arrested for sexually soliciting an undercover male cop in New Orleans in the late 1920s. A woman suddenly recalled, years after Hoover's death, that she'd seen Hoover and Tolson holding hands in a car on their way to a New York nightclub in the 1930s. That sort of thing. Some critics made much of the fact that among the many drawings and sculptures in Hoover's house were a number of male nudes, including a copy of Michelangelo's *David*. But if you look at the full inventory of his estate, there were at least as many female nude artworks as male ones, including a plaster statue of Lady Godiva and the famous nude calendar shot of the young Marilyn Monroe. As a trained investigator, the only solid conclusion I can draw from this "evidence" is that the man liked nudes.

Nor are Hoover's critics willing to accept a possible alternative explanation. In these highly sexualized times, it's difficult for many people to imagine that Hoover might have been asexual, that he simply wasn't interested, or that perhaps he was physically dysfunctional sexually. The thinking is that if he wasn't provably heterosexual, then he must have been gay.

But even if he was gay, the question arises—so what? The usual objection is that Hoover was hypocritical about it, that he publicly condemned homosexuals as "deviates," that he persecuted gays within the US government and beyond. It was true that known or even suspected homosexuals were barred from Hoover's FBI and remained so until 1993, long after his death. But under a 1953 executive order signed by President Eisenhower, gays were barred from employment in any US government agency, on the theory that their sexual orientation made them prime targets for blackmail by foreign espionage agencies. In fact, until the early 1960s, homosexual acts were actually illegal in every state. If Hoover's FBI persecuted gays, so did presidents, the Supreme Court, Congress, the American public, and every police department vice squad in America. It wasn't fair, and it wasn't right, but that was the tenor of the times, and you can't single out Hoover for being part of it.

Then there's the second thing people ask me about J. Edgar Hoover. It's some variation of "Oh, yeah, Hoover. He's the one who wore a dress, right?"

That one really annoys me.

Again, I don't get mad at the questioner, but I'm furious at the people who started and propagated this story. And I can give anybody who asks the question a straight answer.

The answer is no. J. Edgar Hoover was not a cross-dresser. It's a preposterous story and a damned lie.

In the two decades after Hoover's death, not even Hoover's most strident enemies ever tried to spread such a ridiculous accusation. They may absurdly have compared Hoover to mass murderers like the Nazis' Heinrich Himmler and the Soviets' Lavrentiy Beria, but they never tried to put Hoover in a dress. It wasn't until 1993 that a British "journalist," whom I won't name, made the allegation in a book, whose title I won't mention. According to this "journalist," he had an eyewitness who said she'd seen Hoover wearing a wig and a short red dress and a black feather boa at a gay sex orgy with young male prostitutes in the Plaza Hotel in New York City in the late 1950s; she said Hoover was introduced to her as "Mary."

And who was this alleged eyewitness? She was the broke and embittered ex-wife—the fourth ex-wife—of one of Hoover's wealthy friends, a woman who for some reason blamed Hoover for her many troubles and, by the way, was a convicted perjurer. She'd tried for years to peddle the Hoover dress story to various journalists, for cash, but found no takers until the British writer paid the fee and put her in his book.

That was it. That was the alleged journalist's alleged "evidence." Before or since, no one else who ever knew Hoover ever publicly claimed to have seen him engaged in homosexual activities, much less while wearing a feather boa. No one.

And how do I know the woman's story isn't true? The same way I know that Abraham Lincoln didn't walk the halls of the White House wearing a pink tutu. It's ridiculous on its face. I didn't know Lincoln—I'm not quite that old—but I did know Hoover, at least well enough to know that this rigidly self-controlled man, a man whose reputation meant everything to him, would never have entrusted that reputation to a bunch of male prostitutes and the ditzy wife of one of his pals. And anyone else who knew him would have said the same.

Nevertheless, the British writer's book was a bestseller, almost solely because of the scurrilous dress allegation. I suppose it was the delicious incongruity that gave the story its appeal: the image of the dour, beefy, bulldog-faced J. Edgar Hoover in a red dress and a feather boa was too hilarious for most people to resist. The story was widely repeated—sometimes skeptically, sometimes not—in the press and in a "documentary" on PBS, which should have known better.

The ludicrous tale quickly became a staple of late-night talk show humor. Making a joke about a certain elderly politician, one late-night host quipped, "When this guy first went to Washington, J. Edgar Hoover was still wearing a training bra." Even a president of the United States got into the act. When looking for a replacement for fired FBI director William Sessions, President Bill Clinton told reporters he was "having a hard time finding someone to fill J. Edgar Hoover's pumps." Clint Eastwood, usually a fine actor and director, alluded to the dress story in his questionable 2011 Hoover biopic, *J. Edgar*. As recently as 2017, when James Comey was fired as FBI director, among the jokes on late-night TV was "If J. Edgar Hoover could see what's going on in the FBI, he'd be rolling over in his dress."

Those are just a few examples. This absurd story, based on nothing, just won't go away. And with it, Hoover's many critics have succeeded in doing what they could never quite accomplish when he was alive. They've turned him into both a villain and a joke.

I considered not even mentioning the story, lest I add to its longevity. But in writing this book I've tried to dispel some of the many absurd myths that surrounded J. Edgar Hoover, and finally I decided to do what I can to dispel this one.

I know, Hoover critics may argue that Hoover and his Bureau spread smear stories about other people. So why not do it to him? I don't agree with it, but I understand their argument that J. Edgar Hoover doesn't deserve the truth.

But history does.

They're all gone now.

Hoover has been dead for going on fifty years. In his will he left almost his entire estate to Tolson, which, including his house, was valued at about $500,000—a not inconsiderable sum at the time, but in line with someone who was paid the same as a US senator and who ate most of his meals for free. In the will Hoover also bequeathed $5,000 to Miss Gandy, $3,000 to Annie Fields, and $2,000 to Jimmy Crawford, while his nieces and nephews got nothing.

When I heard about it, I was angry at the Director for the meager amounts he left to the three people who'd served him so loyally for so long. But I don't think any of them complained.

Clyde Tolson moved into Hoover's house on the day the Director died and never left. Annie and Jimmy took care of him as his health further declined, and he spent his days watching TV game shows and soap operas, a reclusive, cantankerous, feebleminded old man who was disliked by the neighbors and almost everybody else. He had Hoover's dogs, Cindy and G-Boy, put down and sold many of the antiques and artworks in the house. He died in 1975 and was buried near Hoover in Congressional Cemetery. No doubt at the insistence of J. P. Mohr, who was his executor, Tolson's will left an additional $20,000 each to Annie and Jimmy, as well as, somewhat embarrassingly, $26,000 to Mr. Mohr himself. But Tolson's estranged brother, who received nothing, contested the will and some of Tolson's bequeathments were later reduced.

The other men around Hoover are gone as well. Mr. Mohr spent much of his immediate post-Bureau time under investigation for alleged improprieties and testifying before various congressional committees; he died in 1997. After denying it for almost three decades, in 2005 Mark Felt publicly acknowledged that he was indeed Deep Throat and was widely hailed as a hero for preventing the Watergate cover-up; he died in 2008 at age ninety-five. William C. Sullivan also spent much of his post-Bureau time testifying in courts and in Congress, until in 1977 he was shot and killed while walking in the woods near his home by a hunter who mistook him for a deer. Local police investigated the killing and concluded it was an accident, unconnected to any of Sullivan's Bureau activities—a conclusion his family and friends accepted.

Miss Gandy lived quietly and comfortably in Washington for a number of years before finally moving to Florida to be close to family members. We continued to exchange Christmas cards, and we spoke on the phone a few times, but while we were still friends, it was different somehow. We no longer had the Bureau to share. To Miss Gandy, the Bureau without Mr. Hoover was not the Bureau at all.

I was traveling abroad when Helen Gandy died in 1988, at age ninety-one, and in those days before the Internet and email I didn't hear about it until later. But I had to smile when I read a single line in her brief obituary in the *Washington Post*:

"She was an avid fisherman."

As for me, I resigned—without prejudice!—from the FBI in December 1973, after eight years with the Bureau, including five years as a street agent. It was a difficult decision because I still loved being a special agent of the Federal Bureau of Investigation. But I'd turned thirty that year, a time when many men have to choose between what they want to do and what they need to do. I've already explained the drawbacks of trying to rise through the Bureau's supervisory ranks. But if I remained a street agent, I'd essentially be frozen at a midlevel income, and I wanted something better for my children.

And I had an offer for a job that promised to be almost as interesting and exciting as being an FBI agent. Because of my extensive work on skyjackings and airline security issues, United Airlines offered me a position with their Law Department, coordinating investigations into skyjackings and other crimes against the airline, including, in 1980, the planting of a bomb in United president Percy Wood's mailbox by the Unabomber, Ted Kaczynski. Later I became a vice president of Pan American World Airways, again specializing in security issues and working with a host of foreign security services, everything from Scotland Yard to the special operations tactical unit GSG 9 of the German Federal Police. Once, after starting my own successful consulting firm, I even worked with the Soviet KGB—not as a spy, of course, but to help them bring the Russian airlines up to international security standards as the Soviet Union was collapsing in the early 1990s.

Throughout my long post-FBI career I carried with me the things I'd learned at the Bureau, and from Hoover himself—self-discipline, self-confidence, the ability to never hesitate or show fear. Like the Director, I've been a man of strong opinions and never backed down when I was convinced I was in the right.

Today I live near the ruggedly beautiful Oregon coast, a place that seems to inspire both peace and reflection. To pass along some of the things I've learned in my long life, I teach as an adjunct professor and coordinator of the criminal justice curriculum at Tillamook Bay Community College. Many of my students are young and idealistic and eager to serve their communities and their nation in the honorable fields of criminal justice and law enforcement. They remind me of someone from long ago.

And although I've made some mistakes along the way, like Miss Gandy I can say this:

I don't regret my life.

And I've never regretted being part of Mr. Hoover's FBI.

ACKNOWLEDGMENTS

I am grateful to all the people who contributed to this project, none more than the FBI special agents with whom I worked. Although many have passed on, I wish to honor them: Bill Weatherwax, Bill Markham, Henry Goodson, Dick Cleary, Ken Kirwin, Marty Cox, John Love. And two of the most decorated FBI heroes with whom I remain in contact: Jim Siano and Joe Pistone. A special thanks to former agent John Cox, who shared duties with me in the office of the Director.

This book would not have been possible without the dedicated work of Rick Horgan, vice president and executive editor at Scribner/Simon & Schuster. His confidence in my manuscript and skillful guidance throughout the process has been invaluable. It has been a team effort with the folks at Scribner to whom I extend my sincere thanks: editorial assistant Beckett Rueda, copyeditor Steve Boldt, designer Erich Hobbing, and production editor Jason Chappell.

I also offer my heartfelt thanks to Holly Lorincz, of Lorincz Literary Services, whose belief in the book and great assistance helped to prepare the final draft for submission to the publisher. I am extremely grateful to my agent, Chip MacGregor of MacGregor Literary, Inc. He has lent constant encouragement and critical advice throughout the manuscript rewrites and the entire publishing process. Chip has exercised the patience of Job while working with me.

My overriding concern was to present a factual account to preserve history. My talented collaborative writer, Gordon Dillow, was

ACKNOWLEDGMENTS

tireless in his research of historic facts which alleviated even my smallest of concerns. I cannot thank him enough.

Tim Stapleton, a friend, who while suffering and dying of ALS kept pushing and encouraging me to complete my manuscript at times when I was ready to give up, or at least take a break. Tim died the week the manuscript was accepted by the publisher. He will always be remembered. Much thanks to Morgan Callender who eagerly volunteered and helped with a multitude of tasks, both big and small.

My family has been the greatest blessing of all. My children: Stephanie and her husband, James; Rachelle and her husband, Ben; and my son PJ, have been supportive of all I do and have done in the past. My sisters: Pat, Norma, and Judy and their husbands, the Crisciones, DeTollas, and Coopers have contributed in ways too numerous to list. I thank them all.

Finally, to whom my gratitude goes deeper than words can express: Sharon "Shay" Knorr, a professional storyteller, my best reader, greatest friend, and a domestic partner who, as an artist of theater and song, brings to me the joyfulness of life each day.

NOTES ON SOURCES

Most of this book is based on my personal observations and experiences as a civilian aide to J. Edgar Hoover and as a special agent of the FBI. In discussing historical events, or situations not personally witnessed by me, I've relied on a number of primary and secondary sources.

Hoover's FBI was built on paper, millions and millions of pages of documents that accumulated over the decades. Before Hoover's death virtually all those files were considered confidential and thus unavailable to the public. Since then, the federal Freedom of Information Act and the Privacy Act have allowed the release of many thousands of previously classified documents, albeit with frequent redactions. Those declassified files are available at vault.fbi.gov. Sadly, as discussed in the book, most of Hoover's "Personal/Confidential" files, thousands of pages worth, were destroyed by Miss Gandy after the Director's death.

A great many books have been written about Hoover's life, although none were written by Hoover himself. As far as is known he never seriously considered writing an autobiography, which would have made for fascinating reading—assuming this most secretive of men had honestly opened up about himself, which seems unlikely. However, after Hoover's death, several of his former top lieutenants wrote memoirs, including former Bureau No. 3 man Cartha "Deke" DeLoach (*Hoover's FBI: The Inside Story by Hoover's Trusted Lieutenant*, Regnery History, 1995); former assistant director Ray

Wannall (*The Real J. Edgar Hoover: For the Record*, Turner Publishing, 2000); former Bureau deputy associate director Mark Felt, aka "Deep Throat" (*A G-Man's Life: The FBI, Being "Deep Throat," and the Struggle for Honor in Washington*, with John O'Connor, Public Affairs, Perseus Books Group, 2006); and former Bureau intelligence chief William C. Sullivan (*The Bureau: My Thirty Years in Hoover's FBI*, with Bill Brown, W.W. Norton, 1979). All offer insights into the man and the Bureau, but, with the exception of Sullivan, who developed an almost pathological hatred for his former boss, Hoover's men tend to go overboard in their praise for the Director, at times to the point of outright adoration.

Such adoration hasn't been a problem for most other Hoover biographers. Almost invariably they present Hoover as a diabolical figure whose every motivation was suspect and who never saw a constitutional right he wasn't eager to trample upon. Of the anti-Hoover books, the most thoroughly researched—although still heavily biased—is Curt Gentry's *J. Edgar Hoover: The Man and the Secrets* (W.W. Norton, 1991). The absolute worst of the anti-Hoover biographies is Anthony Summers's execrable *Official and Confidential: The Secret Life of J. Edgar Hoover* (G. P. Putnam's Sons, 1993). It was Summers, whom I declined to name earlier in this book, who first claimed without a shred of credible evidence that Hoover enjoyed wearing wigs and dresses; for Summers, no unfounded myth or unsubstantiated rumor about Hoover seemed too absurd to ignore—and unfortunately many of those myths and rumors have found their way unchallenged into other works about Hoover and the Bureau.

Of historical books about the Bureau during the Hoover era, the best and most balanced is Sanford J. Ungar's *FBI: An Uncensored Look Behind the Walls* (Atlantic-Little, Brown Books, 1975), which offers keen contemporaneous insights into Hoover and the organization he created. The best all-around historical reference book on the Bureau is *The FBI: A Comprehensive Reference Guide* (Athan G. Theoharis, editor, Checkmark Books, 2000). Particularly useful to me was *The Director: An Oral Biography of J. Edgar Hoover* by

Ovid Demaris (Harper's Magazine Press, 1975), which features interviews with scores of people who knew Hoover personally, along with balanced commentary by Mr. Demaris.

Quotes from Hoover's correspondence with Melvin Purvis, including the letters concerning Miss Gandy, are from Alston Purvis and Alex Tresniowski's *The Vendetta: FBI Hero Melvin Purvis's War Against Crime, and J. Edgar Hoover's War Against Him* (Public Affairs, Perseus Books Group, 2005). Hoover's relations with John F. Kennedy and Robert F. Kennedy are thoroughly covered, albeit mostly from the Kennedys' point of view, in Burton Hersh's *Bobby and J. Edgar: The Historic Face-Off Between the Kennedys and J. Edgar Hoover That Transformed America* (Basic Books, 2007). The story of the Media, Pennsylvania, FBI office break-in is well told in Betty Medsger's *The Burglary: The Discovery of J. Edgar Hoover's Secret FBI* (Vintage Books, 2014), while the interactions between Hoover and Richard Nixon and his men prior to Watergate are closely documented in J. Anthony Lukas's *Nightmare: The Underside of the Nixon Years* (Viking Press, 1976). For contemporary accounts of various incidents, including the circumstances surrounding Hoover's death and funeral, I've relied on numerous newspapers, including the *New York Times* and the *Washington Post*.

INDEX